$10.00

MW01113917

H. Anthony Ruckel

VOICES FOR THE EARTH

An inside account of how
citizen activists and responsive courts
preserved natural treasures
across the American West

VOICES FOR THE EARTH
Copyright ©2014 by H. Anthony Ruckel.
All rights reserved.
Printed in the United States of America.

No part of this book may be used or reproduced
in any manner whatsoever without written permission
except in the case of brief quotations embodied
in critical articles and reviews.

For information, address:
Entrada Press
2121 S. Oneida Street, Suite 600
Denver CO 80224

FIRST U.S. EDITION PUBLISHED 2014

*Designed by John Ransom and Barbara Mastej
of Odd Man Out, LLC.*

Library of Congress Cataloging-in-Publication Data
Ruckel, H. Anthony
Voices for the Earth: An Inside Account of How Citizen Activists and Responsive
Courts Preserved Natural Treasures Across the American West / H. Anthony Ruckel—1st ed.
p. cm.
Includes bibliographical references and index.
ISBN-13: 978-1-938633-65-2
Library of Congress Control Number: 2014944994

To David, Geoffrey, Jennifer, Gus
and Nancy

Contents

Contents *(cont.)*

Illustrations

Acknowledgments

I faced a very difficult challenge when I sat down to begin writing this book. It seemed terribly awkward, even presumptuous, to tell the story of *Voices* in the first person, a story that is the product of citizens, activists, professionals, lawyers, government officials, courts, and politicians—the product of the whole working within our legal and judicial systems to protect and improve our environment, and to create along the way a new system of jurisprudence: Environmental Law. Especially the citizens, the volunteer activists, their lawyers, and their ably staffed non-profit organizations. It all starts with them, it is maintained by them, and no results advancing the quality of our environment are achieved without them. It is because of them that the *Voices* story exists.

Three people in particular have given me extraordinary aid and must be singled out. Philip S. Berry was a close friend and colleague in environmental law and environmental activist matters for more than forty years. One could not have wished for a better mentor and advisor, a better friend, or a more engaged counselor. Phil, a pioneer in conservation law, argued out most of the book with me and kept me on the path to its final realization. His experience and wisdom were invaluable. Unfortunately Phil passed away last fall. I humbly hope that he would have been pleased with *Voices* in its final form.

Joseph Hutchison has been my professional advisor, critic, and supporter. He knew what the book required, and he saw to it—my own errors, blind alleys, even absurdities notwithstanding—that those requirements were met. Joe's patience and humor were constantly needed to get me through the rough spots. My third principal advisor has been Howard Roitman, also a lawyer. Well versed in the relationships of the environmental agenda and our government agencies, Howard's commentary was always relevant, level headed, and penetrating.

In earlier years, I came to know John Ransom and Barbara Mastej and their manifest artistic talents. What a privilege for me it has been to have them create the marvelous art and illustrations for *Voices*. They have brought life and breath to the words on the printed pages.

I have been blessed with two editors: Myrna Poticha and Martha Firling. Their keen eye and knowledge of the language and its use saved me from more errors than I can count. Melody Madonna proofed the final manuscript and helped with advice in many other matters. Each time these three touched the

Acknowledgments *(cont.)*

manuscript it got better. Three folks gave me the use of their premises for a writer's retreat, sorely needed at pivotal points: Nancy Olmstead, who also gave me constant encouragement—"Write the story; write it the way you think best" —and Frank Borodic and Karen Anderson on the north coast of California.

Many people helped me by providing information, answering questions, discussing matters with me, clearing up ambiguities, reading drafts, and suggesting paths through difficulties that challenged me. It is impossible for me to thank them all individually or even to make a full list of them. I want, however, to express my obligation to a number whose help went beyond the ordinary courtesy of the republic of letters: Larry Bohning, Conrad Firling, Patrick Gallegher, Aaron Isherwood, Alma Lantz, Mary Ann McKiechan, Deborah Perry, Annalee Pogue, Carol Roche, and Mia Yu. Further, it is important that I recognize my other mentor through the decades: Edgar Wayburn, twentieth century icon in the environmental movement, was always there for me and egging me on.

Heartfelt thanks are due Caleb J. Seeling, whose expertise in publishing at Samizdat Press was crucial in launching *Voices* under the Entrada Press imprint. Finally, an author writing a book such as this must have access to a comprehensive law library. I enjoyed use of an excellent one: Westminster Law Library of the Sturm College of Law, University of Denver.

VOICES FOR THE EARTH

Prologue

Deep within the Grand Canyon of the Colorado River John Wesley Powell takes a seat by the campfire. It is morning, August 13, 1869. The river is relatively quiet now—just the low murmur of the restless current washing its banks—but the unexplored heart of the canyon and its tremendous challenges lie just ahead, and these are on his mind. Major Powell opens his journal to a clean page and begins to write—

> We are now ready to start on our way down the Great Unknown. Our boats, tied to a common stake, chafe each other as they are tossed by the fretful river. They ride high and buoyant, for their loads are lighter than we could desire. We have but a month's rations remaining.[1]

The expedition has spent a couple of days here at the mouth of the Colorado Chiquito, the expedition's name for the Little Colorado River. They have been mending equipment, resifting flour and salvaging waterlogged bacon, determining the camp's latitude and longitude, and measuring the height of the immense walls on all sides. Despite intermittent thunderstorms the men have been able to dry and repair the oar-manned wooden boats—dories, they are called—and they are once again ready for the river.

Tomorrow Powell and his men will enter the unexplored, run unimaginable rapids, and face desperate life-and-death decisions. They have 217 miles to run before they break out of the canyon and onto previously explored stretches of the river at Grand Wash Cliffs. Major Powell resumes —

> We are three quarters of a mile in the depths of the earth, and the great river shrinks into insignificance, as it dashes its angry waves against the walls and cliffs that rise to the world above; the waves are but puny ripples, and we but pigmies, running up and down the sands, or lost among the boulders.

> We have an unknown distance yet to run; an unknown river yet to
> explore. What falls there are, we know not; what rocks beset the chan-
> nel, we know not; what walls rise over the river, we know not.[2]

A stocky man with a trimmed beard, Powell lost his right arm fighting with the Union Army in the Battle of Shiloh. A soldier, explorer, field
scientist, public servant, and visionary, he is well suited to lead the first
full exploration of the Colorado River. His men are gathered around the
campfire with him, and as men often do before confronting unknown
dangers, they try to relieve the tension with light-hearted banter. Powell
continues —

> Ah, well! We may conjecture many things. The men talk as cheerfully
> as ever; jests are bandied about freely this morning; but to me the
> cheer is somber and the jests are ghastly.[3]

Well might he say this, considering what lay ahead.

The next two weeks of constantly fighting ferocious rapids would
bring the intrepid group to Separation Rapid. Three of the men wanted
no more hairbreadth escapes and splintered boats. They left the expedition to climb out of the canyon. They climbed the walls and emerged
onto the plateau, but they went no further. For there, the arrows of Shiv-
wits Indians cut them down. Back on the river, the nine who had gathered at the campfire at the Colorado Chiquito were now six, and the four
boats were now two. But the finely honed river skills and the undaunted
courage of the Major and his remaining men brought them through the
last harrowing stretches and the last tumultuous rapids—in Wallace
Stegner's words, "the last big roar from the river dragon"[4]—and on
August 30th they floated past Grand Wash Cliffs and into legend.

Most people have seen pictures of the Grand Canyon of the Colorado. Many millions have traveled to Arizona to visit Grand Canyon
National Park, and today more than four million come each year. See it
in a brilliant sunset, or in a thunderstorm with lightning flashing among
the crags and battlements and rebounding off the cliffs, or in freshly
fallen snow as the clouds slowly disperse and lift from the gorge, and
you will be party to one of the great spectacles nature offers. When the
world contemplates the wonders of America, the Grand Canyon of the

Colorado River is usually listed as among the most extraordinary. In recent decades, hundreds of thousands of visitors have been awed by the inner walls of the canyon as they followed the path of Major Powell, running that silvery ribbon of water that lies in the deepest part, the mighty Colorado River. From there, the rim of the canyon seems unimaginably far away. Again, Major Powell describes the scene —

> Clouds are playing in the canyon today. Sometimes they roll down in great masses, filling the gorge with gloom; sometimes they hang above, from wall to wall, and cover the canyon with a roof of impending storm; and we can peer long distances up and down this canyon corridor, with its cloud roof overhead, its walls of black granite, and its river bright with the sheen of broken waters. Then, a gust of wind sweeps down a side gulch, and making a rift in the clouds, reveals the blue heavens, and a stream of sunlight pours in. Then, the clouds drift away into the distance, and hang around crags, and peaks, and pinnacles, and towers, and walls, and cover them with a mantle, that lifts from time to time, and sets them all in sharp relief. Then, baby clouds creep out of side canyons, glide around points, and creep back again, into more distant gorges. The clouds, set in strata, cross the canyon, with intervening vista views, to cliffs and rocks beyond. The clouds are children of the heavens, and when they play among the rocks, they lift them to the region above.[5]

One hundred years after Powell's great adventure all was not well within the canyon. By the 1970s thousands of visitors—14,000 of them in 1976—unconstrained by environmentally sensitive controls or limitations were floating the river and running its rapids, and there was alarming evidence of serious degradation of the canyon's natural environment. Unfortunately the response of the National Park Service was feeble and ineffective. Powerful political and economic forces held sway, and the future promised only accelerating deterioration. Concerned members of the public stepped forward—as, in fact, they had been doing in defense of the country's storied parklands since the establishment of Yellowstone National Park in 1872—to defend the Grand Canyon. But in the 1970s these concerned citizens were not confined just to traditional remedies questioning candidates for public office, lobbying legislators, and arguing in the printed press or other available media. They had a new and extraordinarily effective remedy: they could seek redress in a court of law. They could request the U.S. District Court of Arizona to order the National Park Service to take action to protect the Grand Canyon.

This is the story of how it came about that in 1977 ordinary citizens could ask a federal court to intercede against another branch of the government—the executive department—on behalf of a national park. It is the story of how appropriate representatives of an environmental interest—a public interest as opposed to a traditional private or economic interest—could successfully pursue legal remedies. It is also the story of people, events, and institutions that brought this about, and how environmentalists continue to this day using this new tool—environmental law—to fight for a better world for all of us.

CHAPTER I

Origins

The circumstances in Grand Canyon in 1977 explain much about the early years of the modern era of environmental activism. Consider: In 1869 the population of the United States was 38 million, while in 1977 it was 200 million; citizens of Arizona Territory numbered 9,000 in 1869, but a little over one hundred years later the State of Arizona counted 2,000,000; visitors to the Grand Canyon surely totaled no more than a couple hundred in 1869, but in 1977 had risen to three million; and river-runners exploded from nine individuals to fourteen thousand.[1] As our population grew and expanded, burdens on our land and our natural and scenic resources—limited as they must be by the bounds of geography—inexorably grew. As the impacts of those burdens became increasingly evident, the public became increasingly concerned.

Since the days of John Muir and Theodore Roosevelt at the turn of the twentieth century, concerned citizens and enlightened leaders have sought to preserve the best of our natural heritage and have spoken out against environmental degradation. More than one hundred years of conservation advocacy has protected many National Parks, National Forests, and National Wildlife Refuges. When conservationists rose in 1977 to defend the Grand Canyon and its centerpiece, the Colorado River, they readily employed tactics that had served them well over the decades: marshaling of citizen activists, legislative lobbying, direct political pressure, and publicity. But in 1977 they had a vital new tool: Environmental Law was taking its early steps toward recognition as a distinct area of jurisprudence and an integral part of the environmental arsenal. So Grand Canyon activists called their lawyers for help; they wished to bring a lawsuit to protect the canyon. A little more than ten years earlier no one was doing this, and controlling law said no one could do this. But by 1977 conservationists were increasingly filing lawsuits across the country in a constantly expanding range of environmental disputes, asking courts to hold the federal government to its stewardship obligations to our public lands and to the quality of our environment. Within a few days of the call from the Grand Canyon activists, we lawyers were on the job.

Of course, environmental law did not come into being simply because a few lawyers and a court or two awoke one morning and decided it would be a good idea. It was not as easy as looking up the address of the courthouse and arriving at the clerk's office with a fistfull of documents lined out in appropriate legalese demanding the judge tell the National Park Service what to do. Rather, environmental law is a process that has grown out of a rising public need, working within a legal system tasked with the obligation to respond to that need in an appropriate manner and with effective remedies. To gain understanding of how it came about that conservationists could file a lawsuit against the National Park Service in 1977 seeking an order from the court directing the Park Service to manage river-running in the canyon in a manner protecting its environment, we should start with review of the background and origins of this new remedy in the context of the times—the 1960s and 1970s—from which it arose.

As history books tell us, and as some of us experienced first hand, those decades were marked by tremendous social and political turmoil, war, traumatic assassinations, and the forced resignation of a president. Today we marvel at the extent of conflicts going to the nation's very core—the rights of our citizens, the structure and powers of our government, and even our identity as a people. But in the midst of this great turmoil there was also hope, hope we could meet the challenges before us and especially that we might change and improve the world we lived in. This included an intensified concern for our natural environment and our relation to it. A critical force in this renewed environmental ethic was the ability of concerned citizens to seek remedies in a court of law. This book is the story of those early years of environmental law as I experienced them. It is the story of how our legal system responded to the new environmental challenges. It is also the story of the environmental clients, the citizen activists and their member-based organizations, for they are inseparable from the development of the law—indeed, they lie at its heart.

I will try to avoid the relatively dry recitations of a lecture or a treatise by using actual events and cases with real people and drawing what I want to say from these experiences. Case books and detailed essays on the law have their place, but they speak more to the legal profession than the interested citizen; I wish to speak to both. Intermittently, we will have to revert to legal or procedural explanations, for they will be needed to explain why events happened as they did or to place a controversy in its legal or historical context. However, these diversions will be as brief as possible, and we will quickly return to the actual case under discussion. In sum, I hope to bring the reader into the process, not just tell him about it.

The contrast between an unspoiled, and in large part unexplored, Grand Canyon in 1869 and the accelerating degradation of the ecosystem of the Inner Gorge of the Colorado River in 1977 is an ideal reference point for opening this story, for it illustrates so well two fundamental realities underlying the origins and evolution of environmental law: the growing impacts of a large developed society upon the country's natural resources—its air and water, and its land—which could no longer be denied in 1977; and building momentum of public concern over this state of affairs together with an insistent intent to do something about it which would not be denied.

For the moment, however, we need to put aside the Grand Canyon—we will give it full treatment later on—and examine the background from which environmental law arose. We will meet some of the people involved—this "public" that would not be denied—and talk about how the legal system began to play its part. To get this conversation underway, we should first visit a small area in southeastern Kentucky, sixteen hundred miles away from the Grand Canyon. The *Beaver Creek Wilderness* case gives us an excellent picture, which can be briefly and succinctly related, of what environmental law can offer the public interest community from the beginning of a case to its final resolution. This view of the whole helps us better understand the more intricate cases and initiatives in the chapters ahead, including extensive efforts to protect the Grand Canyon.

Bulldozers at Beaver Creek

The telephone call from Kentucky reached me at the Sierra Club Legal Defense Fund in Denver in early summer 1979. Two lawyers from Lexington were calling for help. Like many such calls, it was urgent. Earth moving equipment was poised on the boundary of Beaver Creek Wilderness Area in Daniel Boone National Forest in the southeastern part of the state. In a couple of days they would start their engines, lower their blades, and begin to carve up critical parts of the wilderness. The Forest Service seemed paralyzed. Concerned citizens' organizations, however, were not going to give up easily; they were seeking a way to halt the project. Although comprising fewer than 5,000 acres, Beaver Creek is one of Kentucky's real gems, a secluded hardwood forest along the Cumberland Plateau characterized by sharp ridges dissected by narrow ravines, which are bordered by several miles of distinctive sandstone cliffs. Natural arches and rock shelters are found there. The wilderness area was established and dedicated as part of the seminal Eastern Wilderness Act of 1975.[2] In 1979, it was Kentucky's only dedicated wilderness area.[3*]

What could be done? The lawyers met me at the Lexington airport, and we went to work on a complaint and temporary restraining order. We were in the U.S. District Court seventy-two hours after the call. Typical of many public lands, Beaver Creek's subsurface minerals—in this case coal—were owned by a private entity, while the surface, the wilderness land itself, was owned by the U.S. Forest Service. The former has traditionally been called the dominant estate, and its right to remove the coal could not ultimately be prevented. But the law also provided that the subsurface owner must make a reasonable effort to protect the surface interests. Where the surface owner—the Forest Service—holds the surface for the benefit of another, the public, it should be vigorous in asserting its protective rights. This obligation was intensified by the recent Congressional act creating the Beaver Creek Wilderness Area. Unfortunately, traditionally the surface owner seldom prevailed in a material way. The sub-surface owner had the right to his claim, and this right was not easily abridged. But this was Kentucky's only dedicated wilderness, and local environmentalists were demanding the Forest Service take a hard look at all measures that could give maximum protection to the wilderness. It had obviously failed to do this.

The judge was traveling on circuit in the southern part of the state, so we convened in his chambers in Lexington with the judge on speakerphone. Our complaint asserted that the Forest Service must move

---

* Today there is only one other dedicated National Forest wilderness area in Kentucky: Clifty Wilderness in the Red River Gorge area, established in 1985.

decisively to protect the surface of this marvelous wilderness land, that mining development could not proceed until it was shown the miner was doing everything to protect the surface, and that the court needed to issue a temporary restraining order preserving existing conditions until these matters could be addressed. Furthermore, it seemed clear there was no immediate imperative to strip the land before this process could be completed.

The mining interests pressed their traditional rights. The Forest Service begrudgingly committed to do whatever it could but had nothing concrete to propose. We developed and repeatedly hammered on one overriding fact: Beaver Creek was Kentucky's only dedicated Wilderness, a singular treasure of just 7.7 square miles out of the total 39,732 square miles in the State. Carving it up was irreparable and final—it would be scarred for generations. It would no longer be wilderness. We argued that our law was sound, and the court should restrain any action on the ground until it could more fully consider the merits of our lawsuit. There was the usual back and forth, but the judge increasingly seemed to embrace our position, referring in his comments now to the importance of Kentucky's only Wilderness Area. He urged the defendants to hold off for a few days until he could get back in town. After more back and forth, they agreed.

The Forest Service, now recognizing it had good cause to press the position with which it had always had sympathy, stiffened its spine. The mining interests developed a mining plan which avoided the wilderness area, a land exchange was approved where title to the subsurface mineral rights beneath the wilderness was conveyed to the Forest Service, and the integrity of Beaver Creek was protected and remains so to this day. One would assume protection of Beaver Creek would have been automatic, but instead it took a community of concerned citizens, their dedication to see the fight through, and a federal court to achieve that goal.

The chapters that follow tell of the events and recite some of the lessons of many early cases and controversies like Beaver Creek and Grand Canyon. An equal purpose is to show how these experiences fit into the comprehensive fabric of the law and its ability to adapt to the changing mores and needs of our democratic society. We will explore how aggrieved citizens and their lawyers first began using courts in appropriate and frequently definitive circumstances, quickly placing them in the forefront of efforts to preserve, protect, and improve our environment. While they shared center stage most particularly with the legislative branch, I believe the courts affirmed these environmental objectives in a manner reflecting great credit on the structure of our legal system and its traditions of fair trial, due process, and expected judicial behavior. The noted legal philosopher Edmond Cahn expressed this well:

> Some consumers need bread, others need Shakespeare, others need their rightful place in society—what they all need is processors of law who will consider the people's needs more significant than administrative convenience.[4]

Our judicial system, with its rules of procedure and evidence, the open public nature of its venues and processes, and the respect accorded it for fair play and judicious mien can be particularly sensitive to fundamental changes in public needs, attitudes, and beliefs. This is especially true where markedly new areas of broad public concern such as the environment involve fiercely competing interests and values. Moreover, we Americans expect our laws will be followed, including laws governing the conduct of government entities. Thus we expect the judiciary to call the executive branch of the government, the U.S. Forest Service for example, to account when necessary.

Consider again *Beaver Creek*. New laws were to be interpreted, and old laws placed in a new context. A forum—the court—that could handle the traffic, act quickly, and do so in an ultimately decisive manner was available. Traditional and accepted rules of process and procedure served the outcome well. The fundamental approach of temporarily enjoining activities that materially threaten the interest of a party, or parties, was reinforced. Had further proceedings been necessary, they would have been done in deliberate fashion, with full review of the evidence and the law, and unprejudiced by events on the ground. Persistent, committed plaintiffs demonstrated their importance to the protection of a valuable public resource. A previously disconcerted Forest Service began to think about solutions rather than continue to dwell upon its frustrations. Finally, a knotty problem was resolved in a manner advancing a distinct and important public interest.

In the coming pages other cases will be used to develop these points further. I use the Beaver Creek format, with parties, procedures, evidence, and decision in their usual order. The narrative is not strictly chronological, and cases and controversies drawn from a span of roughly twenty-five years are recounted without regard to date. By using the rough format of the evolution of a typical lawsuit, and grouping cases together by their particular environmental or procedural concern, I believe the underlying themes of the book will more easily be recognized and understood. The participants—the players—will seem more real, and the challenges they meet will be better defined. It is particularly my hope the book will be serviceable to the lay reader and the novice as well as the seasoned professional. I also want to recognize and address young lawyers coming into the profession, and available in one capacity or another to do their part to advance us one more step in our endlessly evolving effort to protect our environment.

There is elegance in a system which tackles the fundamental issues of the day, threads its way through the complexities, and arrives at decisions which, for the most part, are accepted and implemented. Naturally, there will be those who decry all this as "judicial activism," a pejorative label in some circles these days. They will accuse the courts of exceeding their jurisdiction and deciding issues beyond their experience and their expertise. To a considerable degree, however, "judicial activism" is a matter of definition. And, of course, it is most frequently invoked by those who perceive that they are on the losing side of recent judicial decisions and trends. Defining "judicial activism," identifying an "activist" judge or court and the alleged dangers this may imply, and determining whether this is good or bad, is beyond the scope of this book. Furthermore, to the extent applicable here, I would prefer that readers reach their own judgments from the pages that follow.

In the 1960s and 1970s there were only a relative handful of us engaged in the practice of environmental law. Legal fees and funding of nascent environmental law efforts and programs were minimal. Quite literally, we were feeling our way. Today there are hundreds of lawyers involved daily on behalf of public interest clients. Specialties have arisen: air pollution, water pollution, local land use planning, to name a few. While financial resources are slim when compared with the private sector, they are sufficient to support a sizeable environmental law docket across the country. Just as important, the sources of these resources now appear reliable enough to support environmental law advocacy and programs for the indefinite future. This is wonderful! The environment and all of us continuously benefit from the tireless efforts of all those who were and are thus engaged. Perhaps this is the best monument of all to both the early decades of environmental law practice and the wisdom and adaptive abilities of our legal system.[5]

It needs to be emphasized that the public, more specifically citizens arguing in the public interest, play a central role in this story. Public involvement is absolutely critical to the legal process. Individual activists and groups of citizens are the steady and reliable guardians of environmental values, the lobby for good legislation and regulations, and the enforcers of the laws and standards that are established. The public and its citizen representatives must fulfill this role, for often there is no one else available to express this interest as their priority. Other participants frequently have their own agenda. Private entities have specific self-interests, and government entities often serve political or bureaucratic ends. This is not necessarily bad, for in a broad context those interests are often legitimate, and in the larger sense we are all "the public." Moreover, there are always a few private entities that readily adjust to a new environmental law and its regulations. There is always a legislator or two, a state or a federal agency, which on a particular issue will subordinate political or bureaucratic concerns to environmental objectives and our collective efforts to advance them. Examples are included in the chapters that follow.

Nevertheless, it is the public-spirited citizen, by himself, with a few comrades or neighbors, or collectively through member-based environmentally dedicated organizations, who must maintain constant vigilance and stand ready to intervene against misguided or lax regulatory authorities and hostile private interests. So it was with Beaver Creek Wilderness. Regrettably, examples abound where this must be undertaken repeatedly regarding the same distinct issue or the same treasured natural area or wildlife resource. The environmentalist can never forget that those who would alter the landscape or degrade the environment usually have the wherewithal, and often have the patience and financial incentive, to advance their interests again in the future when the political or regulatory climate seems more amenable.

The burden on the environmentalist can seem great, for one big defeat often has far-reaching and lasting impact. Consequently, one would think that citizens and their advocates would shy away from the seemingly formidable aspects of a lawsuit, or the day in and day out intense lobbying required to see the job through. It is likely that this sometimes occurs. Nevertheless, there are always others willing and able to persist. When these activists are multiplied across a country the size of the United States, they become a significant force. They seize the legal tools and go to work; truly, they become voices for the earth. They are doing so now, and I am confident they will be involved as the years ahead unfold. From their ranks come the plaintiffs in the lawsuits, the petitioners in the administrative forums, and the lobbyists in the halls of Congress and the legislatures. We will meet some of these activists later and spend some time with them.

Knaves of Yellowstone

Yellowstone National Park—born in 1872 of high ideals of principled men and the prosaic realities of protection from scoundrels. Its birth was controversial, and controversy surrounds it to this day. In its very first year, park "administration" was in thrall to poachers destroying the large game animals, including the bear and wolves, and hucksters defacing thermal features with bath houses and other visitor "facilities."

But the citizens of Bozeman, Montana were on the job. In 1873 seventy of them, a substantial portion of the existing population and one citizen of Central Park, petitioned the Secretary of Interior pleading for effective government oversight of the Park: The Bozeman Memorial. Lines were drawn, and the struggle over Yellowstone grew; but the febrile management of Interior never exercised effective control. In 1886 a despairing Secretary of Interior called upon the Secretary of War for assistance.

Pursuant to Special Orders No. 79, Headquarters, Department of Dakota, General Phillip Sheridan of Civil War and Cedar Creek fame in command —the General was a fierce advocate for protection for Yellowstone, once proposing that the Park be enlarged to five times its size— Captain Moses Harris, on August 17, 1886, marched fifty men into the Park. For the next thirty-two years, "Boots and Saddles" protected Yellowstone—an administration surprisingly ahead of its time and, for the most part, honorably conducted. In 1916 the National Parks Organic Act was passed, and in 1918 the new National Park Service took over.

Thus the role of citizens protecting our parks has been necessary, aggressive, and passionate from the earliest date. Recent activism beginning in the 1960s and continuing today is not new; it is built on a long and illustrious tradition. Today the issues are many—protection of wolves and bison being notable—and environmentalists are working hard; in point of fact they must, for the stakes are the nation's and the world's first national park.[6]

The press and the media play a very important role in this process. Public issues and controversy are their daily fare. Their interest in a particular environmental issue may wax and wane and follow-through may be sporadic, except for the latest and most persistent issues. Accuracy may suffer from the rush to meet deadlines, a need for instant and continuous feed in the electronic world (the "24/7 news churn"), and the complexity of an issue. All too frequently the brevity characterizing our instant-messaging world eliminates coverage in depth and results in error and misunderstanding. However, to environmental activists and their public interest advocates the first rule is usually to get coverage, to gain visibility, and then to engender public concern. Therefore, capturing the attention of the media is a top priority.

In the largest sense, public interest advocacy of any kind, and certainly in the case of environmental issues, is carried out in the common market place. It is inseparable from political and economic undercurrents running there. Often the folk wisdom, "the squeaky wheel gets the grease," is all too true. But consider that this communications world performs some critical functions. At a minimum, it informs the public of the issue and of the brewing controversy. It identifies the players and their motives. The press and the media educate us, at least to a minimal degree, on the general nature of the controversy. They tell what is being done to protect or advance an environmental issue and how serious the threatened harm may be. We will talk more about this later on.

There is also a perception among some people that needs to be dispelled at the outset. Despite any inferences drawn from the above, environmental law is not a mysterious and arcane field known only to a privileged elite and practiced only by well-seasoned experts. Any notion of a select few moving at rarefied levels should be dismissed. There are real people here, using courts or administrative venues to insure laws are properly interpreted and enforced, and that behavior which could negatively affect the environment is undertaken advisedly. This is fundamentally no different from most of the daily business which comes before our judicial system. Of course, experience counts, and ecological science can be highly complex. But this is what lawyers and courts do: investigate, inquire, test, and decide controversies in a rational, appropriate, and explainable manner. While environmental cases may be more complex than a simple trespass action, for instance, this does not make them unexplainable or somehow wholly mysterious. When an environmental case is more complicated than other cases, it usually only means a little more effort is required.

The specific objectives of this book, therefore, are set forth below in an order which hopefully flows logically from the story:

- To relate some basic events in the history of environmental law;
- To introduce some of the people involved: individual environmentalists, the staff of their non-profit advocacy organizations, and experts who explain the science, technology, and economics involved;
- To show that our legal and judicial systems have the institutional capability to adjust to, and then become an integral part of, the pursuit of new priorities arising from the public;
- To inform the public, and especially the interested and active citizen, that lawyers and courts are not necessarily to be feared. As a corollary: to help demystify their methods and operation;
- To lay out a record in a broad sense that may assist present and future litigants and their lawyers in approaching and tackling new issues and expectations as public concerns evolve;
- To emphasize the absolute necessity for public vigilance over envi-

ronmental matters, for governments and individual or commercial interests are always active in their own behalf, and often their agenda are contrary to environmental interests.

But before developing these points in further detail, it is necessary to set the socio-political stage in the 1960s and 1970s, for law does not develop in isolation. It is a product of its times, and it develops and evolves as public needs and circumstances develop and evolve.

Turbulent Decades

Thursday morning, July 30, 1964, Washington, DC, the Chamber of the U.S. House of Representatives; the House was in session. Bill Number 170, "to establish a National Wilderness Preservation System for the permanent good of the whole people," was before the House for a final vote. For nine long years this proposed legislation had been before Congress, but now in 1964 its time had come. Congressman John Saylor of Pennsylvania, a passionate advocate of wilderness legislation, rose to offer an important amendment. He proposed significant language expanding wilderness review of qualifying public lands. After debate, the amended bill was passed and sent to the Senate where, under the watchful eyes of the Senate leader Clinton Anderson of New Mexico and long time wilderness advocate Senator Hubert Humphrey of Minnesota, expected concurrence was readily gained. On September 3rd, in the Rose Garden at the White House, the Act was signed into law by President Lyndon Johnson. Fittingly, standing behind him were leaders of The Wilderness Society and Sierra Club, the citizen champions of the legislation.[7]

A dream more than four decades in the making had come true. The nation had committed itself to the protection of wilderness lands, areas (in the language of the Act) "where the earth and its community of life are untrammeled by man," areas that have "outstanding opportunities for solitude or a primitive and unconfined type of recreation." The priority for millions of acres of qualifying and deserving public lands became their preservation and protection, as opposed to their exploitation for specific commodity resources, such as timber, minerals, industrial development, or their commitment to building roadway networks. It was an outstanding moment in the history of mankind's relationship to his environment that democratically elected representatives of a country would rise to declare that this place, and that place, must be preserved in perpetuity in their natural primitive state.

That summer millions of people were enjoying our national parks, wilderness lands and forests, our wildlife refuges, and our scenic coasts and waterways. They drank in the vistas, hiked the trails, coasted the seashores, climbed the mountains, enjoyed the quiet and peace of the forests, floated the rivers, and shot the rapids. They entered the stillness and the wonder of wilderness. They enjoyed the wildlife and cast a line into a trout stream. They camped under the stars. They had time to reflect, to feel the heartbeat of nature and to hear her music, to recharge their soul and their will. They put aside the daily cares of their working world. Within them was stirring a new environmental consciousness, and Congress and the federal court system would be increasingly called upon to respond. The Wilderness Act, with its radical departure from traditional land management policies governing our public lands, is an excellent example of that response.

New laws and the will to enforce them are the product of the contemporary social and political fabric from which they spring. To fully understand the dynamic behind the surge of environmentalism and the beginning of environmental law, we must first look to the elemental forces at work in the country during the 1960s and 1970s. By any standard these two decades were turbulent. A catalogue includes marches, demonstrations, assassinations, riots, the forced resignation of a president, and the Viet Nam War. The Cold War saw its greatest crisis with the threat of Soviet missiles in Cuba, ninety miles off our shores. Big issues were out in the open, and the public demanded their resolution. Events moved swiftly, and many of us were not prepared for the enormous changes in American life happening all around us.[8]

But not all was grim. We saw citizens insisting on civil rights for all of our people and persevering in their demands regardless of the violence of the opposition—winning again and again in our federal courts and, eventually, in Congress with passage of the Civil Rights Act of 1964. Martin Luther King, speaking to more than 200,000 people at the Lincoln Memorial in Washington, DC in the summer of 1963, told us of his dream. Thousands, and then millions, protested the unpopular war in

Viet Nam. Their protests were heard, and they contributed significantly to our abandonment of that war in 1973. In 1962 the Supreme Court, as it had done throughout the civil rights movement, again led the way with its decision in *Baker v. Carr*, requiring apportionment of legislative districts on the basis of population, rather than political agenda or tradition.[9] This decision was extremely significant for the new environmental movement, for urban and suburban districts, where its political strength lay, were now more equitably represented in legislative bodies throughout the country. Congress followed the court's lead and in August 1965 passed the Voting Rights Act.[10] In the midst of these momentous events, we reached beyond the planet when Neil Armstrong walked on the moon in 1969.

The Wilderness Act was passed. Opposition to two proposed dams in the Grand Canyon reached a climax in the mid-1960s—the conservationists winning after a heated public campaign—and in 1975 Grand Canyon National Park was expanded to include the proposed dam sites.[11] In 1968 Redwood National Park in northern California was created preserving significant stands of the few remaining redwood forests, the world's tallest trees. Ten years later in 1978 the park was expanded, protecting additional stands from the chain saws of the logging industry.[12] A comprehensive statute protecting diminishing wildlife—the Endangered Species Act—became law in 1973.[13]

Congress was engaged on other fronts. In 1969 it passed the all-important National Environmental Policy Act. NEPA mandated that a comprehensive environmental review of major federal government actions affecting the environment must be completed and then thoroughly discussed in a detailed "environmental impact statement," an EIS, before the activity could proceed.[14] Thorough review of environmental impacts, reasonable alternatives, including the "no action" alternative, and appropriate mitigative measures were required. NEPA also created the Environmental Protection Agency, the EPA, to carry out and enforce new pollution control statutes and mandates.

Pollution control was high on the list. Early Congressional efforts to address deteriorating air and water quality dated back to the 1950s, but while the objectives were good, they completely lacked regulatory force and the appropriate government oversight necessary for effective implementation. During the late 1960s, Congress reviewed the existing ineffectual statutory language and the sparse regulatory measures, and by the close of the decade it was ready to act more decisively. Comprehensive legislation, now called the Clean Air Act, was passed in 1970 and strengthened in 1977.[15] In 1972 and again in 1977 Congress similarly addressed water quality in the Clean Water Act.[16] Far-seeing language giving significant protection to the bulk of the nation's critical wetlands was included. The Environmental Protection Agency was directed to begin and then manage and supervise the all-important regulatory processes that would turn statutory objectives into actual and measurable standards of performance and regulatory achievement.

Literature and the arts profoundly increased public awareness of environmental issues. They provide an excellent window into public attitudes and expectations. We turn to the artists, the writers, the poets, the musicians to express what we find difficult to articulate in our everyday lives, but which we long to say. They bring us inspiration, imagination, reflection, understanding, and community. The 1960s were no exception. John Muir's journals and writings of the last decade of the nineteenth century and the first decade of the twentieth were being republished and widely read. Muir extolled wilderness, the thrill of the trail and the campfire, and a sense of profound sensitivity to his surroundings in Yosemite, Alaska, and other lands —

Climb the mountains and get their good tidings.
Nature's peace will flow into you
As sunshine flows into trees.
The winds will blow their own freshness into you,
And the storms their energy,
While cares will drop off like autumn leaves.[17]

There was the empathy of poet Robinson Jeffers at his home, the famous Tor House, on the cliffs above Big Sur, looking out over the vast Pacific —

Integrity is wholeness, the greatest beauty is
Organic wholeness, the wholeness of life and things, the divine
beauty of the universe. Love that, not man.
Apart from that, or else you will share man's pitiful confusions, or

drown in despair when his days darken.[18]

Ansel Adams was publishing his photographs of Yosemite National Park, bringing those amazing images into our living rooms.

Ecology—the interrelationship of living things and their environments; the patterns of these relationships and man's effect upon them—was becoming important, not only to natural scientists but also to increasing numbers of the public. Rachel Carson's seminal *Silent Spring*, first serialized in *The New Yorker* and published in book form in 1962, alerted us to the dangerous ecological impact of man's indiscriminate use of pesticides.[19] The visionary writings and pioneering ecological views of Aldo Leopold from the mid-twentieth century were being reread and reviewed. Who can forget Leopold's old wolf "with the fierce green fire dying in her eyes" as she succumbed to the hunter's barrage? "Only the mountain has lived long enough to listen objectively to the howl of a wolf."[20]

The environment was becoming a priority, and in response, new laws were rapidly being enacted and old laws given new meaning.

But the act of passing a new law often does not alone achieve statutory objectives. Frequently, good intentions, though an obvious step in the right direction, are not enough. There must be an expectation—a will, really—in the body politic that supports the implementation of its new environmental laws. This "will" was manifest in the 1960s and the 1970s, and concerned conservationists began to draw upon that will as they called upon the federal courts to enforce the new laws and, where appropriate, to order parties to comply with them.

We wanted to be heard in those years; we wanted to make our own judgments; we wanted to participate in the great issues of the day. We were emboldened by our commitment, by our potential, and by our successes. Thousands gathered on campuses, in parks and public places, and in coffee houses discussing and arguing the huge questions of the day. All ages were there, and no subject was really off-limits. We sought support, inspiration, and comradeship from each other. And in August 1969 a multitude, representing this generation, rendezvoused at a farm called Woodstock outside of Bethel, New York. Over four hundred thousand came to celebrate themselves, each other, and their causes. They sang, they swayed, they danced to music ranging from the folk idioms of Joan Baez and Arlo Guthrie to the popular rock of The Grateful Dead and Jimi Hendrix. Contrary to the expectations of many who feared demonstrations and riots, the pervading themes were love and cooperation. A few months later, in the spring of 1970, the first national celebration of Earth Day took place across the country.

> ## "Only the mountain has lived long enough to listen objectively to the howl of a wolf."

This is not a picture of people who would easily bow to outmoded tradition and quietly await the slow evolution of needed social and political change; who would passively witness further degradation of the Colorado River in Grand Canyon or the piecemeal destruction of Beaver Creek Wilderness. While we did not always agree with one another, we would seize the initiative when and where we thought we could. In the context of these times, it was natural that those of us increasingly concerned about protection of our environment organized and went to work, vigorously arguing before Congress, state legislatures, and government agencies and officials. It followed that when someone said we might find effective remedies in a court of law, we had the will to go there. Actually, looking back at those times, it was probably inevitable. We believed firmly in the credo of "Vinegar" Joe Stilwell, that complex mid-century four star General of the Army: "We can't expect to be told about the future. If we want to find out, we must march toward it."[21]

For my generation there was a magic to the sixties and the seventies. Americans still went to work, to school, and took care of their families. We went to ball games, and we enjoyed our weekends. But the energy abroad in the land, especially in the young, was palpable. Society was trying out new and different ideas, crafting changes in old ones, and beginning to measure its future with new standards. The times were exciting! We were participating actively, and we believed we were doing some measure of good. There was a kind of intimacy with one's fellows. Of course some of this is nostalgia and yearning for the vigor and passions of youth. But reflect for a moment on the sweep and scope of the events recited above. In the context of the immense social upheaval, the 1964 Wilderness Act may seem less significant. Nevertheless, it was indicative of developing and growing environmental concerns. And these growing concerns and the desire to do something about them were an integral part of the dynamic of the times. This energized public would protect its parks and its wilderness and the quality of its air and water and, if it had to, would go to court to do so.

Historians and political scientists have had much to say about this time in America's history, and presumably they will have a lot more to say, for the turmoil, the conflict, the resolution, and the truly outsized events rivet attention and are fascinating to recount. Their impacts will always be with us. These times were exciting to experience, and some of that excitement breathes in the retelling. What did it all mean for the individual environmentalist and for the environmental litigant? What did we all have in common? Four words seem to me most descriptive and pertinent:

> **Challenge:** We accepted, even welcomed large challenges. If we could oppose the establishment, if we could march for our convictions, we had the temerity to take on the new challenges of environmentalism.
> **Conviction:** We believed in what we were doing.
> **Insistence:** We wanted to be heard; indeed we insisted upon it.
> **Significance:** We thought that individually and collectively we could make a difference in the outcome of the major issues of the day.

We embraced the teaching of Margaret Mead, the world-renowned anthropologist:

> Never doubt that a small group of thoughtful, committed citizens can change the world. Indeed, it is the only thing that ever has.[22]

And all of us, young and old, civil rights advocate and war protestor, seasoned activist and campaigner, and those new to the belief in a better environment and the preservation of our treasured public lands, had begun to sing Woody Guthrie's anthem —

This land is your land, this land is my land
From California to the New York island;
From the redwood forest to the Gulf Stream waters
This land was made for you and me.[23]

How We Got to Court

While it was certainly natural and fitting that the newly enthused and dedicated conservationists of the 1960s would go to court, an initial jurisdictional hurdle stood in our path. Would our status as advocates for a public interest—a conservation or environmental interest—be recognized and accepted? Were we appropriate parties in a lawsuit? Traditionally, this type of case required a demonstrated private or corporate interest in the subject matter—a financial, property, or contractual interest, or a constitutional question of individual rights. The answer came from up-state New York where the majestic Hudson River carves its way through the chain of the Appalachian Mountains. Storm King Mountain rises above the river's gorge north of West Point. Power companies were seeking to build a pumped storage electric generating plant there, and they had applied to the Federal Power Commission (FPC) for the appropriate permits. Local conservationists objected and filed a lawsuit in federal court. Out of this dispute came a decision that would have a far-reaching impact on American jurisprudence. It would mark the beginning of what we now call environmental law.

The distress of the local citizenry is easily understood. The plan was to continuously pump water from the Hudson River up to a large holding reservoir at Storm King and then run the water down through large power generators and back to the river. The purpose was to create a source of "peaking" electric power for many in the region. The citizens were sure the construction activities and the permanent plants, structures, and facilities would ruin the majestic mountain and degrade the beauty and enjoyment of this most scenic stretch of the Hudson River. The citizens banded together and pressed their opposition to the project before legislatures and government agencies.

But in the spirit of the time they pursued a new and untried strategy: they hired lawyers and sought legal relief from the courts. They organized themselves into the Scenic Hudson Preservation Conference, and, joined by other concerned individuals and two local municipalities, they filed a lawsuit in federal court. They asked the court to set aside the FPC order licensing the project. Plaintiffs objected that the FPC had taken the traditional approach of emphasizing economic interests and had not investigated scenic and recreational values and the effects on wildlife. Plaintiffs cited provisions of the Federal Power Act calling for the FPC to consider "beneficial public uses, including recreational purposes," when reviewing a project. Upon appeal the U.S. Circuit Court of Appeals for the Second Circuit ruled in 1965—*Scenic Hudson Preservation Conference v. FPC*—that these phrases encompassed "the conservation of natural resources, the maintenance of natural beauty, and the preservation of historic sites."[24]

Defendants maintained that nevertheless this did not give plaintiffs "standing to sue" in a court of law. "Standing" at that time meant that a plaintiff bringing an action before a court in a civil case must show actual personal or economic harm. In the words of Supreme Court decisions from the 1920s, a plaintiff, the "aggrieved party" in legal parlance, must show "he has sustained or is immediately in danger of sustaining some direct injury as the result of [enforcement of a law] and not merely that he suffers in some indefinite way in common with people generally." This was the traditional economic and self-interest interpretation of the "case and controversy" language used in Article III of our Constitution, which sets forth the scope and the limitations of the judicial powers of the United States courts. The Court of Appeals opened an expanded interpretation:

> In order to insure that the Federal Power Commission will adequately protect the public interest in the aesthetic, conservational, and recreational aspects of power development, those who by their activities and conduct have exhibited a special interest in such areas, must be held to be included in the class of "aggrieved" parties [under the Federal Power Act].[25]

Consequently, the *Scenic Hudson* plaintiffs had "standing to sue." While they did not allege traditional economic or personal harm, they did have a "special interest" in the matter at issue, this interest was set forth in the relevant statute, and thus they could bring their grievances before the court. This was seminal; it opened the door for aggrieved parties to go to court and argue issues of public interest. The body of environmental law could begin to build. And it all began in a hotly contested but very specific and local environmental issue on the Hudson River midway up the State of New York.

The reader may be wondering why the court could not move directly to the merits of the case without all this procedural folderol. A complete answer is multi-faceted, but suffice it to say here that lawsuits need litigants with firm recognized interests in the issues before the court. That interest need not be economic, but it must be identifiable and distinguishable. Cases need parties who will frame arguments cogently and, driven by their particular concerns, will persevere to a final judgment. The courts need parties who demonstrate such attention to their purpose that they will construct and argue the real issues of the case. This is reasonable. Consider the chaos which would ensue from unrestrained and undisciplined access to the courts.

While the citizens were successful and the Storm King project was never built, the *Scenic Hudson* case made few national headlines. After all, there were a lot of momentous events occurring at the time, and the public and the press were inundated with issues. Nevertheless, conservationists across the country, and particularly their member based nonprofit organizations, learned of the decision and began to grasp its potential. For a couple of years environmental cases were few and dispersed; California, Colorado, Maryland, New York again, and Texas saw early efforts. The federal court for the District of Columbia heard about important matters in Alaska. Environmental cases were soon brought in courts in Arizona, Michigan, Minnesota, New Mexico, and West Virginia. It was evident that the issue of "standing to sue" in one of these cases would come before the U.S. Supreme Court, for fundamental changes in our jurisprudence must eventually have that Court's imprimatur. The case which found its way there was brought by the Sierra Club over a proposed massive all-season resort development in the wild Mineral King Basin in the Sierra Nevada Mountains of California.

In 1972 the Supreme Court ruled on the *Mineral King* litigation. Although remanding the case to the district court for more evidence that Sierra Club members themselves had a particular interest in the Mineral King area that would suffer from development, the Court set forth the constitutional rules in *Sierra Club v. Morton*. For the plaintiff to have standing to sue, he must show he will suffer injury to a demonstrated interest, that his claim is raised within the zone of interests of the law in question, that his injury is fairly traceable to the defendant's conduct, and that a favorable decision is likely to redress the injury. The Court recognized that citizen organizations dedicated to the purposes at stake may sue on behalf of their members, provided at least some of those members satisfy these standing requirements.[26]

Regardless whether *Sierra Club v. Morton* is directly contrary to the opinions of the Court in the 1920s, or is viewed as a logical and natural expansion of those earlier opinions—argument can be made either way— I think Chief Justice John Marshall's view of constitutional provisions defining the powers of Congress in the formative years of our Constitution is particularly apt. In the seminal case of *McCulloch v. Maryland* in 1819, regarding critical language in our Constitution, and interpreting that language as conferring broad powers on Congress, Marshall wrote convincingly of the need for expansive interpretation of important language in the Constitution —

> [The] provision is made in a constitution intended to endure for ages to come, and consequently, to be adapted to the various crises of human affairs.[27]

And so it was with *Mineral King*, opening a fundamental channel for citizens to use for the implementation and enforcement of the new environmental laws these same citizens were working so hard to pass.

Environmental cases and decisions began to increase. We few early environmental lawyers—known as conservation lawyers at that time— now grew quickly in number and in breadth of issues pursued. Interested individuals, non-profit organizations, and foundations established public interest law firms dedicated to environmental matters, and these grew in number and influence. Financial resources, which had typically been slim, increased. The private bar increasingly appeared, bringing individual cases in diverse jurisdictions. Burgeoning student practice programs at law schools were particularly attracted to the field. Environmental law progressed from an idea, through early formative years of exploration and venture, to a recognized area of jurisprudence with expectations, standards, and remedies.

At The Courthouse

Getting into court—having "standing" to bring a lawsuit to assert or defend an environmental interest—only opens the inquiry. There must be law to apply, and for the public interest advocate laws protecting the environment are almost always statutory laws. These must speak to the environmental harm alleged and measure the protections intended by the legislature. The facts need to be ascertained, and appropriate relief must be determined. When a statute is to be interpreted and the facts of a case assessed in light of that interpretation, the specific language used by the legislature will be the first focus: What does the statute say? The second inquiry is prior judicial treatment of the statute: How have courts interpreted it? How have cases similar to the one before the court been handled?

However, when a statute is new, such as the Wilderness Act, or sections of previously written law have rested unused in the background, such as the recreational values section of the Federal Power Act—the Scenic Hudson case—then a more comprehensive inquiry into the congressional intent behind the statutory language is required. Legislative history—the evolution of the language in Congress—becomes very important. This frequently includes review of the language in the context of contemporary events and the underlying concerns and desires of the public. Such review greatly enhances understanding of the statutory provisions. Commencing with Scenic Hudson, courts were increasingly called upon to do this as the new environmental cases came before them.

It is important to note that this is a process, not a single event; interpretation and implementation often are complex, requiring considerable debate and a lot of adjustment. This is especially true where the objectives of a law—the Wilderness Act, for example—are new to the daily pursuits of citizens, contrary to existing governmental practices, and challenging to the habits and traditions of many of those most immediately or intimately affected. Obviously this includes the lawyers. So the work inside the relatively confined walls of the courthouse cannot avoid the world outside, the evolving democracy beyond the courthouse doors.

Furthermore, when judicial decisions determine critical relationships within our society and lay important ground rules for future conduct, courts must inevitably develop a measure of sensitivity. Thus their mission is to recognize the changing landscape within which they work and the context of new laws, all the while carefully examining and testing each case pursuant to accepted rules of procedure and evidence. Additionally, they must recognize where expanded or new interpretations of existing laws are justified in light of tested facts, whether those laws are long-standing and venerable or recently amended. This is what we hope for in a living system of law. The wisdom of Chief Justice Oliver Wendell Holmes, Jr., is compelling:

> The life of the law has not been logic: it has been experience. The felt necessities of the time, the prevalent moral and political theories, intuitions of public policy, avowed or unconscious, even the prejudices which judges share with their fellow-men, have had a good deal more to do than the syllogism in determining the rules by which men should be governed. [...] In order to know what [the law] is, we must know what it has been, and what it tends to become.[28]

It is important, therefore, that we get this right, that courts respond appropriately to these underlying currents, to the new laws, and to the new realities. They do, after all, "sit in judgment," for their structure, their role in our government, and the expectations you and I have of their operations, require that rulings and decisions be made. Legislative bodies can "pass the buck" to their successors or other branches of government, and the executive branch has a lot of discretion and can often avoid making important or difficult decisions, deciding, in fact, not to decide. Courts cannot easily do this. They must rule on the cases brought before them.

We recognize that often interpretation of the controlling law may be difficult, for the legislative process in a democracy can be messy when it comes to actual statutory language. Most legislation is a result of compromise, and the language used is frequently loosely cobbled together in response to differing views and constituencies. This can substantially affect clarity. But this is what judges do—review the law or the statute, determine legislative intent, identify the objectives, and rule accordingly. If they avoid new and tough challenges and rely too heavily upon a literal reading of yesterday's case, or indiscriminately choose to follow only traditional paths, the legislative solution sure to follow may well be worse, as it emerges from growing frustration on the part of both lawmakers and the public. Furthermore, confidence in the judicial system to provide a forum for resolution of conflicts and redress of grievances of citizens would erode.

But these fateful consequences did not come to pass. I argue that our legal system and our courts did get it mostly right in the sixties and the seventies, and they constructed a vital and lasting environmental jurisprudence. They assisted the legislative process rather than impeding it. They tackled the conflicts that arose, and they ruled on the new issues brought before them. They met the mark.

John Muir in Yosemite National Park. California

CHAPTER II

There Must Be Advocates

Concerned Citizens—The Activists

Who were these people who brought the early lawsuits; who carried their struggles to protect Grand Canyon, Beaver Creek, Storm King, and Mineral King all the way to the courthouse? How did they get the gumption, the wherewithal, and the commitment to bring lawsuits to protect or further environmental interests? How do they do it now? And why? Why do they continue today?

Think about this. You drive to your favorite hiking or walking place. You park the car, get out, collect your day pack, and take a long drink from your water bottle. Then you take a couple of steps, then more. You take a deep breath. Your senses come alive to the sounds, the scents, the peace and beauty of the place. You've just connected with our natural environment. For a moment, hopefully longer, but at least for that moment, you are an environmentalist. And at that moment, you would be angry if you discovered forces were at work to damage or even deprive you of that experience. Assume you are distressed enough that you call the park office and protest. Or maybe you just tell your neighbors or the neighborhood citizens' association. Now you've become, pro tempore, an environmental activist. Next you'll be joining a non-profit public interest group. You discover that when appropriate this organization uses the courts to protect or further its objectives. To be sure, there are some steps in this process. But this evolution of activism occurs simply and logically. Many are following such a course on a daily basis, and you can imagine yourself doing it. You are, in the most real sense, one of the millions of potential party plaintiffs in the country.

I want to introduce some of the most consistently intrepid activists and guardians of parklands, rivers, and wilderness whom I knew in the 1970s and 1980s. Their present reputation suggests that they continue to wear this mantle. These are the citizens of Utah and their legion of supporters throughout the country who defend the incredible lands of the Colorado Plateau in southern Utah. Some of these places are probably familiar to you: the iconic Delicate Arch in Arches National Park; the immense rock walls of Zion Canyon; the arresting Waterpocket Fold in Capitol Reef; the canyons and the glens of the Escalante River; the needles and pinnacles of Canyonlands; the hoodoos at Bryce Canyon; and the legendary, almost unimaginable canyon-carving Colorado River and its principal tributary, the Green River.

When one mentions the wonders of the Colorado Plateau almost anywhere in the United States, one or more of your companions may suddenly seem to square their shoulders, to stand a little taller. They may get a certain look in their eyes, a fierceness even. You will know they are among those who have been there, and who insist this unique and inspiring country remains protected. Through the Southern Utah Wilderness Alliance, Sierra Club, The Wilderness Society, The Grand Canyon Coalition, or others, they may sue and sue again to thwart those who seek to despoil these lands in any significant measure. Terry Tempest Williams calls them "Coyote, a dance upon the desert." Williams continues in her evocative "Eulogy for Edward Abbey:"

> Members of the Clan are not easily identified, but there are clues. You can see it in their eyes. They are joyful and they are fierce. They can cry louder and laugh harder than anyone on the planet. And they have enormous range.

> The Coyote Clan is a raucous bunch: they have drunk from desert potholes and belched forth toads. They tell stories with such virtuosity that you'll swear you have been in the presence of preachers.

> The Coyote Clan is also serene. They can float on their backs down the length of any river or lose entire afternoons in the contemplation of stone.

> Members of the Clan court risk and will dance on slickrock as flash floods erode the ground beneath their feet. It doesn't matter. They understand the earth re-creates itself day after day....[1]

These are worthy people for vigorous advocacy, for lobbying, and for litigation.

One of the tremendous advantages lawyers enjoy with clients like these is their willingness and capacity to work on almost any aspect of a case where the lawyer can use assistance. Indeed, they attack these tasks with enthusiasm. A perfect example was a case we brought in 1973 in the U.S. District Court for Utah. An oil and gas exploration company proposed to grade a twelve and one-half mile road in southern Utah which would cross Glen Canyon National Recreation Area (GCNRA), Capitol Reef National Park, and U.S. Bureau of Land Management land to a drill pad for an exploratory well on a grandfathered leasehold in GCNRA. The road was to generally follow a long-abandoned primitive road track that, by 1973, was really no more than a trail. The plaintiffs were two Utah environmentalists, June Viavant and Ruth Frear, and Sierra Club. This *Viavant* case illustrates perfectly how hard work and telling testimony by the individual plaintiffs themselves became pivotal. In dramatic contrast, it also shows the price paid for the egregiously neglectful attitude and lack of knowledge on the part of the Department of the Interior defendants.[2]

This is surpassingly fine country: towering multi-hued sandstone cliffs—red, yellow, and white—deeply incised canyons, water seeps in hidden alcoves harboring miniature green gardens of ferns and moss, the imposing Henry Mountains to the east, and the incomparable Waterpocket Fold, the centerpiece, rising up in a long cresting wave of white sandstone against the blue sky of southern Utah. This is country to be experienced in its wildness and its remarkable beauty—country to be savored. It should not be degraded by more oil and gas wells or additional roads. The oil drillers planned considerable grading, a large amount of bulldozer work on the right-of-way, and thorough blading of the resulting access road—a long and irreparable scar across this magnificent country.

Plaintiffs alleged that the environmental impact review process mandated by the National Environmental Policy Act of 1969, and the resulting "detailed statement" reviewing all impacts and options before making a decision, had not been carried out. Plaintiffs further alleged that defendants' road construction would compromise the wilderness review section of the act establishing the GCNRA. Work had just started when hikers—no doubt members of Williams' Coyote Clan—discovered it; earth moving equipment was approaching Capitol Reef. We lawyers went to court immediately in Salt Lake City and obtained a Temporary Restraining Order (TRO) from Judge Aldon Anderson against any further activity until a preliminary injunction hearing could be held. Eight days later, on December 11, 1973, that hearing took place.

The old United States Courthouse on Main Street in Salt Lake City's Exchange Place Historic District is typical of a lot of federal courthouses built for mid-sized cities in the early decades of the Twentieth Century. An imposing building in the center of town, it was completed in 1905 in the Classical Revival style and extensively renovated in 1932. You have probably seen courthouses with post offices on the first floor just like this in many of our mid-sized cities. A colonnade of Doric columns spans the front, while flanking the steps are detailed granite railings and two eagles with outstretched wings. Inside, the floors of the main lobby and corridors are marble, tile, and terrazzo. This architecture is intended to impress. The three original courtrooms on the second floor retain their historic appearance. They are two stories high with oak wainscot and paneling, as well as ornamental plaster ceilings with decorative coffers.[3]

We convened in the Chief Judge's courtroom, the most expansive of the three. It has an imposing elevated bench, flanked by tall banks of windows on each side, and to its right against the wall and a window was a bust of Utah's first chief judge of the U.S. District Court. In front of the bar the lawyers have plenty of space and fine large oak counsel tables. Behind the bar were oak benches that could accommodate two hundred to three hundred spectators. Local counsel and I, with plaintiffs in tow, arrived early, and already the courtroom was beginning to fill. This was Utah's second environmental case, and public interest was extremely high. Reporters already occupied prime seats, for the press was covering the case thoroughly. The issues framed the historical conflict between protection of National Park lands and other valued public lands versus development of possible mineral resources: Were any lands of outstanding scenic and recreational value really safe from the degrading and enduring impact of mineral exploration and development?

The energy of the crowd was palpable, typical of gatherings in the 1970s when large public interests were at stake. The seats quickly filled with environmental activists and advocates of oil and gas development, with Sierra Club members and contractors for oil companies, with interested members of the bar, employees of federal land management agencies, university professors and law students, and members of the general public who had heard or read of this event in the newspapers. Chief Judge Willis Ritter was hearing the case. He was widely known as a "character"—an independent thinker, hard on poorly prepared lawyers, with a frequently irascible nature. It promised to be an exciting day.

After the granting of the Temporary Restraining Order the two individually named plaintiffs, June Viavant and Ruth Frear, had traveled to the site, walked the twelve and one-half mile route for the road, and thoroughly photographed the entire locale. We put them on the witness stand, and they proceeded to accurately trace the route on U.S. Geological Survey (USGS) maps they had used at the site. They had taken more than a dozen representative and highly pertinent photographs that documented this impending travesty with precision, and they identified them by location and compass bearing. They pinpointed surrounding geologic landmarks, thus putting everything in appropriate perspective.

Counsel for the defendants cross-examined, hoping to discredit the ability of these witnesses to accurately represent the situation. The court's comments were extremely pertinent to what was soon to follow. First, the court's response to defendants' objection to a part of Ms. Viavant's testimony regarding the subject locale:

> **THE COURT:** I want to find out about this. This woman has been there. She knows what she is talking about. She is giving some information, and it is very helpful.

Then a short time later with the same witness under continued aggressive examination:

> **THE COURT:** All right. I am not going to hear any more *voir dire*,* as you call it, about that. The woman understands the contour map. This is issued by the USGS. She had an exact copy of it out there on the land, and she has located herself very well.

Then came the defendants' case. Their most critical witness was the

---

* In this instance, the examination by opposing counsel was intended to test the adequacy of the foundation for the witness's testimony, particularly regarding an exhibit we were attempting to introduce.

Superintendent of Capitol Reef National Park, the official responsible for daily management of the Park and, most particularly, its protection against degradation. Presumably he would testify to detailed Park Service review of the environmental consequences of the road and the care taken by him and his office to make the best and most sensitive decision possible. More than anyone, he would know the ramifications of a road constructed within the park he managed. Instead, this is what we heard:

> Q: COUNSEL (Mr. Greene for defendants): Mr. Wallace, have you been over the area of this road in the vicinity particularly of the BLM lands and the small intrusion into —
> A: I have not. I have flown it.
> Q: You have flown it. Have you flown it [in] a helicopter?
> A: No, sir, fixed-wing aircraft.
> Q: Have you observed from your aircraft voyage the existence of a road?
> A: Where I assume the road is to be.
> Q: All right. And have you responsibility as supervisor of Capitol Reef in connection with issuance of a permit for going onto a portion of Capitol Reef?
> A: Anything that would go into Capitol Reef National Park, yes, sir.

A few moments later, I seized the opportunity to underscore the extremely damaging nature of his testimony:

> COUNSEL (Mr. Ruckel for the plaintiffs): I'm going to object ... [T]his witness only assumes he knows where the road is.
> THE COURT: That's right. He said he assumes where the road is; he doesn't know. The objection is sustained.

What a contrast this made to the plaintiffs' intimate knowledge of the specific area at issue!

As if this were not damaging enough, during the same ten-minute span with the superintendent still on the stand, his counsel tried to resolve the touchy matter of permit status for that part of the road projected over Capitol Reef.

> COUNSEL (for defendants): It [a document purporting to promise

immediate execution of the requisite permit] bears upon the very right to go into this 660-foot intrusion into Capitol Reef. It has that much bearing, your Honor, and I would like to —

THE COURT: That is the application. Are you going to tell me that it has been granted?

COUNSEL: Yes.

THE COURT: Well, all right, why don't we get to it.

COUNSEL: I am going to tell you that it has been promised.

THE COURT: Well, now, "promised."

COUNSEL: And authorized.

THE COURT: I will tell you, Mr. Greene, I am going to cut this right off … You told me that it was granted not two minutes ago, and then you change your mind and say it is promised.[4]

At this point, I could have folded my hands, leaned back in my chair, and coasted to the end. I shortly did so. But, in a moment of zealous advocacy and disgust at this "guardian" supervisor of one of our treasured national parks, I couldn't resist a superficially obvious maneuver: I moved to strike or, in effect, to expunge, the superintendent's testimony, since he really knew nothing material about the matter. This motion is frequently used by lawyers almost reflexively to protect the record from inadmissible evidence should the case be appealed. The court, no doubt equally put off, granted the motion. Ironically, but with good reason, I had just "struck" the most revealing testimony I could want. Regardless of the court's ruling, the testimony and exchanges actually remain in the record transcript. In any event, of course, there were ample grounds for the injunction in the record, and it was soon granted. However, there is a lesson in this vignette: be quick to probe the vulnerabilities of your opponent, but make sure you have established a good record of testimony and exhibits and maintained it, for these are the real foundation of your case. Remember, an appellant court may be looking at the case later.

One is tempted to observe that defendants were poorly represented here. Actually, this is not the real lesson. Their lawyers had a bad case, compounded by egregious neglect of duty on the part of their government clients. Plaintiffs had good law, strong facts, and excellent witnesses and physical evidence. Defendants had weak facts and poor witnesses, and the combination began to irritate the judge early in the proceeding. Suffice it to say that good facts can frequently carry you a long way. Also important to note is that this case turned on the age-old methodology of questions and answers of sworn witnesses, the traditional testing of facts in a court of law. The judge invoked no unprecedented or esoteric procedures or theories. The government's dereliction was quickly and clearly revealed, and its case collapsed all on its own. The oil drillers filed an interlocutory appeal to the U.S. Court of Appeals for the Tenth Circuit. When this was unsuccessful, they abandoned their effort.

Other Participants

We have talked about individual conservationists, or environmentalists, and their member-based non-profit organizations and touched upon their roles, capacities, and achievements. It is also important to appreciate the role of the staff of these advocacy organizations. Most national organizations and many well-established regional entities have professional and administrative staff. I am continually impressed by their abilities, individual talents, and accomplishments. From close association with, and frequent observation of, these professionals, it is apparent that their achievements are the result of their competence and sustained enthusiasm. They are eager to help members organize, articulate the issues, and fight effectively for a worthy environmental objective.

In litigation or in administrative actions, staff members keep the players focused. They handle innumerable seemingly mundane tasks that collectively are critical to successful legal outcomes. Coordinating the gathering of evidence and sifting through documents become well-honed skills. Staff members help to raise money, always in short supply in the non-profit world. They handle necessary publicity. They frequently become de facto experts on one or more specific issues before the court or the administrative tribunal. In large conflicts involving several jurisdictions and venues, a staff person may be the person with the best view of the total picture. Often they are witnesses on a particular matter or issue. From years of observing and working with these professional environmentalists as they effectively and cheerfully perform this multitude of tasks, I conclude they can usually go farther on beer, pizza, and minimal rest, than most of the rest of us.

"Staff" also means management and administrative staff. All too frequently these individuals do not get the recognition they deserve, even from their own constituents. And the larger the organization, the more critical they become. Who ever heard of an effective non-profit organization with comprehensive goals, a long-range view of issues important to it, and the capability to carry out extended campaigns that did not have some level of professional administration? The ability to raise money and keep track of it, to keep office supplies on the desks, and to take care of membership service matters? Somebody to keep the computers and other electronic systems working and reasonably up-to-date? The presence of mind to pay the office rent and look after the leasehold? And, naturally, all of this also applies to the staff lawyers.

The larger non-profits have publishing programs, regular newsletters, magazines, pamphlets, and even books. All have web sites. Critical to the strength and vigor of any organization is keeping members both informed and involved. Activities such as educational forums, political involvement, and guided outings programs or day hikes are offered by many of the conservation organizations. Individual and foundation donors are always crucial to maintaining financial health, and they must be kept advised and current on the issues important to them. All of these endeavors count, for it is the whole entity that brings the lawsuits, and the more vigorous and organized the operation the more comprehensive and effective the legal program is likely to be.[5]

It is past time to recognize co-counsel and local counsel. Only two or three of the cases discussed in this book were handled solely by myself, and these were resolved quickly without the need of prolonged case development. Co-counsel are attorneys who assist the principal lawyer. But to say that they "assist" is not to place their role in a subordinate or secondary capacity; assuredly, this is not the case. The public interest lawyer is almost always under-funded in comparison to his adversaries. This was especially true in the early days when we were feeling our way and financial resources were minimal. Participation of other lawyers at reduced fees or pro bono to assist with important aspects of a case and its preparation was often crucial. This spirit of public interest, of participation in matters of significance, so illustrative of the 1960s and 1970s, has served environmental law extremely well.

It reflects clearly a participatory attitude found at all levels of society during these transformative years. This critical role and this spirit are present today. Indeed, I believe the bar will continue to rise to the occasion where and when it can for the litigant seeking to advance a recognized public interest.

Local attorneys are crucial as well. When a lawyer who is admitted and practicing in one state conducts litigation in another state, he must associate with a lawyer of that state. This gives the court a local lawyer for easy contact when needed. It also helps assure the court of the bona fides and the professionalism it expects. Local counsel participates in the same manner as co-counsel, and their knowledge of the local court and its individual practices and procedures is invaluable. Again, as with the clients, words are inadequate to express my heartfelt thanks for the absolutely critical contributions of the distinguished lawyers whose association I have enjoyed.

We should not ignore the roles, interests, and motivations of some of the defendants. In my environmental practice, and in the experiences related here, the principal defendants were usually government departments or agencies. Indeed, it is likely that this continues to be the case today. However, private interests have increasingly been involved as defendants or as intervenors, i.e. as interested parties on the other side. We will look at some private interests further on. At this point it is sufficient to say that they generally advocated their particular economic positions and points of view well, and occasionally they argued with telling force.

The presence of government entities as principal actors in environmental matters is ubiquitous. Daily they make important, even critical, decisions affecting the environment. When environmentalists sue over what they regard as a bad or harmful decision, they allege that the action taken was arbitrary, capricious, contrary to applicable law, or without legal authority. Alternatively, environmentalists may argue that defendants failed to act where required by law to protect the environment. It is important to emphasize that these government defendants, with rare exceptions, are not outright malevolent. In our view, they are simply wrong. This can happen more frequently, of course, when the administration they serve is hostile to the environment. There is a hierarchy, and for periods of time high-level political appointees of a hostile administration can direct the adoption of unfortunate and harmful policies and positions.

Government Defendants

Government officials may rightly argue that the public is not sensitive to the bureaucratic and political pressures to which they are continuously subjected. In a sense, only the civil servant truly experiences these influences and pressures. But, understanding the environmental law dynamic requires at least some familiarity with all the principal parts, and this surely includes the principal defendants. However, extended association with these agencies or departments on environmental issues, and advocacy against them, are instructive, and the observations and opinions expressed here are the product of more than two decades of active involvement with these agencies and their lawyers.

Since the cases cited in this book were almost all brought against these government defendants, it is instructive and fair to relate some of the difficulties they face in the execution of their jobs. First, and maybe foremost, agencies charged with protecting the environment, or with managing public lands, natural resources and wildlife, are chronically under-funded. The effects of this are pervasive and could be the subject of an entire book. It would be helpful to see more press and public attention given to this issue. The shortage of personnel and resources manifests itself in all operations. A lack of adequate scientific information and review frequently flows from this deficiency. Many of the sciences—biological, chemical, physical, ecological—come into play in the environmental arena. It may be argued that the plaintiffs, with their significant initial ability to select the fight to be made and its subject matter, have a considerable advantage. Initially, of course, this may be true, but this is not an excuse for insufficient scientific expertise, nor an excuse for muddled and ill-considered scientific analysis and work, throughout the life of a particular controversy.

A different series of problems arises when applicable law and regulations are in a state of rapid change. Customary approaches and traditional standards are replaced by something entirely new. It takes time for government agencies to adjust, and this can take a lot more time when the administration in charge is recalcitrant. How much of the old and familiar is still in effect, and how much, and to what extent, has a new agenda or a different management structure or imperative replaced the old? How does an administrator quickly find or develop the new skill sets required of the agency's personnel? How should the administrator deal with the common phenomenon of conflicting statutory and regulatory language? And often new statutory language or new regulations are not particularly clear or may be subject to differing interpretations. Understanding what is really meant may take time.

It needs to be reiterated that a major problem for government agencies is the always present and frequently dominant influence of politics. Whether the issue at hand is a complicated national pollution regulatory process or a question of particular management of protected public lands, political agenda can influence and even determine the position of the decision makers. Legislative control over the appropriations necessary to run a government agency is also a favorite point of leverage. Arguably this is no different from most other public affairs involving the legislative or executive branches of government, but that does not diminish its effect. The views and prejudices of the legislative or executive branches can be so influential as to render an agency almost completely ineffective in the exercise of its environmental or conservation jurisdiction. And because of political agendas, a particular agency may be just plain hostile to environmental concerns and obligations when its top-level administrators come from the very industries or trade organizations it is supposed to regulate.

Political pressure has an effect on agency function in at least three critical areas. First, the applicable law or regulatory system may be weakly written, or it avoids important aspects altogether, or it is written so obscurely that it is subject to differing interpretations. In some instances institution of an appropriate and forceful regulatory structure is ignored completely or rendered a nullity by neglect. Secondly, previously skimpy funding is further reduced. Among other serious ramifications, this makes management of multiple conflicting interests increasingly difficult. Finally, enforcement becomes lax or non-existent. Indeed, without enforcement, well-written laws and well-crafted regulatory structures may ultimately be worth little.

When the management or status of parks, forests, wildlife refuges, and other protected public lands and their resources is at issue, local businesses, mineral development proponents, the timber industry, agricultural and ranching operations, and tourist service enterprises frequently enter the dispute, and often seek to control or manage the outcome. A perfect example is a lawsuit Sierra Club and Defenders of Wildlife brought against the U.S. Department of the Interior in May 1982 in the U.S. District Court for New Mexico. The Department had just approved "hot pursuit" by local ranchers of depredating mountain lions, pursuing the animals across park boundary lines into Carlsbad Caverns and Guadalupe Mountains National Parks.

This affair began in the autumn of 1981 when the New Mexico Natural Resources Department wrote Assistant Secretary Ray Arnett of the Department of the Interior requesting permission for ranchers to run down depredating mountain lions inside Carlsbad Caverns National Park. In January 1982 Arnett agreed, stating that he would institute this as the policy of the Department of Interior. Sure enough, such permission was readily granted in early April 1982, when a lion allegedly struck the flock of a sheep rancher near Carlsbad. Actually, we learned later, this particular catamount escaped. The National Park Service, although charged under its Organic Act to preserve parks and their resources, including wildlife resources, was seemingly powerless to resist. The Secretary outranked it, and thus the Secretary's office "called the shots."

From the beginning, this *Carlsbad Mountain Lions* case had a classic Hollywood western feel. We could not avoid the image of word going out to the sheepherder camps on the open range, the herders saddling up and galloping in to ranch headquarters for instructions. We could taste the dust as the boys milled about forming up their *posse commitatus*. And then what a sight they were, thundering off through the purple sage, passing through that thin green line of park rangers, and scouring the mesas and canyons of two of our great national parks, in pursuit of the swift, the elusive, the predaceous *felis concolor*.* We could imagine them riding into town at the end of the hunt, the slain lion strapped to the back of a saddle, lathered horses pulling up to the hitching rack in front of the Secretary's Saloon, and the boys trooping in for a couple of rounds on the house and a spot of raucous bidding for the lion's hide.

Sierra Club and Defenders of Wildlife held a contrary view. We

---

* Genus—species name for mountain lions

asserted that the Park Service Organic Act mandated protection and preservation of mountain lions within parklands rather than allowing their pursuit and elimination, except under certain narrowly defined and carefully policed exceptions having to do with public safety and protection of park resources. Counsel for the government quickly agreed that permission for additional hot pursuit would not be granted without adequate notice to plaintiffs' counsel, pending disposition of the litigation. We called this the "cold pursuit" option. Defendants then commenced backing and filling through discovery and motion processes and continued this retrograde shuffle throughout the next twelve months. They were anxious to avoid a trial or have the issues definitively resolved on some summary motion. Despite these tactics, however, it became increasingly clear that the court was not going to let them off the hook.

By the spring of 1983, government lawyers, while admitting the April hot pursuit incident and the existence of Arnett's response to the State of New Mexico, declared that in fact there was no established policy of "hot pursuit," and the Assistant Secretary's declaration of it in January 1982 was actually not the policy of the Department of the Interior. Furthermore, Interior would be preparing an environmental assessment (EA)* regarding possible measures, including hot pursuit, which could be taken in the future to mitigate the concerns of ranchers. Litigation activities were then suspended pending completion of the EA.

Meanwhile the environmentalists themselves had been hard at work in the political arena. New Mexico had an election, and the political tables turned. The newly elected government of New Mexico informed the Secretary's office that the State's policy had changed; it now opposed hot pursuit and the killing of allegedly depredating lions on national park lands. In June 1983, the Assistant Secretary capitulated. The parties entered into a joint stipulation of dismissal that the court signed on July 22. In order that the environmental assessment not be used some time in the future to ease the path for subsequent predator control decisions of this ilk, we urged, and the government stipulated, that the existing EA process be terminated. We then holstered our own weapons and adjourned to our cantina for beer and pizza.

---

* A less rigorous precursor to a detailed environmental impact statement under the National Environmental Policy Act.

There is much useful information to be drawn from this *Carlsbad Mountain Lions* case. Both sides played their political cards with vigor, the plaintiffs even going to the ballot box. The players were significant: the office of the Secretary of the Interior, large well-known national environmental organizations, and ultimately the voters of the State of New Mexico. This was a sensitive matter, involving what amounted to a direct rebuke of the Assistant Secretary. We lawyers for the plaintiffs, of course, had the support of the forceful language of the National Parks Organic Act where Congress declares that the "fundamental purpose" of the national parks is —

> to conserve the scenery and the natural and historic objects and the wildlife therein and to provide for the enjoyment of the same in such manner and by such means as will leave them unimpaired for the enjoyment of future generations.[6]

While politics eventually decided the issue, this language was there to remind the disputants of national park purposes, and the court was always available on short notice to take a hand if it became necessary. The Organic Act language would have been controlling if the case had reached a critical point generating a ruling or decision by the court on the law or on the merits.

This case is another good example of how our laws and our court system, with the assistance of lawyers trained to use them, can be particularly effective. An alarming and precipitous action of a high-ranking government official was suspended until more reasonable thinking prevailed. The presence of the case, and the inevitable role of the judge, if the matter was not resolved prior to trial, reminded the government that it could not postpone its own decision forever. The end result was unqualified and dispositive.

A last comment on this matter is appropriate. There are cases where one party or the other, and very occasionally where both sides, are willing to risk a comprehensive court decision on the merits. We had a feeling that this would have been a good one for the environmentalists. Such a decision could have set a widely applicable precedent covering many aspects of national park management policy favorable to wildlife protection. The Secretary of the Interior's office had muscled aside the National

Park Service and made an overt and practically unconditional political decision, with no reference to the statute that delineates the purposes for which national parks are to be managed. We had reason to look favorably on a trial that would highlight ranchers and their agents in hot pursuit of a whole variety of animals—mountain lions, bears, wolves, wolverines—through scores of our national park lands, while tourists, who had come in major part to see this very wildlife, looked on in shock and amazement. As noted previously, good facts can take you a long way. Needless to say, it is quite likely that some of the Interior Department personnel and some of the lawyers in the U.S. Attorney's office saw this same image.

At this juncture, I must proffer an important admonition. It is often easy to arraign administrators and government managers, especially when their conduct seems outrageous and the environmental stakes are high, and I will continue to do quite a bit of that. But it is important to understand, if not condone, the difficulties faced and the burdens borne by our opponents. Besides, it is always good advocacy to know your opponents' case. Finally, it is important to acknowledge in full measure that I have experienced several examples of competent and even sensitive actions and decisions on the part of my government adversaries. And occasionally, they are the first to point the rest of us in the right direction.

It is time now to return to the Grand Canyon. But before we do, I want to extol one more time the citizen environmentalists, the backbone of the environmental movement and the plaintiffs in these cases. We have talked about them and applauded their dedication and their competence. I believe their deeper motives and their spirit are captured well by the songwriter and singer John Denver in "Rocky Mountain High" —

He climbed cathedral mountains, he saw silver clouds below.
He saw everything as far as you can see.
And they say that he got crazy once and tried to touch the sun,
And he lost a friend but kept his memory.

Now he walks in quiet solitude the forests and the streams,
Seeking grace in every step he takes.
His sight has turned inside himself to try and understand

The serenity of a clear blue mountain lake.

And the Colorado rocky mountain high,
I've seen it rainin' fire in the sky.
You can talk to God and listen to the casual reply.
Rocky Mountain high (in Colorado)....

Now his life is full of wonder but his heart still knows some fear
Of a simple thing he cannot comprehend.
Why they try to tear the mountains down to bring in a couple more,
More people, more scars upon the land.
And the Colorado rocky mountain high,
I've seen it rainin' fire in the sky.
I know he'd be a poorer man if he never saw an eagle fly.
Rocky Mountain high....[7]

CHAPTER III

The Grand Canyon

Protecting the River Environment

When John Wesley Powell embarked upon his epic journey down the Colorado River in 1869, much of his route was unexplored, and no one had yet run the length of the awesome Inner Gorge of the river in the Grand Canyon. It was truly wild and forbidding—in Powell's phrase, The Great Unknown. But as we have seen, by the 1970s thousands were rafting the river and running its rapids—14,000 in 1976 alone.[1] Critical natural features were being overwhelmed by the impact of too many undisciplined river-runners, and the ecology of the river and the quality of the canyon experience were being critically compromised. Powell's "Great Unknown" was being loved to death.

Increasingly alarmed at conditions in the canyon, the National Park Service commissioned a study and review of the impacts, to be conducted by the University of Northern Arizona at Flagstaff. In 1976 the study team released a comprehensive and scathing preliminary report detailing the degradation along the river resulting from lack of management of river-running practices and activities. The serious adverse impacts identified by the study team included:

- Significant deterioration of areas around heavily frequented attraction sites just off the river itself, such as Vaseys Paradise and Elves Chasm, a charming grotto just off the river with a delicate waterfall in a shady side canyon of ferns and mosses;
- Degradation of thirty prime camping sites on the shores of the river from intense use by river-runners. This included uncontrolled scavenging of logs and large branches for campfires, resulting in the loss of critical habitat for small animals;
- Proliferation of indiscriminate and damaging "social" trails and pathways along the river and into side canyons, which trampled vegetation, encroached on sensitive habitat, and caused severe erosion problems;

- Poor waste disposal measures, including human waste;
- Noise and pollution from the unlimited use of motors on rafts owned and run by concessionaires, particularly on the large rafts (holding up to twenty passengers).[2]

Natural processes and the fragile ecological systems were being overwhelmed by these impacts with no opportunity to recover. The underlying difficulty was the narrow confines of the canyon itself. Everyone floated the same rapids, used the same beaches for resting and camping, and trod their way to the same attraction sites in narrow side canyons. A competent and detailed management system was needed to reverse these effects of unregulated usage. It was past time for the Park Service to manage river use not only for the convenience of concessionaires, but also for the quality of the river-running trips and the environmental integrity of the canyon's ecosystem.

By the mid-Seventies, the great majority of visitors floating the river and running the rapids signed up for trips with a number of licensed concessionaires. These were private guide and outfitting companies working under permits issued by the Park Service. The permits—set to expire in 1977—were up for renewal, but the river study and review was still evolving, and the Park Service had yet to produce the overdue river management plan. No significant protective regulations had been promulgated, and no detailed environmental review and impact statement had been completed as required under the National Environmental Policy Act (NEPA). This did not deter the Park Service from stubbornly proceeding with apparently automatic renewal of all existing permits for terms of three years! This would have allowed the damaging behavior and practices to continue far too long, and degradation of the canyon environment was certain to accelerate.

Consequently, early in 1977 Sierra Club and its allies decided to seek legal remedies. In the spring, we filed suit on their behalf against the Park Service in the U.S. District Court for Arizona. Our complaint sought relief directing the Park Service to carry out its statutory and trust responsibilities to the public and the park. Specifically, we sought an order requiring completion of the study, adoption of a river management plan, completion of an environmental impact statement (EIS) under the requirements of NEPA, and the inclusion of specific operational provisions in the concessionaire contracts which would protect the river environment. The large river-running outfits intervened on the side of the Park Service. Naturally, they defended their newly granted permits. Concessionaire resentment was so heated that two of the more belligerent filed a counterclaim against the Sierra Club, asserting it was unlawfully interfering with their contractual relationships with the Park Service. This counterclaim was dismissed by the court in the fall of 1978 as groundless.

Inner Gorge, Grand Canyon National Park, Arizona

The major river-running companies made most of their money by using large-capacity inflatable rafts fitted with outboard motors. These large rafts accommodated more paying passengers, and the unrestricted use of motors enabled operators to process passengers through the canyon at a fast pace. The quicker the trip and the more people crowded into each raft, the more customers that could be accommodated during a given period of time, and thus the greater financial return to the companies. The concessionaires viewed regulatory control as anathema, and they particularly fought any restrictions on their use of motors. They argued that permit conditions of this sort threatened the financial core of their business operations, and that the consequences would be to deny a large number of the public the opportunity to experience the very heart of the Grand Canyon and the thrill of running its rapids. They also argued that motors made trips safer—boats could quickly maneuver out of difficult and even dangerous situations.

Sierra Club and the other plaintiffs were superbly positioned to effectively counter these arguments. One of the individual plaintiffs was Ken Sleight, owner of Pack Creek Ranch, a horse and guest ranch outside of Moab, Utah. Described a couple of years ago by a reporter as "lean, dusty-booted, hard of hearing, wear[ing] jeans and long-tailed shirts untucked," Ken was well known among those familiar with activities on the Colorado River. Legend has it that he was the model for the lapsed Mormon renegade Seldom Seen Smith in Edward Abbey's 1975 iconoclastic novel *The Monkey Wrench Gang*, the "eco-protest bible" of present day preservationists.[3] Ken began taking guests on float and rafting trips down the river in the 1960s. He let the canyon's natural features dictate how he would approach the canyon and conduct his operations. In contrast, most of the big river-running companies thought of their operations in terms of maximizing their economic benefits regardless of the impact on the river corridor.

Ken Sleight respected the river's ecology. He believed preserving the river environment in its natural unimpaired state depended upon man's sensitivity to the natural systems, and that these should not be compromised for corporate convenience. He also believed motors on rafts should be outlawed or at a minimum strictly limited. The incessant roar of motors and their accompanying air pollution and dripping gasoline and oil should be left behind. The canyon was infinitely more enjoyable when its true grandeur unfolded accompanied only by the music of the water, the wind, and the storms. Much of the opponents' economic argument and their safety alarms sounded hollow when measured against Ken's years of successfully, safely, and quietly floating guests through the deepest parts of the canyon.

Ken Sleight's importance to the litigation should not be underestimated, even though the degradation and pollution issues commanded more immediate attention. The principal remedy plaintiffs sought—a strong and effective river management plan bolstered by effective regu-lations—would address the problems and would implement solutions. The large rafting companies resisted as vigorously as they dared, hoping for the mildest possible operational regulations and conditions. But, as a consequence of the forcefulness of the Northern Arizona University study, the river-running outfits would enjoy very limited success. Super-ficially, their position appeared weak. However, the concessionaires pre-sumptively had two strong arguments: they were the only entities available that could get large numbers of visitors on the river and through the canyon, and by virtue of their years of experience they were the best "on the river" authorities. They would claim the Park Service and university "experts" could not have that direct knowledge necessary to understand the intricacies of commercial river-running operations in the Grand Canyon. Here Ken Sleight's expertise became critical.

At the beginning of a lawsuit, the judge generally knows little or nothing about the applicable facts, and while he may be familiar with the parties or their lawyers, he does not know the specifics of their rela-tionship to, or positions on, the underlying facts and issues. What the judge does "know" or believes, he tries to put aside when he picks up the papers filed by the plaintiffs—their "complaint." From this point the case forms, the controversy or dispute is defined, and the case proceeds in the usual manner of reviewing applicable law, gathering evidence, and hearing argument. Soon after plaintiffs file their complaint, defendants respond. Parties who have an interest in the outcome of the case, but are not specifically named and joined in the action by the plaintiffs, may move to intervene. The river-runners did this, and, with no objections from the plaintiffs, they were joined as defendants.

Now the importance of Ken Sleight became more apparent. The judge learned there were divergent views within the river-running com-munity itself. In addition, Ken brought to the table his expertise as a commercial river-runner with years of experience—he knew the river and its challenges as well as anyone. The intervenors could not claim they were the only real experts or that their way of running the river was the only option. Ken knew firsthand the degradation of unconstrained oper-ations, and he knew the river could be run in a manner more compatible with its environment. Such details are important. Knowledge of the vul-nerabilities of a party's position, and the ability to reveal and even take advantage of those vulnerabilities, can be pivotal.

In all litigation, few things are more important than the credibility of the parties. Here the force of the concessionaires' arguments and justifications was materially reduced by Ken Sleight's contrary positions. More importantly, the significance of the University of Northern Arizona study to the outcome of the litigation was correspondingly enhanced. Because the Park Service was supine, because the contending environmentalists and large commercial river runners were in their expected positions of opposition, and because the ability of the latter to effectively argue special knowledge and unique experience was credibly challenged, attention increasingly focused on the remaining major players—the authors of the study and their preliminary report and findings. The "preliminary" report became the critical operative evidence.

In all litigation, few things are more important than the credibility of the parties.

I had ample opportunities to emphasize this. Like most environmental cases in the early years of environmental law, there were at least a couple of pre-trial hearings before the court on fundamental legal questions, the scope of pre-trial discovery, or procedural or housekeeping matters. Inside a courtroom, the lawyers sit at large tables in front of and below the judge. These "counsel tables" are the size of a good-sized dining room table. Counsel for the parties are arrayed around their respective table. Files, frequently many files, are spread out, legal pads are in evidence, and boxes with more files, copies of important documents, or transcripts of depositions may be on the floor. Today, laptop computers with their cords and accoutrements are frequently present. In the first hearing before the court in this case, it occurred to me there was a way to keep a degree of constant focus on the river study regardless of the courtroom activities of the moment.

The study results and report were in two substantial bound volumes. If I cleared a spot on our counsel table for these volumes at the foremost edge facing the bench and then deliberately (but of course in a nonchalant manner) reached over—maybe even partially stood—to get a volume and open it for a reference, all the while listening intently to opposing counsel's argument, and then closed the volume and returned it to its place. I would hopefully keep the contents of the study continuously in the forefront of the judge's mind. So I did this intermittently through at least two hearings. Occasionally, of course, I really did need to look something up! Of course, I do not know if this maneuver made the intended impression. However, the judge often referred to the study. He was perplexed that the Park Service itself commissioned the review after concerns about the impacts of river-running operations arose within the agency, but then backed away from the findings and recommendations and renewed the concessionaire contracts for three years with little or no real explanation. We wanted to reinforce this thinking.

This was obviously "acting" of a sort, but courtrooms and lawyers are used to such tactics. The business before a court is serious, and lawyers and judges almost invariably treat it that way, but the setting, the advocacy nature of the process, and the conviction lawyers frequently feel for the merits of their clients' case lend themselves to a measure of play-acting. And while my subtle (or not so subtle) use of the study may seem a bit contrived, it was undoubtedly true that—aside from the Grand Canyon itself —the study was the most important player. Effective advocacy is often more than exhaustive preparation and skilled use of rules of procedure or rules of evidence, necessary as these are; it is also emotion or attitude and creation of atmosphere and even drama.

Our job as counsel was to convince the court that there must be a river management plan. From that plan would flow regulations and conditions that would protect the river and its environment. The strength of our evidence, the Northern Arizona University study, was impressive. We felt confident we would prevail. The Park Service, now prodded into action, finally agreed:

- It released a draft River Management Plan that called for correction of the principal environmental abuses;
- The draft plan recommended phasing out the use of motors on the river;
- It ordered that the concessionaires remove all human wastes from

camping areas and rest spots;

- It banned the burning of wood fires, except with wood brought in by the concessionaires, in order to preserve small animal habitat and help prevent beach erosion;
- And the Park Service began a serious effort to correct the problems created by the multiple and random trails that had been trampled into the environment of the river in many places.

Finally, in the summer of 1979, the Park Service released its final Colorado River Management Plan (CRMP) incorporating these critical mitigative, regulatory, and corrective measures, including a phase-out schedule for motors. In March 1980 the Park Service agreed on the court record to include the regulatory provisions of the management plan in the outfitter and river-running concessionaire contracts as they came up for renewal. At that point, we joined the United States' motion to dismiss the litigation.[4]

Nevertheless, some issues would not go away. In the early fall of 1980, the concessionaires filed their own lawsuit in the U.S. District Court for Arizona against the National Park Service, seeking declaratory judgment from the court that the elimination of motors was invalid on the grounds that it was arbitrary and capricious, or alternatively that it represented an attempt to designate wilderness without congressional authorization. We intervened in the litigation, now on the side of the Park Service, to help defend the plan and its incorporation into the contracts. However, this case reached no resolution because Congress itself "intervened." A rider attached to the FY 1981 Budget Appropriation Act—an "earmark" in today's parlance—directed that a given number of visitor use days would be determined which would provide for the continued use of motors, albeit on a more controlled basis. Motors would be allowed, but their number or frequency would be regulated. This ended the concessionaires' litigation.

Today environmental imperatives weigh heavily in management of the park. After all, if the environment of a national park deteriorates to any significant degree, much of what makes it special and unique is subverted, and the experience and enjoyment of the public correspondingly declines. Indeed it is the special qualities of the parks, their superb scenery, natural conditions, relatively pristine air and water, and the scrupulous protection of their unique features, that makes them worthy of national park status. But recognition of these preservation priorities has not been easy to achieve. It is important to understand why. And to understand where we are now, it is helpful to examine how we got here.

The establishment act for Yellowstone National Park in 1872 stated that a fundamental purpose of the park was to provide a "pleasuring ground" for the public.[5] From the earliest date, emphasis on public access providing for the enjoyment of the parks by the recreating public became the dominant view of the Park Service. Preservation of pristine qualities and protection of the environment of the parks were subordinated to promotion of public use and development of accommodations to facilitate that use. There has been a central rationale behind this: the Park Service has needed the broadest public support to protect these resources as public parks, and to encourage expansion of the National Park System to include a comprehensive representation of the natural wonders of our country. Thus the emphasis on public access and use is explained and justified. This argument was apparently reinforced by language in the National Parks Organic Act of 1916, stating that a basic purpose of the national parks is to "provide for the enjoyment" of them by the public.[6]

The consequences of this policy included, of course, the Park Service's ready renewal of the permits and contracts with the Grand Canyon river-running outfits in 1977, despite growing evidence that the river-running practices of these same concessionaires were causing significant harm to the canyon and the river. Even though the modern environmental movement was gathering steam in the 1960s and the 1970s, and public support of its objectives was accelerating into a strong political force, the Park Service seemed impervious to change. Richard Sellers, in his important 1997 history of the Park Service, *Preserving Nature in the National Parks*, articulated the Park Service attitude and its roots very well —

> The long dominant emphasis on accommodating public use in parks had a profound impact on the National Park Service, leading to the entrenchment of specific values and perceptions. With tourism and the economics of tourism being fundamental to the parks' very existence, the utilitarian, businesslike proclivities of park management

(spawned in Yellowstone and other early parks) thrived as the system grew. Striving for ever more parks and better accommodations, the Service measured its success by indicators such as annual visitor counts; the increasing scope of its programs and size of the park system; and the number of new campgrounds, visitor centers, and related developments....

The ever-demanding construction and development programs relating to public use of the parks ensured the ascendancy of those professions overseeing such work and greatly influenced Park Service funding and staffing priorities. From Mather's [first director of the National Park Service] selection of engineers to fill superintendencies to the present day, the development professions have consistently maintained prominence within the Service's highest ranks, whether in Washington, in other central offices, or in the parks.[7]

However, if we retrace our steps back to the establishment act for Yellowstone National Park and read more thoroughly, we find that Congress was far more expansive in the language it used to protect that amazing place. Congress dedicated Yellowstone as a public national park and intended that it to be enjoyed by everyone, but Congress also directed that the Secretary of the Interior "shall provide for the preservation from injury ... of all natural curiosities or wonders within said park, and their retention in their natural conditions."[8] The Organic Act of 1916 also speaks of preservation and protection ethics, placing the "enjoyment" language in the context of more comprehensive objectives:

[The purpose of the national parks] is to conserve the scenery and the natural and historic objects and the wildlife therein and to provide for the enjoyment of same in such manner and by such means as will leave them unimpaired for the enjoyment of future generations.[9]

The 1970s would see the beginning of portentous change toward this larger purpose. Much of the underlying cause can be attributed to the impact of the many millions of visitor days the parks were experiencing each year—numbers simply unimaginable in the early days of the National Park System. Such a volume of visitors can only be accommodated where the Park Service carefully manages their impact upon park environments. Rules, regulations, and management plans must be instituted to carry this out. Fundamental scientific data must be collected, analyzed, and regularly updated. Visitor activities and their impact upon the environment must be monitored to insure regulations and plans are effective. Despite these realities, accommodation of entrenched interests and old habits gives way reluctantly, and therefore necessary changes must often be forced upon the agency. The status quo is frequently more comfortable than adjustment to the winds of change, with their complexities and uncertainties. Furthermore, for many concessionaires, outfitters, tour operators, and "gate" or entrance communities, the associated traditional revenue streams of the old ways are expected and jealously guarded. Thus this interest group will often fight doggedly to maintain the status quo. The *Grand Canyon River Running* case was a good example of this all too frequent dynamic.

Management of the Grand Canyon was not the only place in the mid-1970s where the National Park Organic Act was being measured and interpreted. As frequently happens in the law, important precedent setting cases that simultaneously address the same fundamental legal issues can be pending in more than one jurisdiction. Events were taking place in California that were to have a profound impact on the degree of protection given to all our national parks, including Grand Canyon National Park. Thus before continuing with the Grand Canyon story, we need to briefly review activities out in the redwood forest country of northern California. The struggle for a Redwood National Park reached a critical stage in the 1970s, as rapacious logging threatened many of the last stands of virgin redwoods—*Sequoia sempervirens*—the world's tallest trees. Entire groves of three hundred foot and taller redwoods were rapidly succumbing to the whine and the bite of the chainsaw, and there were precious few of these groves left. After an epic campaign by Sierra Club, Save the Redwoods League, and others, Congress established a truncated Redwood National Park in 1968.[10]

However, due to drainage patterns and redwood ecology, continued massive logging outside the initial park boundaries threatened redwood stands within the park. The erosion that ensued from denuding precipitous slopes directly upstream from the park sent thousands and even millions of tons of silt and debris into the creeks and drainages, which were then carried downstream into the park. There they accumulated on riparian flats where stood the tallest of all the redwoods. Continued buildup of this silt could smother the roots of these magnificent specimens, eventually killing them altogether. In addition, water runoff from the heavy rains common in redwood country was no longer retained by the absorbent qualities of a healthy thriving forest. The waters increased at flood stage and overflowed into the riparian groves downstream further endangering the redwood stands.

Congress directed the Park Service to do all it could to eliminate this outside threat, even to the point of acquiring additional lands. Once again, the Park Service moved timidly, while trees within precious groves continued to fall and logging practices above the park threatened the redwoods within the park. Sierra Club and allies sought relief in the U.S. District Court for Northern California, citing the affirmative action obligations contained in the statute. Over the course of three years ending in 1976, Judge William Sweigert wrote three opinions, each emphasizing the Park Service duty—a "fiduciary responsibility"—to proactively protect the park. The court reviewed and reached for every remedy available and, in doing this, reinforced the affirmative duties of the Park Service to act aggressively to protect its resources and values. Much was done, but ultimately the court could only take limited steps where large strides were necessary. Consequently, the court's last opinion declared that the Park Service had finally done all it could under existing law.[11]

Congress again intervened. In 1978, it expanded Redwood National Park to include many contested buffer forestlands. But also, thinking of future conflicts between the parks and those who sought to exploit them or ignore their preservation, Congress went well beyond Redwood National Park and amended the National Parks Organic Act of 1916 to include the following language regarding activities permitted in national parks:

> The authorization of activities shall be construed and the protection, management, and administration of these areas shall be conducted in light of the high public value and integrity of the National Park System and shall not be exercised in derogation of the values and purposes for which these various areas have been established, except as may have been or shall be directly and specifically pro-

vided by Congress.[12]

This was a very significant step in strengthening protection of our national parks, including Grand Canyon. And now the National Park Service itself, following the congressional mandate, explicitly recognizes the dominance of the protection imperative in its current Management Policies:

> *Section 1.4.3. The NPS Obligation to Conserve and Provide for Enjoyment of Park Resources and Values.*
>
> The fundamental purpose of the national park system, established by the Organic Act and reaffirmed by the General Authorities Act, as amended, begins with a mandate to conserve park resources and values:
>
>> Congress, recognizing that the enjoyment by future generations of the national parks can be ensured only if the superb quality of park resources and values is left unimpaired, has provided that when there is a conflict between conserving resources and values and providing for enjoyment of them, conservation is to be predominant. This is how courts have consistently interpreted the Organic Act.[13]

The evolution is clear once we have this historical perspective. We have come from a time when the parks were managed to maximize public visitation and use, and where many severe environmental impacts were virtually ignored, through a time of growing sensitivity to environmental concerns, to our present recognition that "conservation is to be predominate." Thus, uses of park resources which result in harm to those resources and the values they encompass are prohibited or strictly controlled. The need for this is explained by Congress "in light of the high public value and integrity of the National Park System," and by the Park Service in terms of ensuring that park resources and values are preserved "unimpaired" for the enjoyment of future generations. This chain of events is also an excellent example of the federal courts and Congress working in tandem to improve protection of all of the national parks.

Nevertheless, despite elevation of environmental imperatives in Park Service stewardship, contention over management of the Colorado River in the Grand Canyon continues to the present day. The River Management Plan was amended in 1989 and again in 2006.[14] Lawsuits have been filed when impasse has been reached on sensitive issues and inter-pretations, decisions have been rendered, and settlements reached. But important issues continue to engender fierce dispute. The use and reg-ulation of motors on river rafts is a recurring issue. Given the limited number of human visitor days the river environment can tolerate without degradation and differing views on the quality of the river experience to be protected, animosity between proponents of generous use of motors and advocates of quieter more serene oar-manned rafts or boats always seems ready to break out. Visitor-day allocation ratios between these groups, and even within them, and the methodologies used to define vis-itor days and to determine allocations, are practically guaranteed to pro-voke friction.

So, have we made any progress? A lawsuit filed in 1977 and the original Colorado River Management Plan that resulted seem insignifi-cant in light of thirty plus succeeding years of perpetual debate over the details of management policies, periodic adjustment and refinement of the Plan, repeated visits to the U.S. District Court, and the impression that many of the larger questions cannot be resolved with finality. This, however, is only one part of the story. There are two overwhelming facts that cannot be ignored: millions of people want to visit Grand Canyon National Park, and more than four million will do so each year; and there is only one Colorado River, and each year thousands will "put in" at Lees Ferry or Diamond Creek and run it. There is no practical way to accom-modate everyone or give each individual complete freedom to enjoy the Grand Canyon without limitations.

In the end, park use and river use must be managed, and this requires scientific study and effective statutory and regulatory provi-sions. Experienced staff must be on hand to draft regulations, develop management plans, monitor impacts upon the park and its resources, and provide enforcement where and when needed. And indeed, the lengthy and detailed thirty-six page Park Service Record of Decision adopting and explaining the 2006 River Management Plan is a far cry from the original 1980 plan. Here is a roll call of topics addressed:

- Determination of visitor day limits
- Allocation between commercial and private visitor days, including lotteries and wait lists for the latter

- Regulation of daily, weekly, and seasonal launch limits
- Group size limitations
- Trail maintenance and its companion obliteration of social trails
- Revegetation of denuded areas
- Campsite delineation
- Monitoring the presence of drift wood
- Erosion control
- Special provisions to protect endangered species
- Removal of human waste
- Continuous monitoring of ecological conditions

So progress has been made. The river and its environment are better protected.[15]

While debate will continue about the extent and interpretation of many of the provisions to protect the canyon and the restrictions on activities they direct or imply, it is at least widely recognized that some basic limitations on use of the canyon environment and practical standards of conduct must be observed.

Reading this history, you may wonder: Why did it take so long? Why the attenuated path? Why doesn't the court just draw up and implement its own river management plan and be done with it? These are fair questions. Comprehensive answers would involve, among other considerations, in-depth examination of the abstruse subject of the separation of powers in our democratic government, a task beyond our scope here. However a brief primer within the context of the River Running case is germane. The fundamental tasks of our three branches of government are familiar to us all: the legislature writes the law, the executive department executes or enforces the law, and the judiciary interprets the law in the context of cases brought before it. Of course, these roles are so broad that overlap and even conflict naturally occur. There is, therefore, an underlying tension between these branches of government, which we often identify as our system of checks and balances.

In the *River Running* case, plaintiffs asked the court to interpret the law governing National Park Service administration of national parks, specifically as applied to Grand Canyon National Park. We believed, on the evidence, that the court would find the Park Service had not acted in accord with its statutory obligations. We further believed the logical and most effective way for the Park Service to comply with these obligations was to promulgate a river management plan and incorporate applicable provisions of that plan into the concessionaire permits. After preliminary maneuvering in court, the Park Service agreed, and the court did not have to rule. The burden of proceeding with solutions to the deteriorating conditions in the canyon then rested firmly upon the Park Service, delay was presumably in the past, and a serious river management plan was to be developed and its provisions implemented. The question at this point was no longer whether the Park Service had acted unlawfully but what was going to be done in the future.

At this stage, it becomes evident that the executive branch—in this instance the Park Service—must carry out the task. The court has neither the resources nor the staff. What was now required was the expertise and ability to refine the Northern Arizona University study and translate it into a published river management plan. Administrative machinery was necessary to draw up a draft plan, receive input from interested parties and the public, and promulgate a "final" plan. Knowledgeable staff was necessary to advise and then to enforce the regulations incorporated. And a continued Park Service presence was needed to monitor conditions in the canyon and recommend changes in the plan as circumstances indicated.

The court, of course, can continue its jurisdiction over the case, require periodic reports, and provide an avenue for a party to return to court requesting further interpretation or even enforcement measures where appropriate. Furthermore, the court has the U.S. Magistrate arm available and the power to appoint a special master to resolve conflicts, review evidence, and make needed rulings or refer measures back to the court for further treatment. But while these powers and authorities are of great utility, in the context of the River Running case they are essentially there to assist and direct the executive department agency—the Park Service—not to replace that agency's appointed functions. The court is always available to explain orders it has made and to resolve important disagreements. But despite the many difficulties that may arise, unless the judge is ready to put on the uniform of a full-time Park Service ranger, and don the iconic hat, he must leave the day-to-day job to the Park Service. This fundamental qualification does not, of course, prevent, or even discourage aggrieved parties from walking over to the courthouse; it only defines the intrinsic reach or limits of the court's jurisdiction. And when it comes to Grand Canyon, the path to the courthouse is well known.

Defending the Quiet and Solitude of Grand Canyon

Another area of park management has required even more judicial review than river running and is seemingly more complex and difficult to resolve. The awe inspired by Grand Canyon is not only enjoyed on the river, on the trails, and from overlooks along the rim. It is also experienced from the air. The first recorded air tour overflight was in February 1919. The first tour operator with regularly scheduled flights began operation in 1927, taking customers up in the classic six-seat Stinson Detroiter. A trendsetter for its time, the Detroiter was equipped with the very latest innovations: a heated cabin and soundproofing! The tour operator flew out of an airstrip on the South Rim of the canyon near Red Butte. Air tours steadily increased over the next sixty years, and their frequency accelerated with completion of Grand Canyon Airport in 1965, three miles south of the park boundary at Tusayan. Today much of the air traffic originates from Las Vegas, Nevada, ninety air miles away.[16]

By 1971, aircraft flights and noise were widespread and often pervasive over many areas of the park. In 1972 an agreement went into effect, requesting—but not requiring—pilots to maintain a distance of 1,500 feet (subsequently raised to 2,000 feet) above and horizontally from all scenic overlooks and trails; but these limitations were completely ignored. A few years later, in 1978, Park Service personnel collected and reported data that aircraft sound was heard up to 95 percent of the time in many places, with up to 58 aircraft observed each hour on some days within portions of the Park. By the early eighties conditions further deteriorated with helicopter use pushing rapidly toward saturation. In fact these craft would hover deep within the canyon and within a hundred feet of attraction sites such as the Inner Gorge, Dear Creek Falls, Thunder Falls, and the Little Colorado River confluence. The noise from helicopters down in the canyon and close to its walls was deafening! One trip would actually land on a sandbar on the Little Colorado. I personally experienced some of this on a sunny July afternoon in 1985 at Cape Royal on the north rim of the canyon. For the approximately twenty minutes I was there, fixed winged aircraft were lined up north of me, then descending in a spaced pattern to rim level and then below, flying a southerly and then westerly course through the canyon. Although intervals between planes varied, the sound was constantly present and often overwhelming. I was appalled![17]

Congress had recognized the severity of noise problems from aircraft operations in 1975, when it passed the Grand Canyon National Park Enlargement Act. In Section 8 Congress declared that the natural "quiet and experience" of Grand Canyon was a significant value and must be protected. Should the Secretary of Interior "have reason to believe" that aircraft or helicopter operation was "likely to ... cause a significant adverse effect on the natural quiet and experience of the park, the Secretary shall submit" to the Federal Aviation Administration (FAA), the Environmental Protection Agency (EPA), and other responsible agencies "recommendations for rules and regulations" he believes appropriate "to protect the ... natural environment within the park." The responsible agency "shall consider the matter, and after consultation with the Secretary, shall take appropriate action to protect the park and visitors."[18]

Nevertheless, Sierra Club and its allies, seeking to achieve some measure of control over the situation, were frustrated at every turn. Meetings with the Park Service went nowhere. The Service felt powerless in the face of the private aircraft lobby and the FAA's adamant defense of its alleged preemptive jurisdiction over Grand Canyon airspace. The legislation was effectively ignored. The Park Service's strongest moment was in September 1985 when it projected that a final aircraft management plan would be in place by the summer of 1986. But, in December 1985, NPS moved the publication of a draft plan scheduled for that month back to February 1986 and dropped any reference to a final plan. In January 1986, calendar references to a draft plan were dropped altogether. The environmental community completely lost whatever patience it still had, and Sierra Club and The Wilderness Society asked us lawyers to seek judicial relief.

We prepared a complaint based upon the language of the Enlargement Act and the Park Service Organic Act, and in May we filed it in the U.S. District Court for Arizona. In this Grand Canyon Airspace litigation, we sought relief ordering an express schedule for draft rules and regulations, a time for public hearings, and a deadline for final regulations.

Within that process, our more specific objectives included:

- A flight-free zone above the Park from all aircraft operations below 18,000 feet, excepting only two expressly drawn corridors where flights could be as low as 2,000 feet above the canyon rim;
- A small "service" area or two and provision for necessary emergency operations;
- Operational restraints, including limitations on numbers, frequency, and time of flights;
- Use of "state of the art" noise abatement measures and equipment;
- Creation of a plan and system with adequate enforcement muscle.

No sooner had we started when tragedy intervened. In June two air tour flights collided in mid-air below the canyon rim and only 2,000 feet above the canyon bottom—one a fixed wing plane and the other a helicopter! Twenty-five people lost their lives. The National Park Service and the Federal Aviation Administration lurched into action. Congress was also alarmed, and it began to move. In March 1987 FAA published the first regulations for Grand Canyon airspace, and in August Congress enacted the National Park Overflight Act. The result of this burst of activity was the very thing environmentalists had sought in the litigation (without the tragic catalyst, of course), so we voluntarily suspended and then dismissed the litigation.[19]

Congress bore down much more emphatically than it had in 1975. Section 3(a) of the Act declared that noise associated with aircraft over flights at Grand Canyon National Park was causing a significant adverse effect on the natural quiet and experience of the park, and Subsection 3 (b) (1) specifically directed the FAA to issue a final plan for management of the airspace. Congress addressed specifics, calling for prohibition of flights below the canyon rim, creation of flight-free zones, and "substantial restoration of the natural quiet and experience of the park." As a result, in June 1988 the FAA promulgated Special Flight Rule Area (SFRA) No. 50-2 which revised flight procedures to prohibit flights below 14,500 feet, instituted four flight-free zones, and set defined routes for air tour operations.[20]

Another chapter began, and more chapters continue to be written today. The four principal players—the FAA, the Park Service, the environmental community, and the air tour operators—regularly disagree on the most sensitive issues, and progress has been halting. Given the twin goals of restoring and maintaining the natural quiet of the park and having viable air tour enterprises, the issues are complex and the parties are often far apart. Nevertheless, one giant step has been taken. Like river-running matters, the fundamental management issue has evolved from whether or not to regulate to the question of what kind of regulations will work best. The alternative of no regulations at all is untenable.

As to be expected, environmentalists and often the Park Service have fought for strong regulations that will best restore and maintain the "natural quiet and experience" of the park. The air tour operators have sought relaxed regulatory strictures and argued that defining natural quiet is difficult, subjective, to be approached gingerly. The FAA, the ultimate regulatory authority in this scenario, has generally leaned toward the operators, has on occasion used misleading or incomplete data to support poor decisions, and has often moved at a snail's pace. The arguments receiving the lion's share of attention continue to be the following:

- An appropriate definition of "natural quiet";
- The closely related issue of the actual baseline level or degree of quiet natural to the Grand Canyon National Park—how quiet is the Park when undisturbed?
- Formulation of an aircraft overflight plan;
- The enforceability of that plan;
- The location and dimensions of no flight zones (where overflights are prohibited altogether) and flight corridors;
- Operational details such as the number, timing, and frequency of flights;
- Use of quiet aircraft technology.

In the decades since Congress wrote the 1987 National Park Overflight Act, the FAA has written, amended, and supplemented many rules and regulations governing Grand Canyon airspace, and the National Park Service has continued to research, explain, and refine the definition or meaning of the "natural quiet and experience of the park." Congress passed three subsequent pieces of legislation addressing the subject, and on one occasion President William J. Clinton personally intervened with a formal "Presidential Memorandum" directing the FAA to issue regulations which would carry out the intent of the 1987 Act. At two critically important junctures the tour operators and the environmental community appealed FAA decisions and regulatory structures to the U.S. Court of Appeals for the District of Columbia Circuit. On both of these occasions the environmentalists' positions largely prevailed. The second case in 2002 pitting the U.S. Air Tour Association against the FAA (Grand Canyon Trust defendant intervenors) is a model of a court's ability to parse and critically review and determine the underlying facts upon which an administrative agency relies in drafting its regulations.[21] Also in 2002, Congress passed the National Parks Air Tour Management Act, directing action requiring quiet aircraft technology and the maintenance or restoration of natural quiet in parklands.[22]

However, a durable regulatory system continues to elude us. Recently, we seemed to come close: the Park Service and the FAA, working with environmental and industry stakeholders, began preliminary work on a comprehensive environmental impact statement (EIS) in 2006 addressing the question of "natural quiet" in the park, and in February 2011 the draft EIS was published. But then Congress intervened once again, this time at the behest of Nevada and Arizona senators, passing amendments to the 1987 Overflight Act which defined "natural quiet" in Grand Canyon by legislative fiat. According to the statutory language, the park would be considered naturally quiet if, for at least 75% of the day (a day defined as 7:00 A.M. to 7:00 P.M.), 50% of the park is free of the sound of commercial air tour operations.[23] This is an extremely lax standard. The environmental community vigorously opposed this action —citing it as a step backward and destructive of Park Service ability to control noise —but to no avail. Clearly, the struggle continues.

I almost hesitate to record three more sizeable issues involving Grand Canyon National Park, which have produced their own share of legal dispute and litigation: water release flows from Lake Powell impounded by the Glen Canyon Dam twelve miles upstream from the park's northern boundary, at the mouth of Marble Canyon; uranium leasing and mining on lands immediately adjacent to the park; and issues involving endangered species, such as the California Condor (America's largest bird of prey), the Peregrine Falcon, and the Humpback Chub, a native fish of the Colorado and Little Colorado Rivers. Indeed protection of the Chub was materially advanced by a federal court ruling in 2005 in litigation brought by environmentalists under the Endangered Species Act of 1973.

Near the close of our discussion of river-running issues I posed a critical question: "So, have we made any progress?" The same question applies to this seemingly endless airspace management controversy. Moreover, many may think that the prodigious efforts on the part of the contesting parties to produce effective and durable regulations governing the airspace above Grand Canyon National Park—or, on the other hand, to preserve as much freedom to the commercial interests regardless of consequences—have accomplished less than the achievements of river-running management at twice the cost in advocacy, litigation, legislative fixes, and regulatory initiatives. Nevertheless, now we do have flight-free zones, including all of the air space below the canyon rim, altitude restrictions, and recognition that natural quiet, the solemnity really, of the Grand Canyon, is to be protected to at least some degree.

> To be effective, activists must engage in the big disputes. [They must] "get down in the trenches."

Admittedly Grand Canyon National Park may be the most disputed 1,904 square miles in the National Park System, although other parks such as Yellowstone, the Everglades in Florida, and, when considered as a collective whole, the five parks in southern Utah, are no slackers when it comes to relentless dispute and conflict. Our national parks are endowed with breathtaking scenery, wonders of geology, fascinating ecological systems and accompanying wildlife, and unsurpassed recreational opportunity. Each year tens of millions of visitors are drawn to them. But extractable or usable natural resources are found in and around them. Opportunities for shortsighted commercial exploitation and development are abundant, and the resulting challenges of management and preservation are daunting. Truly, Grand Canyon National Park, with its multiplicity of management questions and the formidable difficulties in resolving them, gives us a really comprehensive look at what it may take to protect any unit of our justly renowned National Parks System.

This is a good place to summarize some of the important elements necessary for continued protection of Grand Canyon, as well as other treasured park and wilderness lands. First and maybe foremost, those who care should get involved where and when they can—or they must support those who do. To be effective, activists must engage in the big disputes; they must join the contest on the ground and in the applicable administrative and legislative forums. Activists must "get down in the trenches." They also need to keep in mind that the contests do not necessarily play out according to commonly understood rules of fairness and objectivity.

The courts can help in critical ways. Most immediately, they can level the playing field. And their arsenal is impressive:

- They can prohibit unlawful activity and make the prohibition stick.
- They can interpret statutes and applicable regulations whose meaning may not be clear or dispositive when measured against events on the ground.
- Court orders are enforceable—indeed that is their purpose. An order can assure that the law is followed, and it can give specific direction to the parties when necessary.
- Courts can break logjams in administrative processes when impasse is reached among interested parties and order matters to move along.
- Through the use of restraining orders and preliminary injunctions, harmful activities can be suspended until decisions can be made on the merits or potential settlement efforts can mature.
- Often just the realization that a party may have resort to the courts may be sufficient to govern or influence the position or the behavior of an opposing party.

Progress is frequently measured in incremental steps. These steps can create positive momentum, but they can also provide the opportunity for retrenchment. Thus, environmentalists must keep abreast of important governmental actions and significant initiatives from the private and corporate sectors. Of course political considerations are frequently present in environmental controversies. Political interference can derail progress just as readily as it can solve problems. Vigilance is required. Environmentalists and conservationists should recognize they are in for the long haul. The copious revenue streams available to those who will compromise park and wilderness values for commercial advantage are sufficient inducement for their continuing and persistent advocacy. So we conservationists need to remember it is the "good fight" that we make, and the rewards of even partial success may be great and long lasting. We need to celebrate and draw renewed strength from both the struggles we endure and the victories we enjoy.

"Leave it as it is," President Theodore Roosevelt said in the spring of 1903, as he stood at the edge of the Grand Canyon's south rim —

> The ages have been at work upon it, and man can only mar it. What you can do is keep it for your children, your children's children, and all who come after you, as one of the great sights which every American if he can travel at all should see.[24]

Well, Mr. President, we have not been able to "leave it alone" altogether. But we can surely work to keep it as natural and pristine as possible. Today's environmentalists can well say that we are on the job. We will persevere. With the help of the public and this discipline we now call environmental law, we will be at the table when the big issues are laid upon it.

Compadres

May 16, 1903. They laced up their boots and footslogged several miles through a blinding snowstorm to a point above Sentinel Dome. Two men exalting in the storm and the wilderness of Yosemite National Park—Roosevelt and Muir. This was their second camp of the President's three day visit to Yosemite; he came specifically to meet John Muir, eloquent spokesman and writer for wilderness and fierce campaigner for its protection; he came also to enjoy just such nights in the wild as this.

Muir built a campfire and dinner was cooked. They talked of conservation and natural history; they talked of the grandeur of Yosemite. Suddenly Muir sang out, "Watch this!" Seizing a flaming branch, he ignited a nearby pine. As the flames roared aloft, Muir—ever the primordial Scotsman—danced a jig around the burning tree. Roosevelt, not to be outdone, jumped up and commenced hopping around the blazing fire throwing his arms up in the air bellowing, "Hurrah! Hurrah! Hurrah!" The flames leaped, danced, and roared; the wind blustered anew; the storm blew on.... This actually happened! Of course, given the nature of these two exuberant men, one would have wondered more if they had merely passed the moment with only another cup of coffee.

Muir and Roosevelt took each other's measure over the three day trip and forged a bond which reinforced their commitment to conservation and preservation. Important historical moments come in many guises and no one can deny the enchantment of this one. Fortunately the trip has been memorialized in a magnificent—and now iconic—photograph of Roosevelt and Muir at Glacier Point with the granite cliffs and monoliths of Yosemite around them, Yosemite Valley three thousand feet below, and Yosemite Falls thundering across the way. They look confident of their cause and ready for vigorous work—reinforced by their time together. This work they would do with renewed vigor. And we are their beneficiaries. Compadres.[25]

CHAPTER IV

Protecting Wilderness

Earlier I discussed the Wilderness Act of 1964. I noted its unique nature and radical departure from traditional practices of land management. Soon after the Act's passage, it was apparent that wilderness classification procedures and management practices would be complicated and extremely contentious. Decades have been required to create a representative National Wilderness System and to articulate viable management policies for dedicated areas; indeed today, forty-seven years later, impassioned argument over wilderness classification and management continues practically unabated. The work is not yet completed. And, like Grand Canyon National Park, almost every step has involved lawyers representing all sides of the issues.

This chapter reviews an array of wilderness cases dating from the early days of the Act. Each case imparts worthwhile lessons, and I hope each one, in its own way, will broaden the reader's understanding of how environmental law works. Since most of these cases did not reach a level of actual "trial on the merits," a definition of the term "case" is needed. I use it in the broad sense of a substantial dispute between environmental interests and their opposition that has reached a point where legal representation becomes necessary, or at least well advised. After these wilderness cases, the scene of action will shift to the canyonlands of southern Utah—the "Golden Circle" of national parks—and the Grand Staircase–Escalante National Monument. Among other subjects, we will address legislative lobbying—a task familiar to many environmental lawyers—and the role of the media. We will talk about a whistle-blower and his dramatic and timely contribution to a critical case. Then we will delve into the use of expert witnesses, a critical component of many environmental cases, and some surprising and intriguing aspects of this part of the legal world.

We have discussed the energy and ferment of the 1960s and '70s, which provided fertile ground for new ideas and for placing environmental concerns high on the public agenda. We have seen use of the courts rising naturally, logically, and inevitably from this social environment. Observations in this chapter will continue to point out the values of time-honored processes and procedures inherent in our legal system and its ability to grapple with new laws and litigants. Actually, as we shall see in several cases, the simple knowledge that the courts are available to environmentalists encourages and often forces resolution or settlement without the need of a trial on the merits. The same influence is true with administrative appeals.

Indeed, the majority of cases brought to court are resolved at some preliminary level and never get to an actual trial. Many are decided upon motions by one party or the other which bring a case to a point of decision on legal grounds or encourage a dispositive resolution among the parties, as they evaluate the strengths and weaknesses of their position. Other cases respond to the mere fact that a court is available to move toward disposition; that the law will, in fact, be enforced. The inexorable pressures created by a lawsuit, the necessary discovery, pre-trial procedures and motions, the financial costs involved, and knowledge that in due course there will be a decision, focus the parties' attention and may bring one or both to seek agreement and settlement. Serious disputes over management of Grand Canyon have always required repeated and active court involvement, but *Beaver Creek* and *Viavant* needed only a single decisive intervention, and then matters quickly concluded. The *Carlsbad Mountain Lions* required the continued presence of the court over many months, though it was largely passive during the life of the proceeding.

This suggests a second matter that needs discussion before we continue: *Beaver Creek*, *Viavant*, and the *Carlsbad Mountain Lions* may seem to have been relatively easy for the environmental plaintiffs. Only *Viavant* required testimony in open court, but defendants had a bad case, and this was soon revealed. Indeed, as a rule the environmental plaintiff does have some initial advantages:

- He knows where he wants to go—what he wants to get out of the case;
- He is thoroughly versed in the types of judicial relief available in his particular case;
- He is well informed on the statutes and other applicable law from the outset. If these are new statutes, or new interpretations of old statutes, this advantage may be significant, at least temporarily;

Why Wilderness?

Through the years, giants—Henry David Thoreau, John Muir, Theodore Roosevelt, Aldo Leopold—have offered their reasons. I want to offer more recent wisdom from Edgar Wayburn. Dr. Wayburn, great lover of wilderness and extraordinary environmental advocate and campaigner over the last four decades of the twentieth century, tells us —

> The further I have looked, the more value in wilderness I have seen. For wilderness does not merely add to the human condition. In essence, wild places represent possibility, what Wallace Stegner called "the geography of hope." Our curiosity about the unknown has inspired humans to wonder and to wander. We are drawn to the unfamiliar and the uncharted. What will happen to our spirit when every terrain has been mapped, purchased and divided? What will be the value of our freedom if there is no difference between here and there? To where will we escape? Where will we roam? Wilderness is not a luxury; it is a necessity. An ocean horizon, a primeval forest, a mountain pass, an icy fjord each waits, luring us forward with its call to adventure. Without wilderness, there is no adventure. And if not adventure, of what will we dream?[1]

- Judicial review of environmental issues is still relatively new, and, in the legal context, many cases are still unique. Interest is generally high on the part of most courts, and many judges want to carefully review the issues raised rather than summarily dismiss plaintiffs' allegations;
- The interest of the press and media in important cases is usually high. Therefore, the issues are thoroughly and regularly explored, and a large audience becomes interested, or even involved.

These "advantages" seem substantial. However, appearances can frequently be misleading. The defendants have lawyers, and the adversarial requirements of our system give them ample opportunity to be heard. Here are some of the things they have going for them:

- The facts supporting plaintiffs' case must be as represented. To the extent they are weaker in any material aspect, plaintiffs' case becomes vulnerable.
- The new statute, or the old one to be interpreted anew, may be vague in important areas, or it may conflict with other existing and potentially applicable law. In any case, interpretation is required, and defendants will get to make their arguments.
- Plaintiffs carry the burden of proving their case, a fact often overlooked by the casual observer and the media. Plaintiffs must establish that they are entitled to the relief sought. This burden is with them throughout the proceedings.

Now the scales are more evenly balanced. And is not a decision in this context better since it has been tested? These points are not meant to be exhaustive, but they do show that an important degree of balance and fairness is inherent in the system.

We must also be mindful that plaintiff citizen organizations—the predominate force in most complex environmental litigation—can to a substantial degree select the cases they bring and how they bring them. Therefore, they can eliminate at the outset many weak cases that could be filed. In fact, the comparative limits of their financial resources will often dictate their choice of cases to be pursued. I was often in the position of evaluating cases brought to my office and occasionally cases brought to other Sierra Club legal offices. Major considerations included the strength of the case, the extent of local, regional, or national interest and support, and the urgency of the matter(s) at issue.

The wilderness cases we will review here show a logical progression from initial recognition of the new Wilderness Act, through U.S. Forest Service adjustment to the language strongly promoting protection of wilderness, to arguments over more specific details of later interpretation and implementation. We will first identify and describe the wilderness area that was in question in a particular dispute and then focus on the specific "case" that arose and its outcome.

Saving East Meadow Creek From Loggers

Eagles Nest Wilderness Area, in the Arapaho and White River National Forests of central Colorado, was established in 1976 by Public Law 94-352. The Wilderness totals 134,070 acres of the lower slopes and the peaks of the Gore Mountain Range. The Gore is composed of sharp summits and arêtes rising from dramatic serrated ridges riddled with gnarled, tooth-like spires or minarets. Feature names like Prisoner Peak and Ripsaw Ridge reinforce this description. Many headwalls are graced with gorgeous waterfalls with alpine tarns frequently lying just below. The Gore's highest point, 13,534-foot Mt. Powell, is named after our friend John Wesley Powell who made the first recorded assent in 1868, one year before his famous Grand Canyon adventure. The core rock comprising the Gore Range has no known marketable mineral deposits; thus prospectors and miners never laced the area with primitive roads, adits, and mining structures. Consequently, the pristine sub-alpine part of the wilderness is relatively extensive, with untracked mature spruce-fir forests and aspen, interspersed with natural meadows, sparkling streams extending out several miles on all sides of the range, and marvelous mountain lakes. The forests provide a wonderful introduction to the alpine lands above.

In the spring of 1969, the Forest Service engaged to sell 4.3 million board feet of timber on 1200 acres in the East Meadow Creek drainage on the west side of the Gore Range. Construction of a substantial road, probing deep into the forest, was a part of the sale. The wilderness character of the affected lands would be totally destroyed. In fact, long-range plans of the Forest Service projected the road continuing for many more miles, serving many more timber sales. At that time, much of the alpine topography of the Gore Range was managed and protected as the Gore Range Primitive Area, but the sale area was more than a mile from the northwestern boundary of the primitive area.

On April 4, 1969 several individuals, a wilderness guide and outfitter, the Town of Vail, Sierra Club, two local conservation organizations, and Colorado Magazine combined to challenge this timber sale in the U.S. District for Colorado. The *East Meadow Creek* case was the first litigation under the 1964 Wilderness Act. Initially, the statute sets forth a definition of wilderness that describes perfectly the nature of the lands in East Meadow Creek that plaintiffs sought to protect:

> Sec. 2 (c). A wilderness ... is ... an area where the earth and its community of life are untrammeled by man.... [It] is further defined ... [as] an area ... retaining its primeval character and influence without permanent improvements or human habitation, which is protected and managed so as to preserve its natural conditions and which (1) generally appears to have been affected primarily by the forces of nature, with the imprint of man's work substantially unnoticeable; (2) has outstanding opportunities for solitude or a primitive and unconfined type of recreation....[2]

An integral part of the Act is language mandating that certain public lands, including particular Forest Service lands, which meet this definition be reviewed by the President and Congress for their suitability for inclusion in a National Wilderness System.

Plaintiffs asserted that harvesting timber and building the accompanying road would destroy the wilderness character of the land affected, thereby violating the wilderness study requirements of the Act. Consequently, the subject lands had to be maintained in their existing wilderness condition until Congress and the President could review *East Meadow Creek* for possible inclusion in a designated wilderness. The review sections of the Wilderness Act and their origin are critical here, as well as in the two cases that follow. Like most of our important laws governing public lands, the Act is almost as much a product of history and tradition as it is of reasoned logic and the most recent Congressional efforts to fulfill evolving needs and desires of our citizens. Thus, an historical digression will be helpful in achieving proper perspective.

The wilderness movement dates back to the 1920s and actions by the U.S. Forest Service. In 1924, the pioneering ecologist Aldo Leopold, whom we met in Chapter II, then a district ranger for the Forest Service in New Mexico, convinced the regional forester for the Southwest to put more than half a million acres of the headwaters of the Gila River in Arizona and New Mexico into a Gila Wilderness Area. While this was a purely administrative action and could be readily reversed or revised, it was the earliest attempt at some formal wilderness dedication. Leopold was a persuasive and persistent man, and he recruited others to his views. In 1926, and again in 1927, the Chief of the Forest Service endorsed the wilderness concept for certain national forest lands. This led to Forest Service promulgation of the "L-20" regulation in 1929. The regulation adopted the term of "primitive area" for selected lands and directed that they be managed to —

> Maintain primitive conditions … to the fullest degree compatible with their highest public use with a view to conserving the values of such areas for the purposes of public education and recreation.[3]

During the 1930s, a number of these primitive areas were established, including three relevant to our story here: Gore Range and Uncompahgre Primitive Areas in Colorado, and the Idaho Primitive Area in Idaho. This was an impressive beginning. However, regulation was weak, incompatible incursion into primitive areas regularly occurred, and implementation was left to the discretion of local Forest Service personnel. Furthermore, the entire concept was vulnerable to the whims and viewpoints of higher-level Forest Service officers. In response to these weaknesses, the U.S. Secretary of Agriculture* revoked the L-20 regulation in 1939 and adopted the "U-2" regulations. These regulations created a new classification of "wilderness areas" for protected areas over 100,000 acres and "wild areas" for smaller units. Existing primitive areas were to be re-evaluated through a reclassification process. It was assumed that some of these would achieve wilderness status after appropriate review.

For a while there seemed to be progress. Protection of wilderness areas and primitive areas awaiting reclassification was apparently strengthened. However, from the perspective of wilderness advocates the review process became increasingly disappointing. The allegedly increased protection of wilderness was illusory in too many instances. Traditional Forest Service missions of marketing timber, building transportation networks, and encouraging exploitation and development of natural resources continued to dominate. Doug Scott, in his excellent comprehensive history of the Wilderness Act, *The Enduring Wilderness*, describes the situation as the decade of the Sixties opened. The history

---

* The U.S. Forest Service is an agency of the U.S. Department of Agriculture.

and attitudes he relates were not only significant inducements for the Wilderness Act legislation, but also critical in the thinking behind at least the first three cases discussed in these pages. In Scott's words —

> Conservation groups welcomed the newly strengthened Forest Service policies [U-1 and U-2], but over the next two decades they were increasingly disenchanted by the crawling pace of the promised reclassifications. More alarming was a pattern of decisions that realigned the boundaries, removing areas of timber from one primitive area after another for logging....
>
> Even though the gross acreage might remain the same or even be expanded a little, the quality and biological diversity of wilderness was whittled away...
>
> To wilderness leaders, it was unacceptable to see wilderness policy lurch along in such an impermanent, haphazard way. Wilderness had to be saved, securely, once and for all—in perpetuity. A stronger means simply had to be found to save it, something inherently more permanent than the unfettered administrative discretion that ... the Forest Service so jealously guarded.
>
> In fact by the war years, the wilderness classification process was almost completely stalled. Then in the 1950s the Forest Service lifted the wilderness designation of old-growth (mature) forests in the French Pete Valley in Oregon to allow potential logging. And in New Mexico, part of Leopold's Gila Wilderness area was removed from wilderness status.[4]

Legislation would have to be the solution, and by the early 1960s, committed advocates for Congressional protection of wilderness were gaining the upper hand. The debate intensified as public awareness grew and new activists joined the fight. Thus in 1964 the Wilderness Act became law. Congress defined wilderness and decreed the protection and permanent status of "wilderness areas" already designated by the Forest Service. Additionally, in Section 3(b), Congress specifically required the Secretary of Agriculture to review areas still classified as "primitive" for possible preservation as wilderness. The Secretary's findings were to be submitted to the President, who in turn would advise Congress of his recommendations. Section 3(b) of the Act further provided —

Nothing herein contained shall limit the President in proposing as part of his recommendations to Congress, the alteration of existing boundaries of primitive areas or recommending the addition of any contiguous area of national forest lands predominately of wilderness value.[5]

Once lands became formally dedicated as wilderness by statute, their management had to be compatible with preservation of their wilderness quality in perpetuity. This condition could not be changed by administrative fiat.

In retrospect, it is evident that the wilderness review process would quickly reach the courts. Battle lines were clearly drawn between wilderness advocates, the Forest Service, and commodity interests such as logging and mining. While conservationists sought secure protection of wilderness under the law, the Forest Service labored to maintain the broadest possible discretionary authority over wilderness classification and management decisions. Interested industries, particularly the timber industry, fought to keep the maximum number of acres available for commercial purposes. As we have seen, in 1969 it was not yet an obvious course of action to resort to a federal court for guidance, interpretation, and resolution of wilderness classification conflicts. It was an altogether novel approach, and it carried the risk that government arguments in favor of then pervasive Forest Service management discretion could receive judicial approval. Potentially millions of acres of deserving Forest Service lands would be denied consideration for wilderness designation. Moreover, the idea of litigating a case, for which there was no existing precedent, against the resources and experience of the U.S. Justice Department, the U.S. Attorney's office, and the Department of Agriculture's Solicitor's Office, appeared daunting.

On the other hand, conservationists feared that if the Forest Service got away with the sale of timber in East Meadow Creek, a critical part of the Wilderness Act calling for wilderness review of qualifying lands contiguous to existing primitive areas across the West would be emasculated. This was how things were done in the past; it was no longer to be tolerated. The challenge of the Forest Service was accepted, and the lawsuit was filed. After all, it was the 1960s. As we have discussed, large challenges of the day were commonly met by committed individuals and groups of concerned citizens. The exploration of new processes, of new means to worthwhile public ends, was welcomed and pursued.

I attended the lengthy meetings and deliberations of the *East Meadow Creek* plaintiffs prior to filing. They were intense. The Wilderness Act was brand new. There were no precedents for what we were contemplating. Even our right, our "standing," to bring our grievances before a court was still in question. The pioneering Scenic Hudson decision on standing was only four years old and the Supreme Court's decision in the Mineral King case lay three years in the future. Other questions were posed: Could the necessary financial support be found? What would I actually do as the lawyer in the case? How long would it take to get a decision? But it soon became apparent that these were concerns to be pondered and discussed; they were not disqualifications. The conversations and the discussion began to focus on what the individuals present could do to help: who would be available for necessary tasks, who else could be recruited, who knew where—and from whom—money could be raised? Serious questions, surely. Yet, as time wore on, a determined feeling of common purpose and warming camaraderie prevailed. Risky? Of course. But worth taking on? Absolutely. This was the mettle of the *East Meadow Creek* plaintiffs. It is not overreaching to borrow from that earlier conservationist, President Theodore Roosevelt, an eloquent spokesman in his own era of great socio-political change—

> It is not the critic who counts; not the man who points out how the strong man stumbles, or where the doer of deeds could have done them better. The credit belongs to the man who is actually in the arena, whose face is marred by dust and sweat and blood, who strives valiantly; who errs and comes up short again and again; because there is no effort without error and shortcomings; but who does actually strive to do the deed; who knows the great enthusiasm, the great devotion, who spends himself in a worthy cause, who at the best knows in the end the triumph of high achievement and who at the worst, if he fails, at least he fails while daring greatly, so that his place shall never be with those cold and timid souls who know neither victory nor defeat.[6]

The Forest Service, consistent with its tradition and supported by timber industry intervenors, adamantly argued that it maintained its traditional broad discretion over the present status and the future management of the wilderness qualifying areas contiguous to the Gore Range Primitive Area. While it was clear existing primitive areas themselves were to be preserved in their wilderness condition pending Presidential and Congressional review, the Forest Service saw no mandate in the Act to protect the contiguous lands pending completion of the process. It might recommend such areas for wilderness, but this was completely discretionary. The Forest Service thought it retained unfettered discretion to alternatively manage the contiguous areas for other traditional uses, including the sale of timber and associated construction of roads.

The court, Judge William E. Doyle presiding, disagreed. He held that the wilderness review language of the Wilderness Act was not ambiguous, and the intent of Congress was clear. Judge Doyle found the Act contemplated "the President shall be in a position to exercise a meaningful decision with respect to contiguous areas."[7] It necessarily followed that cutting timber and building a road were prohibited until the review process was completed, for they would clearly destroy the wilderness character of the lands involved. The District Court's decision was unanimously affirmed on appeal, and the U.S. Supreme Court declined to review this decision. East Meadow Creek, and thousands of other acres contiguous to the Gore Range Primitive Area, were preserved in their wild state. In 1976 Congress included them in the Eagles Nest Wilderness Area. *East Meadow Creek* was a critical precedent, for there were many other primitive areas in the western states in various stages of review, all of which had contiguous wilderness qualifying lands.

This case illustrates well the importance of a thorough and comprehensive review of all the issues before the court. Over the course of a year, the court endured at least nine motions or hearings prior to the weeklong trial. Judge Doyle first wrote a published opinion on central legal issues in response to preliminary motions of defendants seeking dismissal of the case or outright "summary judgment" in their favor. This was followed by his lengthy opinion after the trial. The protracted nature of the case weighed heavily on both the plaintiffs and us lawyers. In how many more hearings and motions would we have to prevail? Would we ever get to trial? However, throughout this period the Judge consistently emphasized in his responses to defendants' pre-trial motions the importance of the issues, the need to review as much evidence as possible, and the duty incumbent upon him to hear all arguments and consider them thoroughly. To do that, he would not be "rushed." He turned the "unprecedented" arguments defendants were making against them, noting that this was all the more reason to proceed deliberately.

An extremely significant result of Judge Doyle's steady hand was the assembly of one of the most extensive evidentiary and documentary records I have seen in a case of this nature. This was obviously another factor contributing to the thorough judicial analysis and affirmation upon appeal; comprehensive review in the trial court gave increased credibility to the result. Regardless of the perspective of subsequent reviewers, there could be no doubt that all the issues were fully aired, all relevant and material evidence was brought before the court, and defendants were given ample opportunity to present their arguments. This extensive record, the numerous motions and other opportunities defendants had to present their case, and the careful deliberation of the court, are particularly important in a case of first impression, such as *East Meadow Creek*. The case would come to have a critical impact on future interpretations of the Wilderness Act. The thorough treatment of the issues and the arguments would give the case added force as a reliable authority on this new law.

This result would soon be tested. And hard fighting lay ahead for the protection of the Gore Range and East Meadow Creek in public hearings and debate, in the press, and in the halls of Congress before we would obtain the coveted wilderness area status. But for the moment we could celebrate. A boisterous party was held in Vail, and to raucous cheers principal actors were awarded survey stick markers—orange ribbons still attached—pulled from the now defunct timber road survey line. Experiences were relived, anecdotes recounted, and celebration ruled far into the night. The mood is captured well in these lines from Nancy Newhall's poem "This is the American Earth":

> You shall see mountains rise in the transparent shadow before dawn.
> You shall see—and feel!—first light, and hear a ripple in the stillness.
> You shall enter the living shelter of the forest.
> You shall walk where only the wind has walked before.
> You shall know immensity,
> and see continuing the primeval forces of the world.

You shall know not one small segment but the whole of life,
Strange, miraculous, living, dying, changing.[8]

The victory was sweet, but we would get little rest in these early years of interpreting the Wilderness Act. The protected status of magnificent wilderness lands in the San Juan Mountains of southwestern Colorado was soon in peril.

Government Maneuver in Uncompahgre Country

Uncompahgre Wilderness,* at the crest of the expansive San Juan Mountains, was established in 1980 by Public Law 96-560 and was enlarged in 1993. Formerly known as the Big Blue Wilderness Area, this 102,000-acre wilderness is dominated by two spectacular 14,000-foot peaks, Uncompahgre Peak at 14,309 feet and Wetterhorn Peak, an abrupt igneous intrusion—most likely the neck of a vanished volcano—rising to 14,015 feet. Uncompahgre is a massive block of a mountain and the highest summit in the San Juan Range, with cliffs up to 1,500 feet on three sides rising above undulating alpine meadows. It has been likened to a great ship on a rolling sea. Lower rock castles and sweeping ridges complete a splendid alpine scene. The precipitous and practically impassable Cow Creek Canyon with sheer rock walls and tumbling cascades coming off Wild Horse Peak nearby is so deep, rugged, and densely forested that no trails have been carved in its depths.

We learned of the Uncompahgre matter on a Thursday in the early summer of 1971. The Forest Service was going to formally *declassify* Uncompahgre Primitive Area on the following Monday! This was an obvious dodge of the wilderness review mandates of the Wilderness Act. If allowed to proceed, it would return the Uncompahgre area to traditional multiple uses in common with other forestlands. The immediate threat was unrestrained access for large equipment to work mining claims. Our information was that trucks and earth moving equipment were due to enter the primitive area immediately upon declassification. We had papers prepared by Friday noon, and we called the court and the United

---

* Uncompahgre is a Ute Indian word meaning "dirty water" or "red spring water," likely referring to the many hot springs nearby.

States Attorney's Office, informing them that we were applying for a temporary restraining order (TRO). Of course we were using Judge Doyle's decision in *East Meadow Creek* as authority for stopping both the mining incursion and the declassification. We filed the papers in late afternoon and drew Judge Hatfield Chilson, by all accounts the most difficult draw we could make.

The U.S. Attorney could not accompany me to Judge Chilson's chambers, so I went alone. His secretary showed me into the Judge's office. I gave him a copy of the papers that had been stamped by the clerk's office showing the case had been filed. The Judge gave me a baleful look—it was now about 4 p.m. Friday afternoon. I told him that the U.S. Attorney, Jim Treese, could not be present but had no objection to my seeing the Judge. I also relayed to the Court that the U.S. Attorney had not had a chance to review the materials, and that he was not taking a definite position on the TRO at this moment. I argued the immediacy of the matter and the harm that would ensue if activities on the ground proceeded Monday morning. Handing the Judge a copy of the *East Meadow Creek* opinion, I summarized the cause of action and cited parts of Judge Doyle's ruling. I did note that the case was currently on appeal to the U.S. Court of Appeals for the Tenth Circuit.

Judge Chilson seemed unimpressed, and indeed, he was getting ready to leave for the weekend. He listened, but it was clear that I was getting nowhere. I continued pressing the need for a TRO, emphasizing the irreparable harm the plaintiff, Sierra Club and its members, and the public interest would suffer if these events proceeded on Monday. Under the Federal Rules of Civil Procedure, a party who properly brings a motion for a temporary restraining order before the Court is entitled to an immediate ruling. Several times I pointed this out. A specific ruling, even if adverse, would at least open the difficult path to the appellate court upstairs. Of course, the party bringing a motion for a TRO must have serious and weighty grounds for doing so, but I had no real fear of that.

Judge Chilson told me that he would do nothing until the following week. I could return to his court, bring the U.S. Attorney, and he would consider our motion. Of course, the Forest Service planned to declassify on Monday, and mechanized equipment could be moving in by early afternoon. It was highly doubtful that the appellate court, the Tenth Circuit U.S. Court of Appeals, even if it heard our plea, could move before significant physical damage occurred. Uncompahgre would instantly suffer grievously, and subsequent success in the lawsuit could not, in all probability, cure or relieve the damage. The Judge was standing now, packing his briefcase. I was continuing to press our need for a TRO, and our conversation had become heated. I continued arguing as he moved around his desk, grabbed his coat and put it on. He opened the door to his chambers, strode across the reception area, and on out the door. I was hanging right on his heels, practically tripping over my own feet, still arguing, but it was for naught. I then turned to his secretary, who was sitting there at her desk with an interested look on her face, and told her I wanted time Monday to continue my argument for a TRO. She was neither hostile nor friendly, but merely nodded and told me to call her early Monday morning.

It was a tough weekend. We could not let this go, for presumably if the Forest Service tactic succeeded, portions of many primitive areas across the West could be declassified, and much of the impact of the *East Meadow Creek* victory would be lost. On the other hand, we did not want to spawn a Colorado District Court opinion contrary to Judge Doyle's opinion while the latter was on appeal. This was a very real concern, for we evaluated our chances of success to be much lower in Judge Chilson's court than they had been before Judge Doyle. We prepared appeal papers for filing in the Tenth Circuit on Monday, renewing our request for a restraining order at that level. Of course this would be a highly unusual proceeding, but we obviously needed to be prepared should the worst scenario unfold.

My secretary came in early Monday and began typing up the papers drafted over the weekend. This was before the era of computers and word processing. Some of you can remember the click-clack of the old IBM electric typewriter, and the "whack" followed by the ring of the little "bell" each time you threw the carriage back to the left-hand margin. While she was preparing the papers, I was going over the arguments I would again make to Judge Chilson. As eight o'clock approached and we were preparing to call the U.S. Attorney's Office to inform them of what we would be doing, my secretary called out that Judge Chilson's office was on the phone. I picked it up to hear the Judge's secretary saying that the Judge wanted to see me and the U.S. Attorney in his chambers right away. I hurried over. The secretary greeted me with a cheerful smile, poured me a cup of coffee, and told me the U.S. Attorney was on his way. Sure enough, Jim Treese arrived within minutes, and we went into the Judge's office. I was anticipating the worst. In fact I expected a lecture from the court regarding my conduct on Friday. Whereupon I received one of the great surprises of my legal career!

The Judge warmly welcomed us and told us to take a seat. He called to his secretary for more coffee, and we briefly exchanged pleasantries. Then the Judge addressed the U.S. Attorney saying he had read my papers and Judge Doyle's opinion on *East Meadow Creek*, and that this *Uncompahgre* matter seemed very closely related. He told Mr. Treese he was inclined to grant the Temporary Restraining Order but first wanted to know the government's position. Mr. Treese replied that he had called the Department of Agriculture's Solicitor's Office, and they would be getting back to him with more instructions and detail just as soon as they could. They had instructed him to oppose the motion and to remind the court that the government had appealed Judge Doyle's decision. Judge Chilson responded that he was not inclined to do anything to counter Judge Doyle's ruling, he was a fellow judge and a friend of his, and he appeared to have reviewed the *East Meadow Creek* case with a great deal of care and had crafted his decision well. The U.S. Attorney said he had not had time to do more than briefly peruse the papers himself and so, at least for the time being, he would have to abide by the views of the solicitor's office.

Judge Chilson responded that he was granting the temporary restraining order, and he wanted Treese to make sure nothing would happen in Uncompahgre pending further order of the court. He then suggested that Jim and I repair to the U.S. Attorney's office and work on finding a time for a preliminary injunction hearing. With a smile for us both, he stood and ushered us out. Jim needed to use the phone in the secretary's office to call the solicitor's office in Washington and tell them to back off. Completely dazed, I mumbled to the secretary something to the effect that I was startled by the outcome, given my experience on Friday. She smiled and told me that sometimes the Judge did that; he appreciated lawyers who argued vigorously and passionately— as I had on Friday—and he did not hold our heated exchanges against me. She ended by adding that sometimes the Judge changed his mind.

As Treese and I walked down to his office, I was feeling much more confident about our position. Nevertheless, having become familiar with the Forest Service's tenacious defense of its traditional authority and discretion, I reflected that we still had a lot of work in store. At any rate, the morning had started well.

We walked into Jim's office and sat down. After attending to the coffee ritual, Jim asked his secretary to get the solicitor's office on the phone again. Little did I know that I was about to absorb the second surprise of that Monday morning. Jim related to the solicitor the meeting in chambers in some detail. The solicitor's office was not pleased; that much was evident from the answers Jim was giving to the questions that were apparently being thrown at him. It was also obvious that the solicitor's office was reminding the U.S. Attorney that the *East Meadow Creek* decision was on appeal, that the Forest Service completely and fundamentally disagreed with it, and that the United States should vigorously oppose the Sierra Club. The dialogue continued—I, of course, hearing only the U.S. Attorney's end of the conversation.

Suddenly I heard my name and Jim Treese saying, "Why don't you folks talk to Mr. Ruckel? He knows more about this than I do. He's right here in the office." Whereupon Jim handed the phone to me, told me to come around and sit in his chair, and he would go see about more coffee while I talked to the "lawyers in Washington." Needless to say, our conversation was not productive. Other than briefly stating our position, the only thing I could actually add was that we had to get a date for the preliminary injunction hearing. The solicitor's office wanted no more of me and requested I get Jim back on the phone. He came back in with the coffee, sat down across from me, set about getting the phone line untangled, and then I handed the receiver over to him. There was more conversation—mostly on the other end. Jim maintained that *East Meadow Creek* seemed directly on point—I was not aware until then that he had read it that carefully—his office had a full docket, he did not particularly want to take it on, and that the solicitor's office would have to come out to Denver and handle the case themselves! For the second time that morning, I was flabbergasted. Treese's refusal was likely to be extremely significant...—

But I'm getting ahead of the story. It was beginning to sink in that we were probably going to win this.

Jim hung up the phone muttering about the value of Colorado's mountains and of wilderness, and that these things were significant and important. We exchanged a few more pleasantries, and talked a bit about the San Juan country,* for which he obviously had high regard. We compared calendars and arrived at a couple of options for dates and times for a preliminary injunction hearing. Jim told me he would have his secretary get in touch with Judge Chilson's secretary and would let me know the preliminary injunction hearing date by the end of the day. I hurried back to the office to spread the good news. Jim's office called at the end of the day. The hearing had been set for two weeks hence. We began preparing our witnesses, assembling documents, and arranging for photographic exhibits. We did not get far. At the end of the week Jim called me on the phone and informed me that the Forest Service was not going to revoke the primitive area status for Uncompahgre Primitive Area after all, and that no mining equipment would be moving in. Complete victory!

> # By administrative edict, there could have been an end to any possibility of dedicated wilderness in the Uncompahgre country!

I think the lessons here may be more personal than they are legal. Based upon "courthouse talk," it was easy for me to assume that Judge Chilson was, in the vernacular, a "hostile" judge from the conservationists' point of view. I have no real references to the judge's thinking—indeed, he never had to write an opinion or hold further proceedings on the case. His secretary was gracious, but all she divulged was that Judge Chilson liked vigorous advocacy and occasionally changed his mind. One hopes that any trial court judge will have these characteristics.

Solely as conjecture, let me offer several possible reasons for the Judge's apparent change of heart. First, as I mentioned earlier in this

---

* The very name San Juan (Saint John) is synonymous with wilderness: John the Baptist "wandered in the wilderness" for most of his life.

chapter, the interest of the courts in this new environmental law was, I believe, quite real. Intangible though this may be, cases have turned on less. Secondly, and here I am likely on firmer ground, collegiality among judges sitting in a particular U.S. District Court is important. Indeed, Judge Chilson mentioned his colleague Judge Doyle at least three or four times (of course, I mentioned him practically all the time) and had obviously reviewed his *East Meadow Creek* opinion. Besides, all of the judges sitting on the district court bench on the second floor of the U.S. Courthouse in Denver have only to lift their eyes to see the Tenth Circuit U.S. Court of Appeals looking down on them from the fourth floor. Such intangibles cannot be measured, but they are frequently there, and lawyers do well to keep them in mind.

One arresting moment in the short number of hours at the courthouse those two spring days was the precise timing of the court's dramatic change in tenor early Monday morning. Judge Chilson abruptly halted declassification of the Uncompahgre Primitive Area just as the papers were to be signed in Washington. Maybe, just maybe, there was yet another intangible working here: Judge Chilson admired and enjoyed Colorado's mountains.... This was surely in the mind of Jim Treese, the U.S. Attorney, when he told the solicitor's office in Washington they were going to have to handle the upcoming preliminary injunction proceeding themselves.

There is more to this "passing the baton" than appears on the surface. Actually, it proved quite significant. Court cases against the United States Government are usually handled by the U.S. Attorney's office for the district involved, or by the Justice Department itself. Generally speaking, solicitors' offices provide yeoman assistance but are not lead trial counsel in high visibility cases that may involve a full-blown trial and controversial law, such as the *Uncompahgre* case. This is especially true when such a case is on an accelerated calendar like *Uncompahgre*, for the U.S. Attorney's office is usually much better equipped to move quickly in response to rapidly developing events.

Finally, the Forest Service was at least a trifle disingenuous—declassifying a whole primitive area to side-step wilderness review altogether, a review specifically called for by an act of Congress. By administrative edict, there could have been an end to any possibility of dedicated wilderness in the Uncompahgre country! If the case had continued, the court, the public, and the media, would probably have increasingly focused on this. Nevertheless, the outcome was not certain, and thus we were delighted with Judge Chilson's handling of the case. Once again, however, our celebration was pretty brief. We were now tracking primitive area reviews throughout the West, and portentous events were clearly unfolding in the Northern Rockies.

River of No Return

Central Idaho is home to the legendary Middle Fork of the Salmon River, more than one hundred miles of wild river with fierce Grade IV* rapids. If you have been in this kind of water, reflect for a moment. You can probably still feel the waves rolling over you, the certainty that your next breath will be mostly water, the wild cork-screwing motion of the raft, the ache in your arms and shoulders from gripping so tightly to the restraining rope, the strain on your legs bracing your body as you wield your paddle, the momentary fear as you crest the water near a rock, or a vertical drop, and look straight down on the swirling turbulence below. And all this time you are shouting and screaming in response to the exhilaration and the danger!

Then comes slower water. You can catch your breath, rest your muscles, look around, and enjoy the dramatic scenery of the canyon. Perhaps a Bald Eagle or an Osprey will be flying above, hunting the river, his piercing cry clearly heard above the murmur of the water. The boatman may relate a brief anecdote about the rapids you just ran or the ones to come. An off-color joke is not uncommon. But just as you really begin to relax, a distant low thunder intrudes. The boatman checks his oars or grabs his paddle, adjusts his position, and gets ready. The water begins to swirl and boil. This time you are already a veteran; you know what is ahead; your heart beats faster. The exhilaration builds earlier, and the cheering and shouting are more prolonged. The Middle Fork is in fact widely acknowledged as one of the premier white water rafting

---

* Grade IV (American Whitewater River Ratings, 2009): Intense, powerful but predictable rapids requiring precise boat handling in turbulent water. Depending on the character of the river, it may feature large, unavoidable waves and holes or constricted passages demanding fast maneuvers under pressure. A fast, reliable eddy turn may be needed to initiate maneuvers, scout rapids, or rest. Rapids may require "must" moves above dangerous hazards. Scouting may be necessary the first time down.

and kayaking rivers in the world. And in several places the canyon slopes and walls rise toward six thousand vertical feet above the river.

The Middle Fork and part of the main Salmon River are the heart of the Frank Church-River of No Return Wilderness (RNR), an area comprising 2.36 million acres, established under the Central Idaho Wilderness Act of 1980, Public Law 96-312. The smaller 205,000-acre Gospel Hump Wilderness borders the River of No Return to the northwest, and together they form the largest continuous dedicated wilderness land in the lower forty-eight states. To the north, a single track dirt road known as the Magruder Corridor—the old Nez Perce Trail—separates the River of No Return from yet another wilderness, the 1.34 million acre Selway-Bitterroot Wilderness Area.[9]

The Salmon River Mountains dominate the interior of RNR, and four other mountain ranges comprise a vast array of ridges, deep canyons, glaciated peaks, and meadows. Deer, moose, mountain lion, bighorn sheep, elk, mountain goats, black bear, lynx, and now the grey wolf, inhabit this country. It is also one of the most important remaining habitats of the wolverine in the lower forty-eight. The singular Big Horn Crags form a jagged series of summits and are surrounded by fourteen strikingly beautiful, clear lakes. Rivers like the Middle Fork and their tributaries carve their way through in deep canyons—"rivers of no return"; you may get down them, but you cannot return upstream. In August 1805 the Lewis and Clark Expedition, that incredibly fearless and rugged group of explorers, came through near the southern part of the RNR, took a look at the Salmon with the thought of floating down to its confluence with the Snake River, pronounced it impassable, and detoured around. This region was also the home of the Nez Perce Indians and that legendary band led by the remarkable Chief Joseph. In the early 1970s, the heart of this magnificent country was the 1.03 million acre Idaho Primitive Area, established by the Forest Service in 1931 under the L-20 primitive area regulations.

It was apparent from the beginning that the struggle to achieve Wilderness Act classification for these superb forests, rivers, canyons, and peaks of central Idaho would be long and hard fought. The timber and mining industries had a great deal at stake, and rural Idaho citizens at that time were overwhelmingly opposed to wilderness status. Conservationists were equally committed to the need for wilderness protection for most of this marvelous region.

The Forest Service, still taking a minimalist approach, adopted a new strategy for review of the Idaho Primitive Area and its contiguous lands—a strategy completely different from those used in *East Meadow Creek* and *Uncompahgre*. In 1973, it preemptively forwarded a truncated wilderness proposal to Congress, leaving out several hundred thousand acres of the highest scenic and wilderness quality lands on the ground that a mineral survey of those lands, required by Forest Service regulations, had not been completed and published. Having tried unsuccessfully to avoid wilderness review for contiguous wilderness qualifying lands in East Meadow Creek, or negate it altogether in the Uncompahgre, the Forest Service decided to preempt the review process for the River of No Return country and get to Congress first with a terribly flawed wilderness proposal.

The Service simultaneously advised that it was going to administer the lands outside its very limited proposal for "multiple use," including logging and attendant road building, thus threatening destruction of their wilderness potential before Congress could act. Initial efforts by citizens and conservationists, and even the State of Idaho itself, to dissuade the Forest Service from this path were unsuccessful. The proposed logging tracts were huge. The Clear Creek-Garden Creek sale unit immediately adjacent to the primitive area was approximately 50,000 acres in size. Since it appeared to be first on the calendar, and the Forest Service had announced that it was ready to execute a contract, Clear Creek-Garden Creek became the focal point of the administrative legal efforts that followed.

Idaho conservationists had been keeping us informed as debate over the future of the primitive area grew. It was already clear we would have to make a stand at some point. Sale of the timber in the Clear Creek-Garden Creek unit would be the prelude to sales in additional units, and soon tens of thousands of acres contiguous to the Idaho Primitive Area would no longer qualify for wilderness review. Under similar circumstances in *East Meadow Creek*, we had gone directly to court. The lines between the parties were drawn, a timber sale contract had been executed, and the lawyers and parties went to work in their various adversarial roles. But here the Forest Service, despite stating its intentions in unmistakable terms, had arguably not yet taken definitive action. Logging contracts had not yet been signed. Courts are reluctant to accept jurisdiction when there is no definitive act for them to review, and where the complaining parties have not yet been injured. The matter is not "ripe" for judicial review. It does not yet constitute the "case or controversy" necessary for federal court jurisdiction. While we could have argued that the Forest Service was moving ineluctably toward massive sales of timber, and that this itself constituted legitimate grounds for judicial review, we thought that there might be an alternative short of the courthouse steps. After all, we could always go to court when direct government action actually took place, such as a specifically announced and identified sale of timber.

Review of Forest Service regulations showed us the possibility of an alternative direction to pursue. Agency-wide published regulations have the force of law in many instances. They require certain procedures and spell out appropriate standards to guide important Forest Service actions. Within this regulatory framework, we found provisions for formal administrative appeals to the Forest Service itself of its own decisions and actions. Maybe we could argue the issues at stake through a formal administrative appeal to the Forest Service. Today such appeals are commonplace. But in the early seventies these regulations slumbered in the regulatory structure, as yet unused by the conservation community for resolution of their issues. We decided to take a chance and see if we could effectively use them. Since the timber sale plans involved several national forests—the Boise, Salmon-Challis, Nez Perce, and Payette—we filed our petition with the Regional Forester's Office, the regional supervisory entity in Ogden, Utah.

We asserted that the holdings in the *East Meadow Creek* case were directly on point and authoritative: the Forest Service must complete proper review of the wilderness qualifying lands contiguous to the Idaho Primitive Area, and preemptive action—such as timber sales and attendant road building—must not take place until the President and Congress have had a chance to decide whether these lands would be part of the wilderness area. We believed this was the opening round of what would be a long and perhaps bitter legal fight. Idaho fell within the jurisdiction of the U.S. Court of Appeals for the Ninth Circuit, so the Tenth Circuit's affirmation of *East Meadow Creek*, while important authority, was not binding in Idaho. Thus, the U.S. District Court for Idaho could consider the Wilderness Act questions from the beginning and arrive at a totally different conclusion. And we had every reason to believe the Forest Service would adamantly oppose us in court all the way to final judgment.

> [T]here would be many wilderness heroes, sung and unsung, whose efforts were critical in this undertaking.

The Regional Forester docketed our petition for review and soon set a date for our appearance at his office in Ogden, Utah. I rendezvoused with my friend Doug Scott—the Wilderness Act historian cited earlier—in April 1974 at the Salt Lake City Airport, and we drove up to Ogden. I was counsel and representing the Sierra Club, and Doug, a senior staff person with The Wilderness Society, was appearing on its behalf. As we convened in the conference room, we found ourselves surrounded by Forest Service personnel. We were expecting a day of frustration and argument. We surmised this would be the first of many formal legal confrontations over the future of wilderness in central Idaho. But, it quickly became apparent this was not to be the case. The Forest Service had not come to fight; it had come to listen, to talk! The Regional Forester, Vern Hammer, wanted to talk about the lands we thought should be reviewed and studied. There was none of the earlier Forest Service demeanor that implied, "We know best." Quickly getting over our shock, we got out the maps, and soon maps were laid out everywhere. Fortunately, Idaho conservationists, Sierra Club, and The Wilderness Society had been busy, and we had a competent wilderness proposal showing and explaining the areas for which we sought wilderness review.

Discussion continued for another two or three hours. Everyone had something to say; the dialogue cleared the air, tensions were relieved, and issues developed and debated. Acreages, drainages, timber sales and road building plans, and existing conditions on the ground were thoroughly addressed. It was clear the Forest Service was taking our wilderness review issues seriously. We made no compromises, and the

Forest Service made no concessions. It was not that type of meeting. Wide-ranging and thoughtful discussion of the germane issues, such as we enjoyed that day, and which promised amicable feelings at the close, should rarely be concluded on a discordant note of argumentative posturing or insistent demands. This was our first such meeting in a formal context, and no interest had suffered any new or additional harm.

Mr. Hammer told us that the matter had high priority, and everything we said would be carefully considered. We would hear from him shortly, and timber sales and other activities would be suspended until that time. Doug and I celebrated all the way back to Salt Lake. We had no definite indication of what the Regional Forester would decide, but the change of Forest Service attitude was extraordinary, and we had every reason to believe we were better off than when we drove up to Ogden that morning. Our administrative appeal and the resulting discussion would likely lead to an important decision, and Forest Service concern over our issues seemed genuine. True to his word, the Regional Forester ruled within two weeks. Again, we were wonderfully surprised. He announced that no timber sales would be scheduled within the entire area of the citizens' *River of No Return* proposal for the next five years! The Chief of the Forest Service quickly approved this ruling.*

Six long years of debate, campaigning, public hearings, and legislative efforts in Congress ensued before the Central Idaho Wilderness Act was signed into law in 1980. But the Regional Forester's moratorium held firm; indeed it was extended until Congress acted. There were to be many more tense moments, and there would be many wilderness heroes, sung and unsung, whose efforts were critical in this undertaking. The conservationists held firm, and their persuasive arguments ultimately prevailed. The treasured Frank Church-River of No Return Wilderness is now 2.36 million acres, more than twice the size of the original Idaho Primitive Area. The Wilderness includes the old Clear Creek-Garden Creek timber sale unit.

Before Continuing…

Before continuing with these wilderness cases, a review of salient

---

* The head of the U.S. Forest Service is called Chief.

points of the *River of No Return* administrative appeal is instructive. At the outset, it must be recognized that the Regional Forester's friendly and thoughtful reception of this unprecedented administrative appeal laid the groundwork for what was to follow.

- The Forest Service changed direction and opened a previously parochial legal and policy interpretation to a broader platform.
- This was made easier by the nature of the meeting in Ogden. No concessions of important legal positions on the part of either party were discussed or sought. It was understood that management circumstances on the forest land involved were at issue and at a critical juncture, but it was unnecessary at that particular moment to dwell upon this.
- Both parties came prepared to discuss specific proposed timber sale units and specific areas for wilderness review; thus the discussions on these central topics could be meaningful.
- The State of Idaho was not present, but its known position of seeking a full review of most, if not all, of the wilderness qualifying lands in and around the Idaho Primitive Area, made the political context friendlier than it would have been otherwise.
- Using the moratorium approach enabled the Forest Service to preserve its discretion to recommend what it thought best at the end of the Wilderness Act review process. It had made no concessions affecting this discretion.
- The moratorium worked for the conservationists as well. After all, Congress was going to make the ultimate decision about which areas would be designated as wilderness and which areas would not. As long as the moratorium was honored, the conservation community retained the freedom to advocate wilderness status for the qualifying lands at stake. The duress of pending timber sales and road building was removed. And, the conservationists could use the time won to build their political strength.
- Both parties avoided protracted litigation with its uncertain outcome and its attendant expenses. They also avoided the unfortunate tendency of litigation to lock parties into entrenched positions, making the whole process more complicated, attenuated, and potentially more hostile.

Finally, Forest Service handling of the *River of No Return* appeal, and the decisive nature of its resolution, indicated that Forest Service administrative appeal options could in the future lead to substantial opportunities and success for the conservationists.

Citizen Campaigns for Wilderness—A Look Inside

By the early 1970s, review of primitive areas and their contiguous lands was accelerating across the West. Each area was the subject of a wilderness designation campaign led by local conservationists and assisted by national conservation organizations. Conservationists were exploring every ecological zone and mapping the boundaries of the wilderness qualifying lands—the alpine crests, ridges, and cirques, the rolling alpine meadows, the sparkling mountain streams and waterfalls, the forests and meadows stretching out below the high country, the lakes and wetlands throughout.

Let me introduce you to a wilderness campaign headquarters. We are entering a couple of rooms characterized by a sort of orderly chaos—confusion with a purpose—in a typically low-rent office building. Topographical maps of the U.S. Geological Survey cover the walls. Several maps are taped together in order to cover an entire area encompassing tens of thousands of acres under review. Different colored markers delineate boundaries and identify different jurisdictions and existing land classifications. Problem areas and non-conforming uses and structures such as roads and water diversion or storage structures are identified. Overlays show proposed timber sales, Forest Service wilderness boundary proposals or reviewing areas, and proposed transportation corridors. At all hours of the day and evening volunteers and staff are likely to be here, poring over the maps, discussing strategy, and figuring out what else needs to be done. In fact, most usable surfaces seem covered by the USGS maps. Where a map cannot be spread out, there is likely to be a stack of reports, surveys, advocacy papers, or brochures. Scattered amongst all this you can usually spy discarded pizza boxes and used soft drink cups. Wastebaskets in the corners, beside desks, and under tables are likely to be overflowing.

Wherever there is a gap between the maps covering the walls, there will be a picture or two of wilderness scenery, but usually the most noticeable item is a large calendar of upcoming deadlines and events: deadlines for filing comments with the Forest Service, dates of important public hearings and congressional committee or subcommittee hearings, scheduled trips to the field to get more information on particular areas, and various task assignments. Here and there are old, rather beat-up desks. Large collapsible tables with folding chairs for volunteers stand in open areas, and on top of them—you guessed it—maps and more maps. Some people are reviewing photographs for a slide show. And phones—there are several phones scattered about with long cords stretching across the floor, ready to trip the unwary. When these phones ring, folks often have to "follow the sound" to find the right receiver. When events are jumping it can be difficult to move around, with eight or ten people crowded into the room. Navigation requires careful attention to objects stacked on the floor or casually strewn about. In a corner there will be an old coffee pot at work—some of the worst coffee imaginable. But we all drink it.

Let's visit such an office on a typical evening. A group of conservationists is gathered around a large table stuffing envelopes with a brochure describing Garland's Great Arete Wilderness Candidate Area and apprising readers of a forthcoming Forest Service public hearing. The envelopes are pre-addressed to local activists, people on membership lists of conservation organizations involved, volunteers in the community, and various public officials. Two telephones are being used, one by a volunteer and the other by a part-time staff person talking to potential wilderness supporters, alerting them to the coming hearing. Let's listen in:

Thanks for calling me back Margaret ... Yes, I was calling about the Garland's Great Arete wilderness hearing coming up week after next. You signed up to volunteer at our booth at the People's Fair a few weeks ago.

[...]

Wonderful! ... It's Friday, September 21st, at the Town Hall, starting at nine A.M.

[...]

Good. So you got the printout describing the citizens' proposal, contrasting it with the Forest Service proposal....

[...]

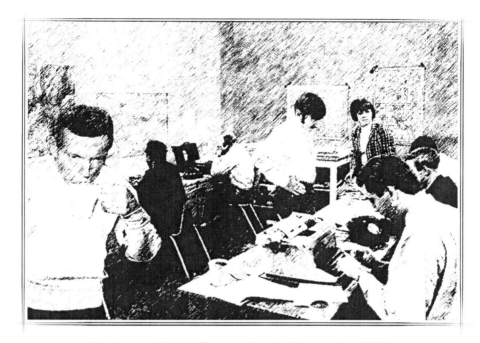

Environmentalists' office anywhere in the country, 1970s

Yeah, the Forest Service's proposal is pretty small. It is leaving a lot of forest, creek drainages, and lakes out—typical—a "wilderness on the rocks."

[...]

Can you get to the Town Hall around 8:30? We want our supporters as high up on the list of public witnesses as possible in case the hearing is on the evening news. The press may only stay for a short while, and we need to get as many supporters as we can into the record.

[...]

Probably not right away....

[...]

You know how it is—all the public officials get to go first, and that's after the Forest Service introduction.

[...]

Sign up and then run over to Hutchison's Bakery across the street. Their coffee and cinnamon rolls are great! You'll have time....

[...]

Actually, there may be a couple of county commissioners supporting us, or at least saying the Forest Service proposal is inadequate.

[...]

That's the point, with the election coming up in six weeks....

[...]

And we can expect the state wildlife people are going to be critical of parts of the Forest Service proposal.

[...]

Listen, I know how it is with kids. If Alan can't stay home with them, I understand. The record remains open for another thirty days for written statements, so—

[...]

Yeah, they're not as good as oral testimony backed by a written summary, but they're better than nothing.

[...]

There's no question the press will be there. They've been covering this from day...—hold on a minute, Margaret—

[...]

[*covering the mouthpiece*] HEY! Will you loud mouths keep it down over there! I'm on the phone with a supporter.

[...]

I'm back Margaret. The volunteers ... they've got an old TV going in the corner. The CU-Nebraska game is on. I think CU just scored.

[...]

Go Buffs, right! Anyway, the press has been covering this from day one. Howard—you know Howard, he's the one with the great slide show of the wilderness. Well, he's working on our publicity—

[...]

Yes, yes ... you're reading that right....

[...]

They really are! They are leaving out Switchback Creek! The Forest Service is leaving out the whole drainage....

[...]

I hear you, but we need to go easy on the invective. We need to marshal our facts here. What we really—

[...]

Yes, that means that the Forest Service is really leaving out Poticha Hot Springs.

[...]

I agree! We all agree. Switchback Creek is the most beautiful drainage. The citizens' proposal has the entire drainage in it.

[...]

Sure, the whole drainage ought to be wilderness on the facts. But you know about Green Brothers' Lumber Company. They've had their eyes on Switchback for years.

[...]

Yes, and the Kootenai Construction Company wants to build a road for hauling the timber out. But—

[...]

Margaret! Anyway, we expect company representatives and some of their employees will be testifying. That's the way it's done, you know. They get to say their piece. That's why—

[...]

Yes, we're going for the whole thing. If we get Crystal Lake, Poticha Hot Springs, and down Switchback to Madonna Cascades, we will be doing pretty well. But we're going to have to fight hard.

[...]

Right. We'll get help from the state wildlife people. That's a great trout stream, and it's great lynx habitat. Good elk calving and summer range. The fishermen and the guides and outfitters are on board....

[...]

That's right, if we get the Creek at least down to the cascades, we'll get the best beaver dams and ponds. And those marvelous aspen stands in there—you know, Nancy's grove....

[...]

We can get them—but our people have to show up....

[...]

Absolutely! And one more thing. Members of the House of Representatives' Wilderness Subcommittee are coming out in a couple of weeks. Keep that in the back of your mind. I expect they'll have a staff person at the hearing checking things out....

[...]

Well, we just heard this yesterday: Congressman Younger says he's

going to look our proposal over carefully! Apparently, he thinks the
Forest Service proposal is too limited....

[...]

Yeah, it's about time. I think that trip Phil and Carla led for him and
his staff and some of the press up there last summer may have got to
him. He was really impressed with the hot springs—took his boots off
and waded right in.

[...]

You're right. The press coverage we've been getting, and the letters
and calls he's received from voters, are helping a lot.

[...]

I've got to run, too. It's been great talking. I'll see you at the hearing.
And let us know if you need a ride there. Martha is arranging rides.

Notice the details in the volunteer's conversation: the conflicting proposals, the existence of explanatory and illustrative materials, good on-
the-ground familiarity with the area, important events and dates,
attention to the formal administrative record, recruitment and use of
volunteers, press and media, the political factor, both local and national,
wildlife aspects, allies, the opposition, and the most critical areas in the
citizens' proposal. Equally important is the enthusiasm of the volunteer.
All of these are necessary elements of a wilderness campaign.

The conservationists' agenda is usually to get as much acreage of
wilderness in a given study area, or in proposed legislation, as the quality and unity of the lands in question permit. Proposals are generous,
but they are rationally reached and rarely excessive. A growing population on a finite land base with only a small fraction of that land of wilderness quality, coupled with the likelihood that the Forest Service and the
commodity-use interests will urge a minimalist approach, are two of the
principal justifications for these generous proposals. In fact, millions of
people are visiting wilderness areas each year. There are other cogent
reasons for sizeable wilderness areas: protection of large ecosystems to
insure the presence of suitable habitat for large wide-ranging carnivores,
watershed protection in terms of both water supply and water quality,
and preservation of extensive and diverse plant communities in an
untrammeled state which can remain self-sufficient and self-regenerat-
ing. Awesome scenery and beauty are practically a given. Then there is

the intangible spiritual quality, the essence of wilderness. Perhaps this is most succinctly captured in David Brower's words: "Real wilderness is big wilderness—country big enough to have a beyond to it and an inside."[10]

From the beginning, conservationists did not confine their efforts to the old Forest Service primitive areas. There are many other extraordinary areas within our national forests which qualified as "wilderness," and which were worthy of formal wilderness area protection. As we have been discussing, conservationists marshaled wilderness campaigns across the West, beginning in the late 1960s, and from an early date they incorporated into their efforts a well-selected group of what came to be called *de facto* wilderness lands—eligible areas of wilderness quality, which at the time had no statutory wilderness review mandate.

These candidate lands were initially championed by concerned members of the public. Wilderness advocacy organizations were in place with their trained staff and avid volunteers, and public support of the wilderness preservation concept was clearly growing and broadening. In fact the first citizen-initiated de facto wilderness bill was introduced in 1965, one year after adoption of the Wilderness Act. The Forest Service had planned to road and log a wonderful area directly south of the existing Bob Marshall Wilderness in Montana. Organizational support for the wilderness was strong in Montana, and the congressional delegation was committed to protecting the area. As a result, the Scapegoat Wilderness Area Act was passed in 1972.[11] Other efforts for de facto wilderness lands were underway.

While these events were unfolding, Congress passed the National Environmental Policy Act (NEPA), and it was signed into law by President Richard M. Nixon in January 1970. NEPA requires comprehensive environmental review and a detailed written environmental impact statement (EIS) for any major federal action significantly affecting the environment. NEPA clearly applies to the Forest Service, and most certainly any timber sale of significant size has to conform to its mandates. Specifically included in any EIS is a thorough review of alternatives to the proposed federal action. This includes the "no action" alternative—in other words the proposed federal action harmful to the wilderness character of subject lands, such as a proposed timber sale, would just not take place. NEPA procedures would become an important part of the wilderness equation, as we shall see in the next section.[12]

Evolving Forest Service Procedures

Even before the *River of No Return Wilderness* accommodation in Idaho, it was increasingly apparent to the Forest Service that it had lost the initiative in wilderness review matters, and it could lose practical control of the situation, as wilderness classification contests and the review processes continued to gain momentum. Conservationists were increasingly well organized, and their proposals were usually well constructed. Congress was actively interested. The Wilderness Act and the National Environmental Policy Act clearly changed life as the Forest Service had known it in previous decades. Seeking to once more be a real, if not dominant, entity in this burgeoning process, the Forest Service initiated the 1971-1973 Roadless Area Review and Evaluation (RARE) process to inventory roadless areas and select those worthy of further review for potential wilderness classification.

Once again, however, the Forest Service severely limited its horizons. It seemed locked into its traditional role of actively managing forestlands for commodity development and comprehensive road systems. Out of 56 million acres which were inventoried as physically qualified, it selected only 12.3 million for further study. Consequently, Sierra Club lawyers in San Francisco brought suit under NEPA in the U.S. District Court for Northern California. From Denver we assisted this important litigation by gathering supporting evidence and affidavits from the Rockies and from the Southwest. I have always enjoyed organizing evidence into a cogent presentation for a court, and here I could devote my entire attention to this part of the case. Local wilderness advocates, wilderness guides and outfitters, hikers and climbers, and knowledgeable staff members of national conservation organizations all had their input. Under the leadership of able counsel they carried the day. Settlement was reached, and the Forest Service agreed to evaluate the wilderness potential of any significant roadless area in an EIS under NEPA before approving activities that would disqualify that area from future wilderness status.

As the RARE process unfolded, however, the Forest Service seemed to continually resist the intent of the public to have a representative, well protected, and expansive National Wilderness System. Again and again the Service would apply a rigorous standard of "purity" for lands to qualify for wilderness study. This standard rejected lands where evidence of man's previous activities had grown faint over time and old roads had reverted to trails, where old timber cuts had substantially grown over, or where old mining structures were abandoned long ago and were deteriorating into the landscape. The Forest Service ignored the more inclusive definitions of wilderness in the Wilderness Act. The inevitable result was to preclude from wilderness consideration large tracts of overwhelmingly wild land, which could then be returned to eligibility for logging and road construction. This flawed RARE inventory was released in 1972. Declaring that many of the inventoried lands had no wilderness value, the Forest Service immediately offered some of them for timber sales.

> The Wilderness Act and the National Environmental Policy Act clearly changed life as the Forest Service had known it in previous decades.

Again, Sierra Club promptly sued, and a preliminary injunction was issued arresting such sales until an EIS pursuant to NEPA was completed. A few months later the Forest Service settled the case, agreeing to complete an EIS before letting any new timber contracts on inventoried roadless areas. Congress was involved by this time, and after congressional "oversight" hearings and further debate, the Assistant Secretary of Agriculture announced that the Forest Service was embarking on a new effort to better inventory roadless lands. This became known as the RARE II inventory and review. As a part of this reformed process, the wilderness "purity" standard was abandoned. Wilderness review and advocacy continue in many locales today with strategies and procedures reflecting contemporary conditions, issues, and objectives. And court decisions continue to play a critical role.

Contradiction in Indian Peaks

The purity issue highlights the lengths to which strained interpretations of statutory language can be carried. This was illustrated perfectly in the review of the Indian Peaks area west of Boulder, Colorado. The Indian Peaks Wilderness Area in Roosevelt and Arapaho National Forests was established by Public Law 95-450 in 1978. The Wilderness totals 76,486 acres of the Front Range of the Rockies from the southern border of Rocky Mountain National Park south to Rollins Pass, a distance of eighteen miles. Serrated ridges and jagged peaks sculpted by glaciers characterize this wilderness. Lying in glacially carved bowls are nearly fifty clear, sparkling lakes, many of them a beautiful turquoise blue color. Located just west of Boulder and the Denver metropolitan area with easy road access, Indian Peaks is one of the most frequently visited wilderness areas in the country.

Over 110 miles of trails bring hikers, back-country skiers and snow-shoers, photographers, backpackers, and rock climbers into the wilderness. Trails in glacial basins such as the Middle Fork of the St. Vrain River are heavily used. Lake Isabelle and Blue Lake are gorgeous alpine lakes at the base of soaring ragged peaks lying a relatively easy hiking distance from the trailhead. At the time of the wilderness review in 1976 and 1977, controversy had swelled to a crescendo over the Forest Service decision to exclude such heavily used areas from a congressionally mandated wilderness review. The Forest Service felt that easy urban access to, and very heavy use of, the trails along the Middle Fork and in other nearby areas disqualified these areas for wilderness status. The Forest Service concluded these areas lacked the feeling of "solitude" necessary for wilderness. Mark Pearson, a veteran of Colorado wilderness, ably summarizes the controversy and its rather obvious solution in *Colorado's Wilderness Areas*:

The question was this:

[H]ow can the requisite opportunities for solitude demanded by the Wilderness Act be met by an area as popular as Indian Peaks? The answer was much the same as for most wilderness areas: some parts, such as readily accessible lakes short distances from trailheads, will continue to be heavily used while undisturbed quiet and solitude will still be found in trailless drainages, such as those west of the Continental Divide. The challenge for managers would be to mitigate resource impacts where large numbers of people congregate and to distribute use to lesser visited portions of the wilderness or even into nearby non-wilderness areas.[13]

The Forest Service at first resisted such common sense thinking. After all, there was potentially much room for maneuver by using such an imprecise measure as "solitude." Like the closely related concept of "purity," the Forest Service might be able to retain broad management discretion over larger parts of its forests by using indeterminate concepts to counter overwhelming facts on the ground. We were asked by Sierra Club and local environmentalists to intervene. We quickly pointed out to the Regional Forester and the Chief of the Forest Service that their interpretation of the Wilderness Act's definition of wilderness was far too restrictive. The statutory definition of wilderness indeed mentions solitude, but this must be viewed in the more complete context of the Act:

> Section 2 (c). A wilderness is an area ... which (1) generally appears to have been affected primarily by the forces of nature, with the imprint of man's work substantially unnoticeable; (2) has outstanding opportunities for solitude or a primitive and unconfined type of recreation.[14]

The qualifiers used and the congressional intent for a broadly inclusive interpretation of the Act's definition of "wilderness" are obvious.

The Forest Service soon relented, and the regional forester agreed to publicly explain that heavy use of trail systems was legally compatible with wilderness designation, and that Forest Service final review reports and findings would be revised accordingly. While this controversy was quickly resolved, it is instructive. Practically no legislation can be written which is so absolute, precise, and at the same time all-encompassing in its terms, that it can address every circumstance, situation, or variation which may subsequently arise. Reasonable interpretations are required; this is the teaching of the law and the courts. Thus one must be wary of those who pick out a single word or term in a statute and attach to it a dispositive meaning regardless of context.

Application of a standard whereby existence of a wilderness area, a park, a wildlife refuge, is conclusively defined by the management agency's ability to maximize its solitude would lead to folly: an area of absolute "solitude" would be preserved for public enjoyment, but only a tiny fraction of the public could use it at any time. And the boundary of the protected area would be as far removed from public access points as necessary to assure maximum "solitude." Mark Pearson's solutions are obvious: accept the existence of congestion at trailheads, accept that particularly striking or accessible areas may be heavily visited, but mitigate the impacts of such visitation to the extent you can. Be tolerant where you must, manage the area so that trails disperse visitors over larger areas, and then keep some areas trailless altogether.

For all that, this argument over the meaning of the single word "solitude" may still seem gratuitously technical. After all, it was likely the Forest Service would manage the headwaters of the Middle Fork of the St. Vrain for recreational purposes even without wilderness classification. There are persuasive responses to this supposition. The boundary of a wilderness area demarcates those lands that will be managed for wilderness and those that can be used for multiple purposes. As you cross the line into wilderness, all management practices become dedicated to wilderness protection. The developed recreational activities and facilities just downstream from the Indian Peaks Wilderness boundary—the improved campground, the trailer park for seasonal Forest Service personnel, access roads and parking lots, entrance and information huts, road pullouts and parking around Brainard Lake—will not expand upstream into the wilderness. And beautiful Long Lake—Indian Peaks' largest; within the wilderness but touching the boundary line and readily accessible to the public—will remain in its practically unblemished condition. Finally, there is the intangible value of knowing wilderness is there; that after parking your car and grabbing your day-pack you will step into wilderness, to be greeted by Long Lake, or by the equally pristine Mitchell Lake a half-mile in on the northerly trail to Blue Lake. Thus, a narrow literal interpretation of that one word—*solitude*—completely ignoring the context of its use in the statutory language could have had far-reaching consequences.

To those of us living in the Denver-Boulder area it is difficult to imagine Indian Peaks as anything other than protected wilderness. Countless mornings over the years I have risen at dawn in Denver, driven my car the less than two hours' journey to the St. Vrain trailheads, and hiked the two plus miles to Lake Isabelle—passing Long Lake on the way—or three miles to the truly alpine Blue Lake with the stunning waterfall at its head. The aromatic smell of the spruce-fir forest and the vibrant fields of wildflowers—particularly the large spread of blood-red Parry's Primrose in the cascades above Mitchell Lake—sharpen my senses. When mid-day arrives, I seek out a good vantage point to sit and relax just beneath the peaks for an hour or two, contemplating the scene and the wonder of it all. As the afternoon wears on, I return down the trail with heart and spirit renewed, with a "spring" in my soul—if not necessarily in my legs—and with an agreeable fatigue at the end of a wonderful hike, a true escape into a moment of wilderness. By the way, Congress included these trails as part of the Indian Peaks Wilderness Area in its establishment act of 1978.

Holy Cross Wilderness—Petitioning the Chief

This wilderness controversy had an absolutely unique finish. The Holy Cross Wilderness Area in San Isabel and White River National Forests in central Colorado was established by Public Law 95-560 in 1980. Totaling approximately 122,000 acres, the wilderness includes twenty-five summits over 13,000 feet and Mount Holy Cross itself at 14,003 feet. The ultimate "water wilderness," this area abounds in emerald green lakes, countless streams, pools, and cascades, and impressive expanses of glacially carved valleys. The Seven Sisters Lakes, stair-stepped one above the other amidst towering rock cliffs, are a favorite destination. This wilderness glistens and shimmers with water. Historically this water has been coveted by the cities of Aurora and Colorado Springs. Consequently, controversy, conflict, and litigation have been frequent fare—the municipalities seeking maximum water diversion, with the state, federal government, and environmental community all fully engaged attempting to protect their particular interests.

The headwaters and mountainous core were part of the Forest Service RARE process discussed previously. At the same time (1974–1975), the Beaver Creek Ski Area, now a large destination ski resort, was on the drawing board, and its proponents were pressing for Forest Service permits in the northern reaches of the Holy Cross study area. The ski area developers, Vail Associates, wanted the permits to extend far into the backcountry toward Holy Cross Mountain itself.

Environmentalists* wanted a reasonable buffer extending away from the immediate presence of the mountain and the early stretches of the streams born in its glacial cirques and on its heavily watered slopes.

The fact remains that the Wilderness Act was unprecedented and incredibly far-seeing and wise.

Fellow counsel in our local Denver office organized the case. First, we forced the Forest Service to reconsider the project's air, water, and growth-inducing impacts pursuant to the National Environmental Policy Act. This achievement accomplished important environmental and wildlife mitigation measures, but it did not protect the threatened wilderness country. For that we used the now familiar administrative appeal process, arguing that regulations and administrative directives governing the RARE process were not being followed by the Regional Forester's office, which was conducting the review and would ultimately recommend or grant the requisite permits. We lodged our appeal with the Chief's office. We discovered a previously unused provision in the regulations outlining administrative appeals, which permitted appellants or petitioners—Sierra Club and The Wilderness Society were our clients—to request an appearance before the Chief to argue their case. Our request was granted, and we flew to Washington, DC The Executive Offices of the Department of Agriculture were in the old Department of Agriculture building on the Mall, just across from the Washington Monument. At the appointed hour we arrived at the Chief's suite of offices.

Chief John McGuire, a tall, distinguished gentleman with an outdoor look, ushered us into his office. It looked out over the Mall, and by walking to the windows and looking northwest you had an uninterrupted view of the Washington Monument. It was a large room with lots of wall space, and the history of the Forest Service emerged from the pictures hung there. Classic bookcases and period furniture and chairs were dis-

---

* By the mid '70s, conservationists were increasingly being called environmentalists, so I generally use this terminology for the remainder of the book.

tributed about in comfortable fashion. At the "working end" was a rather small desk. Chief McGuire proudly related that it was the original desk used by Gifford Pinchot, Theodore Roosevelt's confidante and the first chief of the U.S. Forest Service. At the other end of the room was a sitting area with several chairs around a coffee table. We sat down and opened with friendly conversation—the mundane topics of weather, the trip out from Denver, a little more of Forest Service history. We were joined shortly by a staff person and by a lawyer from the Department of Agriculture Solicitor's Office. Good china cups and saucers were brought in for coffee. The atmosphere was friendly, even convivial.

The Chief finally brought us to the subject matter by remarking that this meeting or "appearance" was brand new to him, and, he thought, probably new to the Forest Service. He hoped we would understand if he was feeling his way. We talked a bit about the RARE issues and the ski area. We got as far as expressing our view that Beaver Creek Ski Area did not need all the land it sought in the permit application, when McGuire interrupted and said he wanted to get the Regional Forester on the phone. His secretary placed the call, and the connection was soon made. The Chief picked up the phone at our sitting area. He told the Regional Forester that we were there with him in his office, and that our arguments seemed cogent. He believed we were probably correct that the ski area did not need so much "backcountry," and the proposed permit boundary was too close to Mount Holy Cross. To us that pretty much covered it. There was no point then in launching into a detailed argument and presentation. Chief McGuire said he assumed we had heard everything he said, and that he or the Regional Forester would return the area in question to the roadless area review process for further wilderness study. A few days later this was done and the bulk of the contested area is now in the Holy Cross Wilderness Area.

As we saw in the *River of No Return* case, your opponent can become your ally. I had occasion to see Chief McGuire on a couple of subsequent occasions. He was invariably cordial and interested in what our office was doing. Of course we were almost always involved in some controversy with the Forest Service in those years, so our conversation would sometimes be a bit oblique, but he was always friendly. As noted, by this time in the mid-seventies wilderness reviews were taking place in all the western states. None was a simple matter, and given the extraordinarily diverse and rich resources found in our public lands, competition between competing interests was constant and intense. The fact remains that the Wilderness Act was unprecedented and incredibly far-seeing and wise. For the first time a people had declared through a law passed by their elected representatives that preservation and protection by law of some places on the earth in a wild uncompromised state is an important objective. They declared there were values in these lands beyond minerals to be extracted, timber to be harvested, road corridors to be established, or intensely developed recreational facilities to be constructed.

Wilderness area review and establishment of new wilderness areas is a continuing process. In 1975, eleven years after the Wilderness Act, the Eastern Wilderness Act was passed establishing wilderness areas east of the Mississippi River, such as the Beaver Creek Wilderness in Kentucky.[15] These are generally smaller areas than those in the West, for the ravages of an industrialized nation are more widespread. Additionally, important public lands previously used by man for other purposes were returning to their natural state, were appearing less blemished and increasingly wild, and were worthy candidates for a crowded populace to enjoy and appreciate. In 1976 the Federal Land Management and Policy Act extended wilderness review and potential classification to vast unreserved public lands managed by the Bureau of Land Management.[16]

President William J. Clinton's administration promulgated the Roadless Area Conservation Rule in 2001, which temporarily protected 58 million roadless acres of National Forest land, barring non-conforming uses until these areas could be reviewed for potential wilderness status. President George W. Bush worked to reverse President Clinton's action, for the Bush administration was adamantly opposed. At this writing, the administration of President Barack Obama is vacillating about reinstating the Clinton Rule. As always, the federal courts are at the center of the process, with court rulings continuing to have a critical impact. These administrative and legal processes continue today, each major step challenged and tested, and slowly a National Wilderness System is emerging which even now is the envy of the world.

The Maroon Bells and a Marble Quarry

The Maroon Bells-Snowmass Wilderness Area in White River and Gunnison National Forests was established directly by the Wilderness

Maroon Bells-Snowmass Wilderness Area, Colorado

Act of 1964 and substantially enlarged in 1980 by Public Law 96-560. The Wilderness now totals 180,962 acres of the Elk Mountain Range. The whole area is spectacular. North and west of the Bells, Capitol Peak, with its famous "knife-edge" ridge with dangerous exposure on each side leading to the last scramble to the summit, and Snowmass Mountain, with its enormous snow field on its eastern flank, lie at the crests of long waves of jagged rock ridges gracefully curving above alpine lakes and meadows below. Located east and a little south of the Bells is Castle Peak, the highest summit in the Elks, guarded by its surrounding battlements and its companion Cathedral Peak. Below these are Castle Creek and the esteemed Conundrum Creek Hot Springs. Some of the most extensive stands of aspen in the state cover the lower altitudes, and the sub-alpine flower-carpeted meadows and aspen glades are among the most beautiful in the Rocky Mountain West.

In the narrow Conundrum Creek drainage cutting downward from Castle Peak, though, the long shadow of western history intrudes. As you can readily conclude from these pages, our uses of public lands, the various "rights" to them, and their management, both in the past and presently, are the product of history and politics. And this history confronted and openly challenged the new ethic of wilderness preservation in the Maroon Bells-Snowmass Wilderness Area. Thus in Conundrum Creek, well within the wilderness and just short of the marvelous hot springs, lies an old marble quarry cut. Gold and silver were also sought in the immediate area a hundred years ago. In 1985, 472 acres in the heart of this amazing wilderness, including the quarry site, were still privately owned, patented to private owners under antique nineteenth century mining laws.

Notes from the Field
(A wilderness campsite high in the Colorado Rockies)

Evening is coming on. The wind has died down to just a murmur. The only distinctive sounds are the melodious notes of a couple of Hermit Thrushes coming from the forest. The cooking stoves have been turned off and sleeping gear has been arranged in the small tents—sleeping bags fluffed up and ready for quick occupancy. The last hot water fills cups of hot tea—a couple supplemented with a fine old brandy. We huddle close around the campfire—the glowing embers and diminishing flames warding off some of the colder night air now settling in. Remaining rays of the setting sun momentarily tinge the highest peaks with a reddish or pinkish glow—alpine glow—and then quickly recede leaving the darkening forms of the mountains etched against the evening sky. Stars begin to appear.

Conversation is subdued—the day's climb or hike; that huge bull elk grazing in the alpine meadow. Often we turn to comparisons: the couloir up there today is like the one on Crestone Needle; the basin reminds me of Chicago Basin down in the Needle Mountains. Then someone asks what we think is the finest place in Colorado's mountains; the place with the most dramatic peaks and the finest mountain scenery. The Maroon Bells and Pyramid Peak, each rising above West Maroon Creek to 14,000 feet in the Elk Mountains of central Colorado will be leading candidates.

As the fire dies, the stars increasingly fill the darkening sky, and the Milky Way arches across the vault of heaven. Images of "the Bells" and Pyramid Peak rising straight up from the valley floor fill the minds of these mountain veterans—the deep red color of the Bells against a deep blue sky and the dramatic striations of their rock cliffs which reflect back to the eye from the clean still water of Maroon Lake. Crenellated Pyramid Peak, also of that deep red sedimentary rock and spectacular in its own right, stands sentinel for the Bells across the narrow valley.

The finest superlatives seem inadequate to describe these jewels of the mountains. But soon it is time to turn in; dawn comes early, and tomorrow promises to be another exhilarating day in the mountains. A person can do worse than fall asleep with such thoughts on his mind.

That year the Forest Service purchased the surface interest to these claims, but this failed to give complete protection, for the mineral rights and the timber—the very trees themselves—remained in private hands. Immediately after the Forest Service acquisition, two individuals living in Aspen claiming ownership of the mineral estate announced their intent to open an active quarry on the holding. By 1987 the Forest Service had prepared an environmental assessment, negotiated with the miners, and settled upon a limited access permit for ten trips and the removal of thirty tons of marble—previously quarried blocks which lay on the valley floor. The miners intended to test the marble and explore potential markets for it. Prior to this, the quarry had been briefly worked some eighty years before. In the intervening years, the quarry site and the old access road were steadily returning to their natural state.

We lawyers were engaged by Sierra Club and The Wilderness Society in 1986. Given the incredible damage that would ensue from active quarrying operations, we sought all available remedies. The local Pitkin County Commissioners opposed the quarry as fiercely as the environmentalists, and the County Attorney joined us in all of our legal efforts. Our arguments involved the following:

- We researched titles in the Pitkin County Courthouse, finding title flaws which slowed matters down and gave us a bit of breathing room;
- We asserted NEPA jurisdiction by virtue of Forest Service ownership of the land surface;
- We contested permit applications before the Colorado Mined Land Reclamation Division of the State Department of Natural Resources, and we appealed the Division's pro-quarry ruling to State court;
- The County passed resolutions creating temporary "road blocks";
- We continually urged the federal government to bring condemnation proceedings if an outright purchase could not be negotiated.

The miners were unmoved. The federal government eventually made a ridiculously minimal financial offer to the owners for purchase of their rights, which was promptly rejected. At one point however, the miners, using their lawyer to preserve confidentiality, broached their own thoughts on a buyout to me in my capacity as counsel for the environmentalists. Unfortunately, the Forest Service panned this overture. The miners continued a pattern of quick trips into their claim designed to irritate the Forest Service, the citizens of Aspen and the county, and the environmental community. Despite all the posturing and all the legal maneuvering, this fight could really only have one outcome.

Imagine the explosive thunder of dynamite blasts as miners attack the very heart of the Elk Range. Imagine the ground shaking, the dust rising from the quarry, the roar of machinery, the shrieking of drills, and the rumble of trucks hauling ore out of the valley. Imagine this in Conundrum Creek, below Castle Peak and hard by Pyramid Peak and the iconic Maroon Bells! In Colorado's signature wilderness area! It was more than politicians of any persuasion could endure. The claims would have to be purchased, or they would have to be condemned at fair value. And so they were. The Forest Service rejected the latter route and, given the protracted history and delay, paid far more than the amount implied by the miners when they made their earlier overture to us.

There are areas which are so valuable, so definitive of all a statute or a law seeks to accomplish, that they really cannot be compromised. So it was in Conundrum Creek in the heart of the Maroon Bells. The real question is whether the dance should have lasted so long. This is not easy to answer. In an open democracy, there is a presumption that all interests and all firmly held opinions will be heard. It may seem wasteful at times, and goodness knows the imperative to protect the Maroon Bells- Snowmass Wilderness was clear from the outset. Indeed the Forest Service had already purchased the surface rights. But in a society that recognizes and even promotes the interplay of conflicting interests in the hope that better decisions will be the product, efficiency may not have the highest priority. Regardless, the trail is still open to Conundrum Hot Springs, and the Bells, Pyramid, and Castle still reign over true wilderness. We have every reason to expect they will reign for generations to come.

CHAPTER V

Sculptured Lands

Notes from the Field
(Canyonlands National Park, Utah—June, 1974)

Another Campfire. We are here for a two-day meeting of the Southwest Regional Conservation Committee of the Sierra Club. We call the committee SWRCC, activist and staff leaders from the Four Corners states of Utah, Colorado, New Mexico, and Arizona. Some fifteen or twenty of us rendezvoused last night at Squaw Flat Campground, the end of the maintained road in the Needles District of this recently dedicated Canyonlands National Park.

This morning was tough—coaxing, pushing, and winching several jeeps and pickup trucks up the infamous Elephant Hill. We had to lift the little Volkswagen and carry it up over a couple of the worst spots. After Elephant Hill, we slowly negotiated an old ungraded vehicle track for a mile or two, parked our vehicles, shouldered our packs, and set out on foot. After enduring a sharp but thankfully short rain squall, we passed through a gap in the rock formations and walked out into a broad grassy meadow ringed by the needles of Canyonlands—striking rock spires and tall layered formations of red, white, and yellow sandstone. Chesler Park.

Five small camps have been set up, each in its own alcove beneath the rocks and needles ringing the park, but each within sight of another. Dinner pots and pans are being cleaned and put away; gear is being organized. A couple of folks have found an old fire ring and are building a communal fire. The sun is just dipping below the horizon, and the clouds in the still blue sky—white fleecy ones just above and a dark grey squall line of a retreating storm off to the east—are trying on their red, pink, and orange colors.

The rocks glow vibrantly for several minutes, displaying their own palette, especially the reds, to their best effect. Contrasting with the rocks and the sunset sky, the now dark greens and grey-greens of the juniper, isolated pinyons, and the sage scattered before me provide dark accent points to this marvelous scene. I listen again for a final song from the Canyon Wren, whose clear cascading notes—the song of Canyonlands—accompanied me while I was setting up my own camp.

As the shadows lengthen, the small blue and white flames of the camp stoves flickering in the soft evening breeze resemble fallen stars in the fading light. The smell of sage and juniper lingers in the air. I am thinking of what I have recently heard about this proposed massive power plant project called Kaiparowits. I understand it is probably the single greatest threat in historic time to the parklands of this astonishing corner of the planet.

Tomorrow John McComb, the Sierra Club's regional staff director, is going to tell us about Kaiparowits in detail. It is the subject of our two-day meeting here. This group of activists will begin to develop the broad strategy and get an idea of the effort that will be required to fight it. Legal advice and action will no doubt be needed, so I was invited to come. For now though, the camp stoves are winking out one by one, a friend has brought out his guitar and is tuning it up, and folks are beginning to gather around the communal campfire. I'm heading over to join them.

Kaiparowits Power Plant: An Unprecedented Threat To The Colorado Plateau

What amazing country this is—this land geologists and geographers call the Colorado Plateau! Reaching more than 200 miles north from the Grand Canyon through northern Arizona and encompassing all of southern Utah, the sculptured land of the plateau is a boldly etched landscape of sandstone cliffs, dramatic canyons, petrified sand dunes, swells, reefs, and folds, an expanse of soaring arches, natural bridges, spires, needles, goblins, ribs, and fins. There are painted deserts, petrified forests, and ancient abandoned Pueblo cliff dwellings. This is "red rock country"—predominately red sandstone, but everywhere brightened by pinks, oranges, yellows and almost pure white. "The colors are ... deep, rich, variegated," wrote the pioneering geologist Clarence Dutton in 1880, "and so luminous ... that light seems to glow out or shine out of the rock rather than be reflected from it."[1] Patches of black, grey, and even purple from coal and shale outcrops and the occasional volcanic remnant can be seen here and there across the land. The Colorado River and its tributaries carve deep sinuous canyons through this rock, slashes of green across the turbulent land. Mountain ranges with pine, fir, spruce, aspen, and snow-capped summits provide accent. The ramparts of bold mesas and high plateaus—Markagunt, Paunsaugunt, Aquarius, Kaiparowits—crowned with fir, pine, and pinyon-juniper forests stretch across the horizon. Cottonwood and willow blaze yellow in canyon bottoms in the fall.

There are "hoodoos," weathered rock pillars, each one different from the other, and many startling in aspect. They reach their greatest concentration in Bryce Canyon National Park where they crowd into each wondrous amphitheater, but they are found everywhere on the Colorado Plateau. Geologists call them erosional remnants. I prefer the Paiute Indian definition as related by Scott Thybony in his survey *Canyon Country Parklands*:

> [H]oodoos are the remnants of the Legend People, animals that had the power to appear in human form. Trickster-hero Coyote turned the creatures into stone when they defied him after he invited them to live in the village he had built for them in the cliffs. According to the Indians, Coyote always does the opposite of what he is told—a trait shared by humans since he was the one who taught people how to live. "His tracks are still there in the earth," said a Paiute elder, "and we step in them as we walk."[2]

The fight to protect this magnificent country from the impacts of the proposed Kaiparowits Power Plant Project and its progeny is a grand story. It was a marshalling of all the environmental activism and lessons of the 1960s and '70s, a campaign of truly national scope bringing together environmentalists and an alarmed public from coast to coast. The proposed Kaiparowits Power Plant, to be located in southern Utah on the north shore of Lake Powell not far from Paige, Arizona, was huge. Greer Chesher, in her book *Heart of the Desert Wild*, writes:

If commercial interests had prevailed, in place of the Kaiparowits Plateau's wild, free openness, we would see: a 5,000 megawatt, 9,000-acre coal-fired generating station puffing 316 tons of pollutants every day from its 600-foot towers and slurry and electrical transmission lines snaking toward Southern California. Heavy trucks pound the new sixty-seven-mile road, as below in Wahweap Canyon, a 300-acre gravel quarry exhales white clouds, and 120 million tons of rock waste accumulates on Fourmile and John Henry Benches. Clanking machinery echoes from the Smoky Mountain strip mine while coal trains wind through Escalante to Boulder, then disappear into a long, deep tunnel under Capitol Reef National Park. The 20,000 people living in the new town on East Clark Bench, Bueno Vista, hustle about their lives. [*Chesher's note:* "I made up the town name."][3]

Exaggeration? No. Built out to its originally proposed 5,000-megawatt capacity, Kaiparowits would have been the largest power plant in the entire country. And those air pollution numbers—that's 316 tons of contaminants *each day*. Even at its modified size of 3,000 megawatts, in 1976 it would still have been the largest plant, while today it would rank in the top ten.

Huge fossil fuel burning electric power plants such as Kaiparowits only became economical in the 1960s. Technological breakthroughs made it practical to transmit very large voltage loads over hundreds of miles to the consumer. This encouraged utilities to band together in consortia, share costs and technical expertise, and limit regulatory requirements and burdens. At the same time, California utilities were facing increasingly restrictive air pollution laws and standards which discouraged or prevented operation of large coal-fired plants in California service areas, especially the large population centers. Looking eastward to the Southwest, the utilities saw more relaxed local and state regulatory requirements and active assistance from the U.S. Government, providing cheap coal from plentiful seams and cheap water from reclamation projects. From the industry's perspective, large power plants like Kaiparowits to serve southern California power needs were not just economically feasible, but they had actually become economically desirable.

But the lands at risk? Six national parks, often called the Golden Circle of National Parks, were well within the affected zone: Arches,

Canyonlands, Capitol Reef, Bryce Canyon, Zion, and Grand Canyon. Ten national monuments, several designated and potential wilderness areas, significant state parks, Monument Valley (the widely admired tribal park of the Navajo Nation), and two large national recreation areas were nearby. The Virgin, Paria, Escalante, Fremont-Dirty Devil, San Juan, and Little Colorado Rivers flow through their own awesome canyons — gashes of mystery and wonder carved in rock — in the heart of the region on their way to the Colorado River.

A ruinous impact was certain to follow from development of at least four new coal mines on the wild and dramatic Kaiparowits Plateau.* The power plant site itself would cover more than fourteen square miles. Extensive transportation networks, transmission lines and towers running across the landscape and ultimately ending in southern California, and development of a nearby service town for fifteen thousand people would all have a devastating impact. Water use and consumption would have been in the tens of thousands of acre-feet each year, and serious air pollution would spread for hundreds of miles. Edward Abbey summed up this industrial exaltation as only he could in his quintessential classic, *Desert Solitaire* —

> There may be some ... who believe without question that any and all forms of development are intrinsic goods, in the national parks as well as anywhere else ... There are some who frankly and boldly advocate the eradication of the last remnants of wilderness and the complete subjugation of nature to the requirements of—not man—but industry. This is a courageous view, admirable in its simplicity and power, and with the weight of all modern history behind it. It is also quite insane....[4]

The environmental community was going to fight with every weapon in its arsenal, and it was certain that all would be needed.

Moreover, waiting in line was Intermountain Power Plant, another 3,000 megawatt coal-fired behemoth to be located between Canyonlands and Capitol Reef National Parks to the north and west, as well as the

---

* *Kaiparowits* is a Paiute Indian name meaning "Big Mountain's Little Brother." Big Brother referring to the Aquarius Plateau or its highest point, Boulder Mountain, rising above 11,000 feet to the north.

huge Allen-Warner Valley coal strip-mine complex near Bryce Canyon National Park, with a "relatively small" power plant nearby and a very large one to the west near Las Vegas. Sierra Club and the Utah based Wasatch Mountain Club had been preparing for this fight since the early 1970s. Other environmental organizations across the country were beginning to follow the struggle and were eager to lend a hand. Leadership quickly developed in Salt Lake City, in Denver, and in the Southwest Regional Office of Sierra Club in Tucson, Arizona. Legal remedies and challenges were reviewed and debated in law offices in Denver, Salt Lake City, Los Angeles, and Washington DC. No applicable jurisdiction was ruled out of bounds, no material legal argument or remedy was to be ignored.

Before we get into this battle in detail, it is necessary to revisit the National Park Service, for it would play a pivotal role in the fight. Obviously, the Park Service has not fared well in these pages. From the 1960s well into the 1980s, the Service seldom took aggressive affirmative action to protect park environments from proposed threats arising outside the immediate boundaries of subject parklands. When the Park Service did engage, it was often late to the game and irresolute in its actions and objectives. The massive power plant proposals for southern Utah were different. By the time Kaiparowits became a serious threat, park superintendents and their staff were already alarmed. They recognized the gravity and the region-wide extent of the impacts.

There was obviously concern, deep concern, about the enormous degree of environmental degradation and destruction, given the six national parks and ten national monuments which are found nearby. But there was also the fact that two sister agencies of the U.S. Department of the Interior were important players and presumably favored the project. This was bound to create policy and political tension within the Department. The Bureau of Reclamation had already entered into a contract with Southern California Edison and San Diego Gas & Electric approving long-term use of one hundred and two thousand acre feet of water from Lake Powell and the Colorado River. The Bureau of Land Management (BLM), responsible for rights-of-way, land use, and mining permits on the federal lands involved, was assumed to be amenable to the project. Furthermore, BLM was the "lead agency" responsible for directing and preparing the comprehensive environmental impact statement required by the National Environmental Policy Act before any further federal approvals of the project could proceed.

One of the most important Park Service actions was to establish and maintain an Assistant Regional Director's Office in Salt Lake City. This new office was deemed necessary to fulfill in an able and timely manner the increased burdens of management and review resulting from Kaiparowits, the other proposed plants, and their associated facilities. The mere presence of this office spoke volumes about the level of Park Service concern. Sometimes just being visible on the front line is a more eloquent expression of commitment than a whole stack of reports and administrative directives. Moreover, the office was accessible to the public, the environmentalists, and the press. The press was to play an important role in the prodigious struggle over these massive power plants.

Returning to the legal arena, in early 1975 Sierra Club and others who had been closely following these developments recognized the Kaiparowits Project was gaining momentum. Delay in asserting fundamental legal rights and options could weaken the environmentalists' position. It was time to act. Sierra Club and its allies met with me and local counsel in Denver and in Salt Lake City, and we reviewed in detail the rapidly evolving situation. The projected environmental harm would not only be widespread, but irreparable. These activist leaders emphasized that the matter was of the highest priority and the stakes were enormous. Therefore, they were committing substantial resources, financial and otherwise, to a comprehensive national campaign against Kaiparowits, and pursuit of legal remedies would be a critical component.

The cases and the controversies related heretofore have come down to a single jurisdiction—a specific court or a particular administrative agency. This would not be our approach with Kaiparowits. The size and complexity of the project involved many jurisdictions, the direct and indirect use of many natural resources, and posed many questions of state and national significance. Furthermore, Kaiparowits was the first of several similar proposed projects in the immediate region. Thus, approval and construction of Kaiparowits could ease the path for even more degradation of this magic area of the Colorado Plateau. Every applicable federal and state legal remedy, including administrative remedies, needed to be analyzed and evaluated, and comprehensive legal opinions and recommendations were requested from us lawyers as soon as possible. And wherever jurisdiction could reasonably be asserted and material relief reasonably and appropriately sought, then there we would be.

I quickly found myself coordinating the legal work of lawyers in Los Angeles, Salt Lake City, and Washington DC We focused on six jurisdictions or areas of the law:

- The National Environmental Policy Act (NEPA);
- Statutes governing the use and management of federal lands, particularly the National Park Service Organic Act;
- The federal Clean Air Act and its implementing regulations;
- Federal and State of Utah laws governing water use and consumption;
- The California Public Utilities Code and its Public Utilities Commission;
- The Federal Power Commission (FPC).

We soon abandoned the FPC because jurisdiction was problematical, but we pursued the other venues through the entire campaign.

Promising California and Utah State Remedies

The most intriguing, and potentially the most promising, legal remedy at this stage of the project appeared to lie with the California Public Utilities Commission (PUC). State public utilities statutes typically vest a state commission with authority to determine whether a large capital project such as a power plant is required to serve the energy needs of a utility's service area, the so-called public need. This jurisdiction applies because the ratepayer ultimately pays for the project. Thus a formal determination is required confirming that the power plant is needed by that rate-payer, or more accurately that it will be needed in the reasonably foreseeable future. Other considerations in the equation are the state's interest that its citizens have a reliable power source, the size and scope of the project and its relationship to the recognized needs

---

* The California utilities owned 63.4% of the power expected to be generated. Arizona Public Service Company had a minority share, and the remainder was as yet unsubscribed.

of the service area, and the utility's enjoyment of limited-monopoly status in that service area.

We believed we could show the Kaiparowits utilities—Southern California Edison (the largest participant) and San Diego Gas & Electric*—were grossly over estimating the quantity and timing of future power needs in California. Furthermore, once realistic energy needs had been determined, the utilities had a number of options for meeting that need: a smaller plant or plants, expansion of existing facilities, institution of meaningful conservation measures, a less polluting fuel source such as natural gas, and site locations well away from the national parks. PUC review and proceedings would be a most effective forum for bringing these critical considerations before the commission and the public. Questions of need, alternatives, and costs would be thoroughly explored in proceedings in which the environmental community, the people of Los Angeles, and the State of California could contribute and participate.

The process before the California PUC works—and worked then—in a relatively straightforward way. The utilities involved in a proposed project apply to the PUC for a certificate of "public convenience and necessity." The Commission and its staff then undertake a detailed review, and the staff makes recommendations to the Commission. If the project is large and controversial like Kaiparowits, a hearing examiner is often appointed to review evidence, hear arguments from interested parties, and make findings regarding the facts and the presentations of the parties. Then the Commission makes the decision of whether or not to grant the certificate. Once a project is approved, the utilities involved can fold the project costs into their rate structures.

Before the 1960s state public utilities commissions only dealt with facilities located at or near the customary service area. They saw no reason to assert jurisdiction beyond their state borders, and well into the mid-1970s, both the states and the utilities conveniently ignored the regulatory ramifications of the dramatic recent advances in high-voltage transmission. The Kaiparowits utilities consortium maintained that the traditional, geographically limited base of the PUC's jurisdiction should continue to define the legal standard. Besides, they argued, the Commission would have jurisdiction in the usual rate-setting matters, and this was enough. Of course, this would occur after the utilities had already committed themselves and perforce the ratepayers to the project.

The utilities could enjoy significant corporate benefits, such as reduced regulatory burdens and increased financial return to the shareholders at the ratepayers' expense, by operating beyond the reach of state inquiry. But change was in the air. State public utilities commissions were no longer sure traditional limited jurisdiction was in the best interest of the public.

New Mexico was the first state to formally argue that its jurisdiction extended beyond the state border. In 1973 it asserted jurisdiction over Public Service Company of New Mexico's participation in the Palo Verde Nuclear Power Plant near Phoenix, Arizona.[5] We opponents of Kaiparowits hoped to persuade the California PUC to follow New Mexico's lead. For this we needed some good California lawyers. Consequently, in early May 1975 I flew to Los Angeles to enlist the assistance of the Center for Law in the Public Interest, a new public interest law firm. Together with a Sierra Club staff representative there in Los Angeles, we made our way to the Center's office near Century City. Our inquiry was simple: Would they be willing, on behalf of Sierra Club, to petition the California PUC to assert jurisdiction over Kaiparowits?

> ## [T]he Colorado River and dramatic canyon tributaries ... running through the heart of the Canyon Country could be severely affected.

The Center lawyers were enthusiastic. We pored over the details and discussed the New Mexico precedent. Over the next couple of months meetings took place with PUC staff, but it became clear that the jurisdictional issue would have to be formally brought before the Commission itself. Therefore, in November we filed a petition on behalf of Sierra Club requesting that the PUC require the California utilities to obtain a certificate of public convenience and necessity with respect to their participation in the Kaiparowits Project. The Commission accepted the petition and appointed a hearing examiner to receive evidence and hear argument. The PUC staff seemed to support our position, and after a period of deliberation the California Attorney General intervened on our side. Obviously this indication of the State's concern was very significant support. Preliminary proceedings began.

While PUC jurisdiction was our first line of attack, water issues arising under water laws of the State of Utah were also very much on our minds. A large power plant such as Kaiparowits needs a considerable amount of water for cooling purposes. The development of four coal mines and the construction of a new town would consume yet more water. From the outset, we felt that the utilities' pending application before the Water Division of the Utah State Engineer for continuation of the right of appropriation of 102,000 acre feet of Colorado River water* allegedly required for the project and its many facets was vulnerable to challenge. We believed the amount of water sought was considerably more than the Kaiparowits Project needed, and that the project was not far enough along in securing necessary federal and State of California permits to merit an award of so much water.

The size and ultimate location of the power plant were by no means certain, and change in either could substantially impact the quantity of water needed as well as its source. Either of these factors—size or location—could have caused reduction of the amount of water to be appropriated or even denial or withdrawal of the application. Furthermore, while the utilities seemed to assume that all Utah governmental agencies would endorse Kaiparowits as proposed, together with its associated resource demands, we were not so sure. The pending application was a good opportunity for us to intervene and make our arguments.

Through Utah counsel, Sierra Club filed a formal objection to the application. We also petitioned the Utah State Engineer to conduct proceedings pursuant to a Utah statute providing for water planning which incorporated and hopefully protected a broad range of water uses, including non-consumptive uses for wild and scenic watercourses of substantial recreational merit. This was significant because the Colorado River and dramatic canyon tributaries—the Escalante, Fremont-Dirty Devil, Paria and Virgin Rivers—running through the heart of the Canyon Country could be severely affected by the development of Kaiparowits

---

* An acre foot of water is the volume of water over one acre of surface area at a depth of one foot. In the arid and semi-arid environments of the West, it is roughly the amount required for all the water needs of one or two suburban households over a one-year period of time.

and sister projects already in advanced stages of planning. As with our petition to the California PUC, these water matters were also pending in the winter of 1975–1976.

Far-reaching Procedures of the National Environmental Policy Act

Meanwhile, important reviews and procedures under the National Environmental Policy Act (NEPA) were well underway. Signed into law by President Richard M. Nixon on December 31, 1969, NEPA is one of the most important pieces of legislation of the modern environmental era.[6] The Act requires a detailed environmental impact statement (EIS) reviewing the impact of proposed major federal actions that would significantly affect the environment. The review and the EIS must be completed before the proposed federal action can be approved. But since all the Act seems to require is a study, albeit a comprehensive one, why is it central to so many controversies?

The answer lies in the process itself. First, NEPA is a full disclosure process. Every important detail of a proposed major federal action and how it would affect the environment must be disclosed and thoroughly examined. "Major federal action" means a significant federal role such as use of federal lands or natural resources, actions affecting protected lands and their environments, the involvement of important regulatory systems, and substantial use of government funds. This is a very expansive list; obviously, Kaiparowits easily qualified. Moreover, the NEPA process and development of the environmental impact statement are a public process. It formally begins with a "draft" EIS. The public gets to comment and participate—indeed, they are encouraged to participate. For controversial matters there are usually one or more public hearings. These provide a critical rallying point for the environmental community and focus the attention of the media. The comments of involved or affected federal agencies and of state authorities are sought, and their responses are part of the public record. Then an expanded and more thorough and complete "final" EIS is published. Only then can the federal agency involved proceed with its decision.

All of this is enormously important to the environmental community. In fact, many proposed projects or federal actions bend and even break before this scrutiny by an interested public and its advocates.

While commercial and development interests frequently complain that the NEPA process is just more bureaucracy for them to overcome, a brief look at the principal language Congress uses in NEPA reveals its true value. After elevated recitation about the importance of our environment and the need to protect it, the Act addresses the core duties and obligations of federal agencies:

Sec. 102 (2) (c) [A]ll agencies of the Federal Government shall—

- include in every recommendation or report on proposals for ... major Federal actions significantly affecting the ... environment, a detailed statement [EIS] ... on —
  - the environmental impact of the proposed action,
  - any adverse effects which cannot be avoided should the proposal be implemented,
  - alternatives to the proposed action, ...
  - any irreversible and irretrievable commitments of resources which would be involved ...
- study, develop, and describe appropriate alternatives to recommended courses of action in any proposal, which involves unresolved conflicts concerning alternative uses of available resources.[7]

To the extent this can be burdensome, such burden is far outweighed by the benefits of full disclosure and the more environmentally sensitive decisions that frequently result.

The Act also created the Council on Environmental Quality (CEQ) in the offices of the President to monitor compliance with NEPA on the part of federal agencies, promulgate comprehensive regulations and guidelines for implementation of NEPA, and provide a mechanism for resolution of disagreement between or among federal agencies. Several of the regulations promulgated by the Council which are relevant here include the following mandates:

- Federal agencies shall not take action prejudicing selection of alternatives before making a final decision;
- An EIS shall serve as a means of assessing environmental impacts prior to agency action rather than justifying a decision already made;

- Discussion of alternatives in an EIS must include the no action alternative;
- Appropriate measures for mitigating impacts shall be reviewed;
- The opportunity for public involvement shall be solicited, including holding public meetings and hearings when appropriate;
- The public shall have access to important documents and reports.[8]

The importance of mandated review of alternatives to a proposed project or action needs to be particularly emphasized. Frequently viewed as the "heart" of NEPA, such review draws attention to other less environmentally damaging ways of achieving the desired objective. Thus the EIS process can materially change major components of a proposed action, leading to substantial modifications in its size, scope, or location. And the greater the threatened environmental impact of a proposed action, the more impetus there will likely be to accept a less environmentally harmful alternative.

The review of alternatives was critically important in the Kaiparowits fight. There were several viable options, particularly expansion of facilities already operating in California and elsewhere in the Southwest—plant and mine sites well away from the parklands—and application of significant energy conservation measures and incentives. We believed there were no intrinsic circumstances foreclosing any of these options. Moreover, in particularly difficult situations the agency involved may recommend the "no action" alternative as the best option. If the no action alternative is adopted by the federal agency or agencies involved, no federal approvals are likely to be forthcoming.

NEPA review of Kaiparowits was proceeding apace within the Department of the Interior by 1975. As already mentioned, Kaiparowits would impact thousands of acres of federal land, use or consume vast amounts of public coal and water resources, dramatically affect national parks, monuments, wilderness areas and other protected lands, and would substantially degrade the pristine air quality of the region. The Bureau of Land Management, housed within the U.S. Department of the Interior, was the lead agency responsible for preparation of the environmental impact statement, for it managed a large percentage of the public lands and resources directly involved and had major permitting jurisdiction. Obviously the National Park Service, also an agency of the

Department of the Interior, was deeply concerned. The Bureau of Reclamation, builder and operator of Glen Canyon Dam and Lake Powell from whence the utilities would get the water needed for the Project, had a direct interest in the water resources and management of Lake Powell. The independent Environmental Protection Agency had both air quality jurisdiction and a statutorily designated role in reviewing environmental impact statements.

The scale of Kaiparowits and the mandated environmental review required a prodigious effort on the part of the local, regional, and national environmental communities. Environmental staff and lawyers, scientific, engineering and economics experts, lobbyists, and the always-critical citizen activists were all necessarily involved. As the NEPA process unfolded, participation by this committed community grew each month in the Southwest and then across the country. There was continuous dialogue with local and regional offices of the government agencies involved. However, given the scope of Kaiparowits and the national interests at stake, it was clear federal decisions would be made at the agency director and the Secretary of the Interior levels. We prepared to travel to Washington DC

The Importance of the Media

Before we follow the story to Washington, we need to take a moment to review the role of the media in environmental and public interest law matters, for they were now playing a central role in the Kaiparowits fight. Public interest advocacy, and particularly environmental advocacy, is carried out in the common marketplace, the public arena. After all, the condition of our natural environment affects all of us, and we have an abiding interest in protecting our lands and resources and the quality of our air and water. The natural ally of the environmentalist or the conservationist is the general public, not the commercial or commodity interests with their company-specific agendas, and not the government agencies involved, well meaning though they may often be. Our underlying strength is our passion and our commitment, but we must also reach out to our grassroots base of concerned citizens. We have our magazines, journals, calendars, and books, our booths at street fairs and community festivals where we can distribute T-shirts, water bottles, and information on pressing issues, our local and national outings programs, and our petition drives. While these avenues are necessary and important, more outreach is ordinarily needed to garner broad support on important issues.

To reach a wide audience on a developing environmental issue, the attention of the press and the media is usually helpful, frequently very important, and often vital. At a minimum the press and media inform the public of the issue and the controversy brewing. They identify the players and usually their motives, and they begin to educate the public on the nature of the controversy. They tell us what is being done to protect or advance an environmental issue and how serious the threatened harm may be. This is substantial. But when they give front page or lead story coverage, return to the controversy on a regular basis, and treat the issue with relative objectivity, then the public interest—in this case environmental issues—can benefit even more. As with NEPA, the disclosure aspects and the public education and participation engendered are extremely significant. Moreover, continued coverage keeps the subject alive in the public consciousness and usually recruits new support for the environmental viewpoint. In those instances where coverage of an important issue is continuous and where the environmentalists enjoy even partial success, the public can also see how individuals or groups of individuals can make a difference.

Good media relations can bestow a further benefit. Frequently, when a newspaper or media outlet is regularly covering a story, it will assign a particular reporter to the issue. Over time he or she will likely become well informed and will develop contacts within the government agencies involved and the private sector parties. The reporter's knowledge of the subject matter will grow, and thus his reporting may contain new or expanded information that is not only useful but also increasingly reliable. Conversations with him as he goes about acquiring information and interviewing interested parties may reveal a great deal to the public interest advocate.

Of course, courts are supposed to hold themselves apart from the transient emotions of the day, and indeed our principles of government assume judicial independence. Courts and administrative forums decide issues on the evidence before them and the law that applies. But what if the facts or the law are not altogether clear, or new conditions arise not contemplated before? As Justice Oliver Wendell Holmes, Jr., said, "The felt necessities of the time, the prevalent moral and political theories, intuitions of public policy, avowed or unconscious ... have had a good deal more to do than the syllogism [of the law] in determining the rules by which men should be governed."[9] The guidance of prior judicial rulings on a contested issue is fundamental and must be the starting point for contemporary judicial review. But laws and their interpretation evolve; they are never really frozen in time. They must address the evolving needs and confirmed basic desires of society and the issues and problems of an increasingly complex world. And when the press and the media regularly cover an issue, it is usually a good sign that the issue has become an important public concern.

Obviously, the legislative and executive branches of our government have extensive responsibilities regarding developing issues, and often the executive branch can move relatively quickly. This does not mean the courts can avoid building controversy and difficult new realities. After all, it is likely that aggrieved parties will soon be before them. Moreover the judiciary has important and very useful tools to apply: rules of procedure and evidence, courts of appeal, and lawyers—yes, lawyers— to test facts and to frame, refine, and argue the issues. While these tools may not be perfect, they are nonetheless impressive. They measure the real extent of the controversy, the veracity of the players, the merits of the parties' positions, and the practicality of remedies and solutions. Furthermore, application of these tools will turn away lawsuits lacking merit and reject frivolous actions.

Publicity also influences Congress. Problems of the day are aired and proposed solutions discussed. If a member of Congress suspects an environmental issue has become important to his constituents and has good reason to believe legislation can address or assist its resolution, his interest in the issue is likely to increase. Naturally different legislators answer to different constituencies, and there may be sharply divergent points of view. But this comes back squarely to the disclosure, educational, and participatory roles of the press and the media. Thus while exposure in the press and media can cut many ways, on balance the public interest involved generally benefits and often decisively so. Certainly this was the case with Kaiparowits and other power plants proposed within the Golden Circle of national parks in Utah and Arizona.

Druid Arch, Canyonlands National Park, Utah

The environmental community greatly boosted its campaign against Kaiparowits by giving it special attention in its own publications and publicity efforts. Newsletters, brochures, dramatic photographs of the spectacular scenery, press releases and interviews with the press—all were used to the maximum extent. Particularly notable was a widely distributed special edition of Audubon Magazine exclusively featuring the parks, landscapes, and canyons involved.[9] The Audubon Society pulled out all the stops with comprehensive text on the project and its impact, accompanied by magnificent photographs. Also of great assistance was Sierra Club's coffee table book *Slickrock*, published a few years earlier with text by Edward Abbey and photography by Phillip Hyde.[10] Finally, we lawyers played our part by being accessible to the press and media and ready to explain the legal proceedings and arguments.

Returning to the eve of our departure for Washington DC in March 1976, our coverage in the press and media was all that we could reasonably desire. The Salt Lake City newspapers, the *The Salt Lake Tribune* and the *Deseret News*, gave Kaiparowits detailed and continual coverage. *The Los Angeles Times* treated the controversy in depth, and the stories and reports were often front-page news and almost always prominently featured. And of course any subject that is big news in southern California is important in northern California. On a more national scale, there was conspicuous coverage in the *New York Times*. *The Washington Post* and the *Philadelphia Inquirer* ran significant stories. Television news in Utah gave the subject frequent play. National TV coverage occurred frequently, and our trip to Washington was thoroughly aired. Thus as we organized for our mid-March journey Americans everywhere were becoming aware of the issue.

Petitioning the Government

Our plan was to approach each of the critical federal agencies with a comprehensive presentation explaining our issues with Kaiparowits, the rulings or decisions we felt the federal government should make, and articulating our legal positions. We put together an outstanding team. We were ably anchored by John McComb, Sierra Club's Southwest Regional Representative. We had two experts. First was Michael Williams, a distinguished engineer from New Mexico who was thoroughly grounded in air-pollution-control technology and the atmospheric dispersion of air pollution emissions. Additionally, we had Ronald Doctor, an economist and a commissioner on the California Energy Commission, who was well qualified to address economic issues, such as energy needs in California, as well as the practicality of alternatives to Kaiparowits. Two volunteer leaders—one from Salt Lake and one from southern Utah—were in the delegation, as well as two Sierra Club staff lobbyists from the Club's Washington office. Joining me to help with legal issues and explain the proceedings before the California Public Utilities Commission was one of our lawyers from Los Angeles.

Secretary of the Interior Thomas S. Kleppe was our first appointment when we arrived in Washington. Judging by his one year in office, he clearly favored development interests over environmental interests. Nevertheless, it was very important that we give him and his staff the benefit of the full presentation we had prepared. The other agencies we planned to visit would unquestionably ask if we were communicating with the Secretary. He was going to make critical decisions and it would be expected that we would seek an audience with him. Failure to do so might well impair our credibility. How confident could we be in the merits of our positions if we only met with our supporters? After all, we were going to urge other agencies of the federal government to directly challenge the wisdom of the project.

There were other more subtle but nonetheless important reasons for our meeting. Upon hearing our arguments and the opinions of our experts in person, Secretary Kleppe might begin thinking about a smaller project, alternative sites, or approvals conditioned upon rigorous environmental mitigation measures. We felt strongly that we had support in the National Park Service, and there were undoubtedly other mid-level and perhaps even high-level employees scattered through the Department of the Interior who sympathized with us. If our arguments were well organized, and if our experts and the underlying facts were strong, our appearance could strengthen the position of such allies. Furthermore, assuming a good presentation, hopefully the Secretary would get a clear picture of how earnest we and the national environmental community were. And of course there was always the chance that contrary to expectations Secretary Kleppe would decide against any approvals and permits sought for Kaiparowits. Finally, common courtesy called for a meeting with the Secretary. We were in town, and our presence and agenda were widely known.

We rendezvoused on March 19th at the Department of the Interior offices a few blocks southwest of the White House toward the Potomac River. We were scheduled for an hour; we would need all of it. We had five major topics we wanted to address:

- The projected need or energy-demand in the utilities' service areas;
- The statutory obligations of the Secretary of the Interior under the National Parks Organic Act, which mandated protection of the parks from harm;
- The air pollution threat;
- Alternatives to Kaiparowits, including energy conservation alternatives;
- The overarching EIS process required under NEPA.

Secretary Kleppe was a businessman and ex-Congressman from North Dakota. Stern in demeanor, although nonetheless courteous, he did not warm to our premises or our arguments. While attentive, he was largely silent, letting his staff do most of the talking. The Secretary's entourage was as numerous as our own and included several high-ranking department officials. As noted earlier, three agencies directly interested and involved reported directly to the Secretary: the Bureau of Land Management, the Bureau of Reclamation, and the National Park Service. Each had one or more representatives present. Assistants to the Secretary and a lawyer from the department's Solicitor's Office rounded out the government roster.

In briefings of this nature the activist leaders, professional staff, and the experts customarily take the lead; we lawyers fill in with additional information later on. This approach directly communicates the environmentalists' commitment and competence. John McComb, the Southwest Regional Representative of the Sierra Club, led off with introductions and a brief outline of the situation. John was a positive and enthusiastic advocate, and he probably knew better than anyone the total Kaiparowits picture, with all of its elements, circumstances, and ramifications. He had a way of looking right at you and absorbing every word you spoke, regardless of the length of the question or the complexity of your statement. John addressed alternative locations where power plants and extractable coal deposits would be well away from the national parks and sensitive lands of southern Utah. John referred often to an easel-size map of the Southwest, showing the core of the Colorado Plateau—the national parks, some of the national monuments, and Glen Canyon National Recreation Area. Overlays showed the existing power plants in the region, those in the proposal stage such as Kaiparowits, and ancillary developments and mines.

Considerable care had been taken in developing this map and its overlays, for it was being widely used in public meetings and hearings, our own publications, and, very importantly, by the press. The visual representation of the entire picture put the proposed plants and their ancillary developments into a graphic perspective that showed the huge geographical extent of the environmental impact they would have. The map and overlays provided a common reference point for both advocate and viewer, and their repeated appearance and use, particularly in the printed media, increasingly drove home the stakes involved. Such a tactic can be very meaningful, and the map stayed up before the Interior Department audience during our entire presentation. Its alarming details were constantly before the viewers' eyes. Indeed, this map and its overlays became a critical and much-used reference point in many venues during the Kaiparowits campaign.

Our economist, Ronald Doctor, followed McComb. While his credentials were impeccable, the fact that he was also a member of the California Energy Commission gave him additional credence. Ron had an earnestness about him—he would lean forward seeking to personally engage his audience in what he had to say. Upon making an important point he would pause, looking around the room to make sure everyone had heard it. Dr. Doctor addressed California's energy needs, alternatives for satisfying the legitimate needs without building Kaiparowits, and energy saving benefits to be derived from using evolving conservation measures.

Michael Williams, our air pollution expert, came next with technical observations regarding the nature of air pollution emissions, their concentrations at different locales, and the extent of their projected distribution into the environment. An engineer and physicist with impressive credentials, Dr. Williams probably had no equal at that time in understanding the complexities of air pollution emissions and their dispersion into the atmosphere. Tall, lean, and fit, Mike had an earnest delivery and clear explanations that commanded close attention and serious consideration. He also addressed realistic air pollution control technologies that could be installed and the mitigative effect they would have. The utility sponsors of Kaiparowits were planning air pollution control technology substantially below the best then available. We were particularly eager to present the analyses of Drs. Williams and Doctor, for this type of face-to-face setting provided an excellent opportunity for Department of the Interior personnel to hear firsthand very pertinent opinions on critical issues from highly qualified experts not representing the utility companies. Since this was not a lecture format, questions came freely, and we had several opportunities to respond in detail.

Secretary Kleppe and a couple of his associates raised the subject of a pending ballot initiative in California, which, if passed, would preclude further development of nuclear energy in the state. The implication, of course, was that if California could not have nuclear power, it must have coal. They were also worried about the country's continuing heavy dependence upon foreign oil for our energy needs. Seemingly ignored were our arguments regarding several viable alternatives:

- A power plant burning natural gas, which would result in much lower air pollution emissions if Kaiparowits or an equivalent plant had to be built;
- Power plant sites well away from the Golden Circle of National Parks;
- The efficacy of smaller power generating units;
- Building additional capacity at existing plants;
- Promotion of, and reliance upon, energy conservation measures then beginning to gain traction.

The Secretary had no comment regarding the threats of environmental degradation to the parks and wild lands of southern Utah and northern Arizona.

We lawyers took over in the last minutes of the meeting. My colleague from Los Angeles reviewed the proceedings pending before the California Public Utilities Commission, while I addressed the Secretary's obligations to protect the parks and monuments under his charge pursuant to the requirements of the National Parks Organic Act. Several references to the National Environmental Policy Act had already been made, and we had some concluding remarks on the EIS process, which was now well underway. Once more we emphasized the less damaging alternatives and their suitability for addressing California's energy needs. We wrapped up the meeting with a direct request that the Secretary deny the permits and rights-of-way sought by the utilities.

We huddled over lunch to discuss the morning. We thought we had done the job we needed to do and had done it well. However, we also felt that the Secretary was probably already committed to the Kaiparowits Project. The alternatives of a smaller plant or approval of a plant with significantly better air pollution control technology than proposed were still possibilities, but the odds seemed against us. We also had a chance to digest a rather curious document handed to us during the meeting. The power companies had heard about our pending trip and had put together with obvious haste a written memorandum advocating the project. It seemed likely that the Secretary obtained the bulk of his arguments and positions from this document. Although lengthy, the document was unimpressive and repetitive. It clearly did not adequately meet the issues we posed and our arguments. More than anything, the evident haste in its preparation told us the utilities were worried about our arguments and the effect they might have on our audiences.

Friendly Reception at the Environmental Protection Agency

The next morning we met with the Deputy Administrator of the Environmental Protection Agency (EPA). The EPA has jurisdiction under the federal Clean Air Act for setting air quality standards, determining limitations on air pollution emissions, and approving implementation plans established by individual states to achieve and maintain compliance with those standards and regulations. An important aim of the legislative framework is to protect air sheds—geographic areas or regions of measured air quality—that have not been polluted and where the air is relatively pristine.[11] Southern Utah and northern Arizona and their parklands easily qualified as a pristine air quality region. Just as obviously, Kaiparowits and its sister plants could enormously degrade that pristine air to conditions rivaling some of the worst urban or industrial locations in the country.

EPA was just turning to questions of protection of clean air locales in the mid-1970s. In the first several years after passage of the Clean Air Act amendments of 1970, the Agency directed its principal efforts to setting air pollution standards and developing implementation plan frameworks which would begin to address the country's worst areas of existing air pollution. The outline of a potential regulatory system to protect pristine air sheds was only beginning to emerge when the controversy over Kaiparowits erupted. Congress was also addressing the subject and was expected to legislate on it in 1977. The regulatory mechanism being considered began with the proposition that an area having air pollution concentrations below a certain minimum level would be allowed to absorb only very limited pollution from new sources. Thus permitted pollution emissions would result in no significant deterioration of existing pristine air quality. These pristine locales were to be designated Class 1 areas, and the regulatory structure being considered bore the title Prevention of Significant Deterioration (PSD). Clearly the parklands of southern Utah and northern Arizona were pristine air quality areas and thus would be designated as Class 1, and just as clearly Kaiparowits would emit pollutants in such volume that Class 1 levels would be far exceeded.[12]

We specifically challenged the EPA: If the pristine air quality in the heart of southern Utah, with all its magnificent and unique national parks and monuments, could not be preserved, then where could any pristine air quality areas be protected? However, a note of caution is required here. The question assumes the pristine air would be significantly degraded from the operation of Kaiparowits. Assumptions are certainly necessary in legal and administrative arenas; in fact matters could extend almost indefinitely if obvious and warranted assumptions are not made. Of course we were convinced, but when lawyers and parties are dealing with the foundations of a case or disputed matter, they must be wary of assumptions. A successful attack upon these fundamentals may undermine your argument and thus your entire case. What if important assumptions are arguably wrong, or only partially correct? Then the question becomes: Which part is correct? And there is the danger that your adversary or the decision-maker may later reject what he seemed to have accepted earlier. Thus, at least a preliminary showing of the facts behind the assumptions is a good idea. Consequently, Dr. Williams thoroughly covered the technical aspects of air pollution emissions from the proposed power plant, their dispersion in the ambient air, and their resulting concentrations in the surrounding environment.

Another part of the Clean Air Act spells out certain obligations of EPA regarding projects such as Kaiparowits. Section 309 requires that the Administrator of EPA review proposed major federal actions which will affect the environment and which involve EPA responsibilities under the Clean Air Act or any other act giving EPA authority in the environmental field, or which require an environmental impact statement under NEPA.[13] The Administrator must publicize this review, and he must advise the "lead agency"—the agency preparing the EIS and making the operative decisions regarding the proposed federal action—of his views and recommendations. Section 309 goes on to say —

> In the event the Administrator determines that any such ... action ...
> is unsatisfactory from the standpoint of public health or welfare or
> environmental quality, he shall publish his determination and the
> matter shall be referred to the Council on Environmental Quality.

We urged the Administrator to make this referral based upon substantial and irresolvable air pollution problems.

Our reception at EPA was more cordial than we had experienced at the Department of the Interior. EPA's representatives seemed better prepared to discuss the merits of the controversy, although we recognized that Interior Department staff might have been constrained by the policy and political differences among the Interior agencies involved. While the Deputy Administrator and his staff were careful to maintain a neutral stance, their interest in Dr. Williams' presentation on air pollution matters was obvious. EPA had brought a couple of its own air pollution experts to the meeting, and it was gratifying to see Mike respond so comfortably and so well to their questions. There was a useful amount of dialogue throughout the session, and we left encouraged.

Briefing on Capitol Hill

That afternoon we gave a briefing for congressional staff in a large conference room at the House of Representatives Rayburn Office Building. Here we had a large audience, bright lights, and press and media presence. We spoke from a lectern and microphone at the head of the room. The activities of the audience at briefings like this, with comings and goings from congressional hearings, other briefings, and meetings with lobbyists and constituents—the conflicting schedules typical of Capitol Hill—and the low hum of conversation among those standing at the rear of the room can be distracting. But the organized presentation which had served us well at the Interior Department and EPA proved adaptable to the buzz and activity in the room, and our worries about a potential lack of focus soon dissipated.

We had four principal objectives: inform personal congressional and committee staff of the seriousness of the issue and the project's ramifications; emphasize the importance of protection of pristine air sheds, with a view to pending Clean Air Act legislation; feature the depth of our review and the professionalism of our experts; and receive publicity from attending press and media. In addition, the environmental community and interested citizen constituents had been maintaining a steady flow of letters and telephone calls for some time to most of the members of Congress and their offices. Many representatives were becoming aware that the Kaiparowits Project was extremely controversial and might be an important political issue in their individual districts. This magnified interest in our briefing.

The importance of congressional staff cannot be over-emphasized. Congressmen and senators cannot possibly inform themselves on every important issue without a lot of help from their staff. This applies equally to congressional committees. And if a congressman is interested in an issue, he may well assign a specific staff member to follow it closely. This person will be reviewing alternatives in statutory language, attending committee hearings, and seeking advice from experts. We want to get to know that individual, provide the information he needs to impress his boss, and be ready to answer his questions.

The event came off extremely well. It was well attended, a number of staff people came to the front of the room after our presentation with pertinent questions, and many expressed their appreciation for the briefing. There seemed to be a consensus that the issues were important. Many mentioned receiving a lot of communications from their Congressman's constituents. (More on the importance of this grassroots' lobbying will be addressed later in this chapter.) We were especially pleased that several congressmen themselves stopped by and listened. A few came up after our presentation, introduced themselves, and thanked us.

The next morning—our third day in town—our appointment was with the Deputy Administrator of the Federal Energy Administration (FEA). The FEA had no direct involvement with Kaiparowits, but its interest in energy matters was undeniable, and the agency would of course be commenting on the pending environmental impact statement.* FEA's views and arguments paralleled those of Secretary Kleppe vis-à-vis our dependence on foreign oil and the pending anti-nuclear initiative in California. As with Interior, FEA saw the argument as a choice between nuclear power and coal. The Deputy Administrator heard us

---

* In 1975 what are now functions of the Department of Energy were vested in the Federal Energy Administration.

out, but he seemed unreceptive to our arguments involving California's legitimate energy needs and reasonable alternatives for meeting these needs. Nevertheless, we "covered the base" and parted amicably, though little common ground was apparent.

The President's Council on Environmental Quality

In the afternoon, we were scheduled to meet with the Chairman of the Council on Environmental Quality (CEQ) and his staff. By now all the unspoken worries which I had harbored at the outset of our journey about our reception and how well we would do had dissipated. We seemed vindicated in our decision to come with a full complement of experts, staff and volunteer leaders, lobbyists, and lawyers, and to organize a comprehensive and detailed presentation at each office we visited. Our audiences were attentive and ready with questions and statements of their own views, and on no occasion were we told that time was pressing and to wrap things up quickly and bring the meeting to a close. Our team had become a well-oiled machine, each person settling into a role that played to his or her strengths, and our two experts had performed at a high level from the outset. Our confidence had grown, and this imparted its own energy to us.

It was in that spirit that we made our way to Lafayette Square across Pennsylvania Avenue from the White House for our appointment with Russell Train, Chairman of the Council on Environmental Quality. As we approached Lafayette Square, this is where matters stood:

- We had a petition pending before the California Public Utilities Commission with an important hearing coming up in April;
- We had intervened in a Utah water rights proceeding and were petitioning the Utah State Engineer to begin a water planning proceeding;
- We had pressed the Department of the Interior to look to its statutory obligations under the National Parks Organic Act and the National Environmental Policy Act;
- We had urged the Environmental Protection Agency to assure protection of the parks from significant deterioration of their pristine air quality and, pursuant to authority in the Clean Air Act and

NEPA, refer the questions of approval of federal actions regarding Kaiparowits to the CEQ; and
- We had thoroughly briefed congressional staff.

Moreover, across the country environmentalists were responding to our message of alarm and the drumbeat of the media coverage—a ground swell that commanded attention and gave us even more confidence.

A group of citizens such as ourselves, in town to petition our government, cannot walk across Lafayette Square without experiencing a moment of reflection. This seven acre stretch of grass and park across the street from the White House may be the country's single most important ground to a citizen who wishes to demonstrate in person regarding a policy of the federal government. Originally planned as a pleasuring ground for the White House, the Square was separated in 1804 when President Thomas Jefferson had Pennsylvania Avenue cut through. In 1824 it was officially dedicated in honor of General Marquis de Lafayette, the gallant French nobleman who gave critical support to the American Revolution.[14]

In the past, Lafayette Square has been used as a racetrack, a graveyard, a zoo, a slave market, and an encampment for soldiers during the War of 1812. In the 1960s and 1970s the Square saw massive rallies for civil rights and against the Vietnam War. Scenes of these demonstrations frequently splashed across our television screens on the evening news as we sat down for dinner or unwound after a busy day. Now hardly a day goes by without someone in the park carrying a homemade placard advocating a favorite cause. And here we were, products of the 60s and 70s, no strangers to dissent and public advocacy, walking across Lafayette Square past Clark Wills' equestrian statue of Andrew Jackson to the offices of CEQ. This was the final meeting of our three-day trip to our nation's capitol to petition the government for relief from the enormous consequences of the proposed Kaiparowits Project to the incomparable parklands and pristine environment of the Colorado Plateau.

Facing the north side of the Square are four-story row houses of eclectic nineteenth century architectural styles. On the inside, passageways have been cut through walls so several of these are joined together as the CEQ offices. Our party made quite a procession ascending in single file the old staircase to the conference room on the top floor. The

Chairman, Russell Train, greeted us, and after introductions we began our well-practiced presentation. We had three objectives: to show how well we had mastered the central issues, to feature our two experts, and to urge the Council to exercise its broadest authority pursuant to Section 309 of the Clean Air Act, the National Environmental Policy Act, and CEQ regulations. As noted previously, Section 309 of the Clean Air Act requires EPA to review and comment upon the environmental impacts of federal actions affecting EPA's statutory and regulatory jurisdiction, including actions for which an environmental impact statement must be prepared. If EPA determines that a federal action under review is "unsatisfactory from the standpoint of public health or welfare or environmental quality," the Administrator of EPA must refer the matter to the CEQ.[15]

CEQ regulations provide direction for handling referrals. The Council first seeks a response from the agency proposing the action under review. If the response fails to resolve the problems, CEQ has a variety of remedies to apply. It may recommend negotiation between the agencies involved, initiate discussion with them with the objective of mediating the disputes, hold public hearings to obtain additional views and information, and publish the Council's findings, "including where appropriate a finding that the submitted evidence does not support the position" of the agency advocating the federal action in question. Finally, Section 1504.2 (7) of CEQ's regulations states that "when appropriate [the Council may] submit the referral and the response together with the Council's recommendations to the President for action," thus laying the controversy directly on the President's desk. We could foresee considerable benefits to our position from one or more of these procedures.[16]

Obviously, CEQ knew we had made arguments in support of referral of the Kaiparowits Project in our meeting with EPA. For the last two days word of what we were about had been traveling well ahead of us to our next appointment. Nevertheless, we gave our full presentation, and we emphasized to Chairman Train and his staff that we fully intended to hold EPA's "feet to the fire." We stressed our belief that EPA could not easily avoid its responsibility to refer any Interior Department approval of requisite permits for the project to CEQ. As we had done with the other agencies, we assured CEQ that we were prepared to provide further information and support for our positions, including additional data, opinions, and conclusions that might be requested of our experts.

We expressed our hope the Council would have no objection to continued communications and status updates from us. We were confident that Chairman Train and his staff realized the scope and gravity of the environmental threats of the Kaiparowits Project. When we took our leave, Chairman Train and his staff urged us to "stay in close touch" with them.

As we descended the old staircase and walked into Lafayette Square, we finally relaxed a little. We could not really know how well we had done at that point. But we did know we had pled our case aggressively and, we believed, effectively for three days and before all the important government players. Our presentations had been comprehensive, covering all the points we intended to address. Our experts had presented impressive testimony based upon solid data and hard facts. Maybe most importantly we knew that our concerns about Kaiparowits were now getting close attention in critical government circles.

Satisfied we had done our best, we flew back to our respective homes in Albuquerque, Tucson, Salt Lake City, and Cedar City, Utah, Denver, San Francisco, and Los Angeles, while thinking of what the coming weeks and months held for us. One thing was quite clear: We would have to be able to move quickly if Secretary Kleppe made an abrupt decision to grant permits for Kaiparowits, thus short circuiting the administrative efforts before the Public Utilities Commission in Los Angeles, the State Engineer's Office in Salt Lake City, and the Department of the Interior's sister agencies in Washington DC It seemed unlikely the Secretary would so defy both the state jurisdictions and the National Environmental Policy Act process, but we could not rest easy solely on probabilities.

If it became necessary, the most direct legal route we could take would be legal action in the appropriate U.S. District Court under NEPA, asserting the Secretary could not legally act in defiance of the procedures spelled out in the statute and the regulations. We would argue that the environmental impact statement process could not be truncated. Procedurally, we would seek immediate preliminary relief from the court enjoining the granting of permits under consideration, and suspending action under permits already granted, to last until a full ruling could be made by the court on the merits of the case. Administratively, success on our part would return the question to the Department of the Interior with instructions to complete the NEPA process. We would also argue that approval of Kaiparowits as planned and proposed would violate the Secretary's statutory obligation under the National Parks Organic Act to protect the national parks under his charge, and would violate the Clean Air Act's protection of pristine air quality regions. With all this in mind, over the next couple of weeks we drafted a complaint and started the process of securing necessary affidavits. Emergency action would probably not become necessary, but with stakes so high we could not afford to take a chance. Furthermore, if the time for judicial intervention came, delay in filing our action could produce difficulties down the road.

Return to Los Angeles—A Startling Victory

Already on the calendar was a hearing scheduled in April (just three weeks away) in Los Angeles before the California Public Utilities Commission's Hearing Examiner, Philip Blecher. While this appearance was important, there was nothing to indicate that it would be in any way out of the ordinary. The agenda was routine: to wrap up any loose ends and provide the parties with a last opportunity to supplement arguments before the hearing officer took the matter under advisement. He would then draft his findings, opinions, and recommendations to the Commission. We had a couple of matters we wanted to briefly expand upon, but nothing critical—just the normal wrap up. Unless the hearing examiner had questions requiring detailed answers, we anticipated a short hearing.

We convened in a nondescript municipal office building in downtown Los Angeles. The hearing room was small, bereft of even a picture on the wall, and altogether drab. The "bench" was a truncated, pedestrian affair, and counsel tables were small and barely serviceable to the lawyers with their files, exhibits, and paraphernalia. To the right of the bench and just opposite the counsel tables was an emergency exit door leading to a stairwell and half-a-flight of stairs, partially roofed over by an iron grill, going up to ground level. This was definitely not the impressive courtroom in Salt Lake City or the Chief of the Forest Service's large history-draped office overlooking the Mall in Washington DC Given the housekeeping nature of the hearing, no important actions were expected. Thus the only audience was Larry Pryor of *The Los Angeles Times*, for the *Times* was covering all aspects of the controversy, even mundane hearings.

The hearing officer's clerk called us to order. We resumed our seats after the hearing officer entered and took his seat on the bench, and we finished arranging our papers and voiced a few last thoughts to each other. Morning greetings were exchanged, and the hearing officer indicated that we, as the moving party—the original petitioner—should proceed. As our Los Angeles counsel rose, the lead Southern California Edison lawyer across from us stood and asked if he could first make a statement. The hearing examiner nodded, and in a clear voice counsel began —

> I have an important announcement to read into the record. Southern California Edison is postponing indefinitely its plans to build the Kaiparowits power project.

This took several moments to sink in. We were truly speechless. Edison's counsel continued with the rest of his short statement, while at our table we fought to remain calm. He related that the formal corporate action taken was to erase the project from the company's future financial and resource plans. Equally surprised, Examiner Blecher declared a ten-minute recess. We were up from our seats, out the door, and into the stairwell. I am sure that stairwell had never before seen three lawyers dancing about, exchanging "high-fives," pumping fists, and yelling "Yes, yes, yes...!" The utilities' counsel and *The Los Angeles Times* reporter looked on.

Our stairwell "dance" and celebration did not last long. Soon the hearing examiner's clerk opened the door and, with a smile on her face at our antics, told us the hearing would resume in five minutes.

We filed back in and Examiner Blecher resumed his seat. The overriding question now was whether the Public Utilities Commission proceeding should continue; whether the PUC continued to have immediate jurisdiction over the questions raised in Sierra Club's petition, since the specific subject of the petition, Kaiparowits Power Plant, had been withdrawn. This was not easy to answer, especially at that moment with no time to reflect. Consequently, all of us agreed that the parties would file briefs on the question at a later date, and additional proceedings would be considered at that point. With that, Examiner Blecher adjourned the hearing. We lawyers phoned our clients there in Los Angeles, and in Salt Lake and Tucson, and told them to begin celebrating. We then returned to our respective offices to contemplate and digest this startling event.

Los Angeles Times

Largest Circulation in the We   THURSDAY APRIL 15 1976   Daily 52

EDISON SHELVES UTAH POWER PLANT PROJECT

Legal, Environment Delays Make It Too Costly, Utility Says

BY LARRY PRYOR
Times Staff Writer

ROSEMEAD, CA—The Southern California Edison Company announced Wednesday that it was postponing indefinitely its plans to build the proposed $3.5 billion [1976 dollars] Kaiparowits Power Project, a massive coal-generated electrical power plant in Southern Utah.

William R. Gould, Edison's executive vice president, said the project has been erased from the company's future financial and resource plans because of an accumulation of legal and regulatory delays that made the plant too costly.

The controversial project, located within a 200-mile radius of eight national parks and three national recreation areas, would have shipped power to Southern California and Arizona starting about 1982.

Environmental groups, concerned about the impact of air and water pollution on the national parks, viewed Edison's decision as a major victory.

"It had become literally a shootout over whether these national treasures would be compromised by an alleged energy shortfall," said H. Anthony Ruckel, director of the [Sierra Club Legal Defense Fund] in Denver.

A chief uncertainty is an amendment pending in Congress that would tighten air quality controls near national monuments [national parks and pristine air-sheds].... [Gould] also cited greater interest by the State Public Utilities Commission and state Energy Commission to supervise out-of-state construction of electric power plants.

[...]

"This plant went by the boards because it was loaded with too many objections from too many sides," Gould said

Utah and California State Remedies II

One might think withdrawal of Kaiparowits by the utilities would have quickly terminated the California PUC proceeding, the review of water appropriation in Utah, and the NEPA review process in Washington, DC After some legal endeavors, we can declare victory and simply walk away, but a party to a legal proceeding needs to be sure the exit is appropriate. Often we have to finish, or at least reasonably lay to rest, what we have begun, even though the immediate cause for our participation no longer exists. This was the case with Kaiparowits. Each of the three actions had additional steps to complete. How this developed provides additional lessons for reflection. In a moment we will take up again the story in Utah before the State Engineer, but first we shall address a recurrent issue with complex and extensive projects like Kaiparowits: the practical problems of multiple state and federal jurisdictions reviewing the same project.

At the beginning of this review of the Kaiparowits Project, I noted that the environmental community would seek every available federal and state legal remedy, including administrative remedies, where material relief could reasonably and appropriately be sought. As we have seen, there was no shortage of applicable statutes and available jurisdictions. This raises a fundamental question often asked by concerned observers: Is it necessary to have so many decision-makers? Would it not be much more efficient to have a single forum —so-called "one-stop shopping"—where all the issues could be resolved? It has been argued that this approach would save time and money and still provide that all environmental and related issues are fully aired and addressed. But let's look at countervailing arguments.

The most basic explanation for dispersion of jurisdiction lies in our democratic system of government. It does not favor having a decision-maker with unlimited power. In a previous chapter, I touched on the division of powers among the legislative, executive, and judicial branches of our government—our system of checks and balances. But our system also disperses power vertically between local or municipal government, state interests, and the federal government. As a general proposition, Americans support meaningful local and state government roles. Who better to decide the energy needs of California citizens, and by extension the appropriate financial burden the rate-payers must assume to satisfy those needs, than a California state agency or commission specifically charged with these responsibilities? Utah citizens are vitally concerned about the allocation and use of the limited available water resources in their arid and semi-arid environment. Is not Utah interested in reviewing the appropriation and use of its water, how water demands of a Kaiparowits would fit with pre-existing water rights and uses, and how appropriation of that water would affect the availability of water to Utah citizens in the future? Would either state or their citizens easily relinquish their roles in these critical areas of public concern? I think not. On the other hand, the federal government, upon whose land Kaiparowits would be built, whose coal would be burned to power the generators, and whose national parks are held in trust to be protected for all of us, also has an intense interest in such a project. The Environmental Protection Agency is vitally concerned about threats posed to the quality of the nation's air.

Of course, the interests of these jurisdictions can and will overlap, but is it wise to eliminate these several jurisdictions and fold the critical matters they address into one all-powerful entity in the interests of greater administrative or corporate convenience? There is also the problem of defining and establishing such a single entity and providing it with the structure and ability to entertain and competently review all the legitimate issues. Who appoints this entity, who supervises it, and where does it find the required expertise to fully address all the issues? Costs and fees to corporate interests, public interest parties, and governments themselves are important, of course, but the cost of erroneous decisions and significant harm to the environment must also be part of the equation. The reality is that governing three hundred million people in a modern democracy, with finite natural resources to support them materially and spiritually, is a complex and difficult process.

Often this multi-jurisdictional system gives environmental or other public interests the opportunity to seek relief in more than one forum and the promise of more opportunities to succeed. This better insures that an important public interest gets fully explored, and that environmental problems are addressed before they get out of hand. For the corporate advocate there are additional opportunities to explain a proposed action and to identify and develop mitigating measures that would make his actions less damaging. Moreover, the corporate advocate should not ignore the advantages he may gain from increased public and governmental acceptance of his proposals as they are further tested and improved.

We left water issues in Utah with the environmentalists' objections to the utility consortium's application for the right to appropriate 102,000 acre feet of water for the project pending before the Utah State Engineer. Also pending was our original petition for initiation of a state water planning process. These matters were still on the active docket. The State Engineer was fully aware of the recent events in California, and thus he was expecting explanatory pleadings from the utilities. Shortly after the Los Angeles hearing, counsel for Southern California Edison initiated a meeting with us in Salt Lake City to inform us of the utilities' new but still "tentative" plans. They were going to abandon application for several tens of thousands of acre-feet of water, but nevertheless they intended to refile for a smaller but still significant appropriation to serve alternatives to Kaiparowits. The utilities emphasized the value of the high-quality coal, together with anticipated appropriation of ample water supplies from Lake Powell, and, of course, their continuing hope to use the coal for electric power generation. Since such alternative developments would still be huge and their impacts severe and widespread, we were firmly opposed.

On July 15, 1976, three months and a day after the dramatic event in Los Angeles, the consortium withdrew its application for 102,000 acre feet of water and refiled for 30,000 acre feet for their proposed alternative operations. These included projects "(i) to provide clean energy fuels through a gasification and/or liquefaction [of the coal] plant, (ii) to construct a coal slurry pipeline or other transport system, and (iii) for power generation utilizing advanced air quality control technology." Kaiparowits had not gone away—it had merely changed its spots! In truth though, the utilities were actually trying to gain time to decide what they really wanted to do next.[17]

While these events were occurring, there still remained the major procedural issue to be resolved by the California Public Utilities Commission. After Southern California Edison's startling announcement at the close of the April 14 hearing, the immediate question was whether the pending action before the PUC could proceed. The utilities maintained that it could not, for the issue "was rendered moot" by withdrawal of Kaiparowits. Thus, they argued, the Commission should not render judgment on legal questions of jurisdiction without a specific project under review. We responded that the PUC should continue with the matter, for it had been well briefed by interested parties, argued before the public through the press and media, and involved fundamental issues which, in any event, would have to be resolved in the near future. Furthermore, the utilities had filed pleadings with the Utah State Engineer declaring their intent to pursue one or more specified alternative projects. The utilities replied that while they had a preferred alternative—coal gasification—the plans were only "concepts," not projects mature enough to form a basis for PUC jurisdiction. PUC staff—previously supportive of exercising jurisdiction—now chimed in that the matter should not be dismissed, but rather suspended until the utilities could more clearly define their plans.

Occasionally a lawyer encounters a puzzle which he cannot explain or solve....

By the end of the summer and by general consent of the parties, further action on *Kaiparowits* was suspended until the utilities decided what course they wanted to pursue. They said this would take at least a year. The environmental community was content to leave it there for the time being, because it was now fully engaged against Kaiparowits's sister project—another proposed monster called Intermountain Power Plant, which was to be located ninety miles north of the Kaiparowits site on the Fremont River, twelve miles east of Capitol Reef National Park and forty miles west of Canyonlands National Park.

An EPA Mystery

Occasionally a lawyer encounters a puzzle which he cannot explain or solve—an unattributed statement, an isolated event out of context, or a document out of place—but which in some manner obviously involves or references the matter at issue. The size and complexity of the Kaiparowits Project and the large number of parties and jurisdictions involved provided many opportunities for just such a circumstance. Our friends at the Environmental Protection Agency and the Council on Environmental Quality seem to have furnished us with just such an enigma.

We have discussed Section 309 of the Clean Air Act which declares that if the Administrator of EPA determines that a major federal action affecting the environment (citing the language of NEPA) "is unsatisfactory from the standpoint of public health or welfare or environmental quality ... the matter shall be referred to CEQ." When we met with EPA back in March we urged the Administrator to make that finding and refer federal approvals for the Kaiparowits Project to CEQ. However, three weeks later, when counsel for Southern California Edison rose in the hearing room in Los Angeles and announced the "withdrawal" of Kaiparowits, the environmental community immediately turned its attention and resources to the proposed Intermountain Power Plant, the new threat to the neighborhood. We knew we had to address the residual open questions at the California PUC and with the Utah State Engineer, but otherwise Intermountain had priority. But there is evidence—"evidence" in a very loose sense—that EPA had not yet finished with Kaiparowits. A faint historical footprint exists in old archives.

Surfing the CEQ web site for references to Section 309 referrals, a researcher will come across a very odd document. Its title, or heading, is straight forward enough: "Referral of inter-agency disagreements to CEQ under the National Environmental Policy Act." The text begins with a summary of the 309 referral process and concludes with a list of twenty-seven referrals from 1974 into the fall of 2001. The fifth referral listed is "Kaiparowits Power Plant, Kaiparowits Plateau, Utah," and EPA is identified as the referral agency. While referral of Kaiparowits to CEQ was what we had sought from EPA, this particular document is a mystery.

First, the "date of referral" is listed as June 8, 1976, almost two months after Southern California Edison publicly announced withdrawal of the project! And this is only the beginning. The document itself bears no date, no signature, and no indication of who prepared it or why. It is a summary recitation and does not seem to be a part of any formal administrative record. Clearly it is not the actual EPA referral itself, nor is it associated with any documents or files which could throw more light on its provenance. The only notation on its pages other than the text itself are the page numbers—numbers one through four. From the phrasing alone, it could be an internal training paper or background for a speech, or it could be a summary written to accompany testimony before a congressional committee—there are other possibilities—but this is merely speculation.

Recent inquiries of EPA and CEQ were unproductive. The agencies were cooperative, but neither seemed to have easily accessed records or information regarding a Kaiparowits referral or an explanation of the document. Of course we could file a formal Freedom of Information Act (the government disclosure statute) request, but a thorough search of administrative archives from thirty-six years ago would likely be tedious and expensive. And it might be completely unproductive. Historians may want to know more, but given the purposes of this story I am going to leave it a mystery—tantalizing, even suggestive, but still a mystery.

Decision of the California PUC

We environmentalists had supposed the California Public Utilities Commission was agreeable to suspension of its proceedings. After all, by the fall of 1977, eighteen months after withdrawal of the project, nothing further had happened. That changed with breathtaking swiftness on October 18th. The PUC ruled—four votes in favor and one abstention—that it had jurisdiction![18] The Commission was no longer going to wait for the utilities to report their intentions. The utilities' argument that the issue was moot and the matter should be dismissed was rejected "because of the urgency of [the] question and its relation to the future energy resources for California." The Commission specifically acknowledged the recent water rights application in Utah. Responding to the delay argument, the Commission ruled that "later determination of our jurisdiction merely delays the day of reckoning until the time of crisis, when a project is already in the works." Then the PUC found:

> (1) There is no distinction between an ... out-of-state plant serving California and [an] in-state plant in relation to its impact on California ratepayers, [and] (2) Public convenience and necessity inquire into the need, convenience, and costs of a California utility's out-of-state plant serving California to the same extent as [a] local plant."[19]

Complete Victory!

From that October day, large energy projects outside the State of California proposed by shareholder-owned utility companies to fulfill energy needs of California would be subject to PUC jurisdiction. The utilities would have to obtain a certificate of convenience and necessity from the Commission before building a plant. This would be a public process, and the environmental community could participate in full measure. The energy needs of California ratepayers and alternative means of satisfying those needs, such as energy savings from energy conservation measures, smaller sized plants, expansion of existing facilities, and the type of plant to be approved, would all be relevant and material to the PUC's determinations. Furthermore, environmentalists would have a full opportunity to present evidence and advance argument in support of their positions.

It may appear that all of this activity, after the Southern California Edison lawyer stood up in the Los Angeles hearing room back in April 1976, was carefully choreographed. Actually, it was the various agencies whose jurisdiction had been invoked bringing their proceedings to a close or, in the case of the California PUC, to a final conclusion. This is appropriate and efficient: it is what we expect and need from our government entities. Moreover, the proceedings and decisions of the agencies on the issues raised would provide useful guideposts for interested parties going forward. In fact, everything we had learned fighting Kaiparowits would be needed right away. Ninety miles to the north of the abandoned Kaiparowits site loomed the threat of another massive power plant proposed at a site just east of Capitol Reef National Park, home of a remarkable one-hundred-mile-long geological warp in the earth's crust, the Waterpocket Fold.

The Fight Against the Intermountain Behemoth

Notes from the Field
(Before Dawn in Capitol Reef)

One of my favorite hikes in the canyon country begins at a trail-head in the Fremont River Canyon. You need to get there early—just before the break of dawn while the sky is still black. Capitol Reef is quiet then. What sound there is—the soft murmur of ripples in the river—seems to make the silence even more profound. The dust from yesterday afternoon's winds has settled out of the air, and it is cool, crisp, and fresh. I am going to be on the trail leading to Cohab Canyon and Cassidy Arch. It climbs steadily up the south side of the canyon where it will strike a contour on top of a bench that heads Cohab Canyon.

Before going very far, I stop for a moment to look back at the river. I'm still within the canyon walls, but looking downstream where the river is cutting its way through the bedrock presents a remarkable scene. The massive white Navajo Sandstone domes capping the Waterpocket Fold on the eastern horizon seem ethereal against the still dark sky—white ghosts riding the horizon above the canyon walls and the formations carved by the Fremont River, now a couple of hundred feet below me. However, I cannot pause long— I must get higher before the first shafts of morning sunlight pierce the gaps between those white domes.

My timing is good today, and as I negotiate the last switchback in the trail and walk out on the bench, shafts of sunlight are beginning to flow through the gaps and play on cliffs across the way, on subsidiary canyons in the foreground, and on large boulders all around me. Intervals of slanting sunbeams point the way down the trail. Little sunbursts break through small holes and crevices in the rocks, both far and near, striking my eyes, then quickly blinking out as I keep walking. But in another step or two—another sunburst!

When I emerged from the canyon, I left its pale yellow and white sandstones and walked into the full color of Capitol Reef. Now formations clothed in many hues are showing off all about me. The deep reds—Kayenta and Wingate Sandstones; and here and there the bold Moenkopi Formation—are particularly striking, vividly coloring the bench on which I am now walking, the walls of Cohab Canyon just ahead, and the cliffs all around. Some of the escarpments in the distance show narrow dark bands—probably coal and shale. I know that on close inspection purples and even lavenders emerge from them. All around me, in sharp contrast, are ledges and individual boulders of that pale yellow and white color found back in the canyon. Pinyons and junipers standing about show their green and grey colors.

The sun has now climbed above the crest of the Waterpocket Fold and bathes the entire scene with its full morning light. The air is crystal clear, and everything stands out in sharp focus. A gentle breeze is blowing as the cool night air grows warmer. I think of a grand symphony, beginning softly, soon trying out melodies and harmonies spiced with instrumental solos, and then building through marvelous crescendos to a dramatic climax.

I walk toward the ledge above the head of Cohab Canyon looking for a good vantage point to sit and soak this all in. Nowhere else on the Colorado Plateau are so many colors so sharply defined - layer upon layer—as here in Capitol Reef. And this morning light shows them to their best effect. The Navajo and Paiute call this country "Land of the Sleeping Rainbow." It strikes me more forcibly than ever that this is no place for an enormous 3,000-megawatt power plant just over the horizon behind those white domes.

The proposed Intermountain Power Plant was another 3,000-megawatt monstrosity—just like Kaiparowits—with coal mines, gravel quarries, transmission lines and towers, a huge transportation network, a power plant site covering thousands of acres, and a related construction, mining, and service influx of thousands of people. As with Kaiparowits, the level of air pollution emissions would be staggering. Intermountain was to be built on the Fremont River near Caineville, Utah. The Horseshoe Canyon Unit of Canyonlands National Park with its famous Indian pictograph panels was forty miles to the east. To the west, only twelve miles away, lay Capitol Reef National Park. Necessary water resources would be drawn from the Fremont River, underground aquifers, and potentially from dams on the headwaters of the Escalante River. The Escalante—considered by many the jewel of the Colorado Plateau—starts at 11,000 feet on the Aquarius Plateau and descends through a maze of side canyons, narrow and twisting slot canyons, glens, and breathtaking amphitheaters until the main stem of the river pours into Lake Powell a couple of miles below Stephens Arch, a total distance of more than a hundred miles.

Intermountain initially appeared to present a tougher legal problem than Kaiparowits. Since the sponsor, the Los Angeles Department of Water and Power (DEWAP), was a municipal utility owned by the citizens of Los Angeles, the California Public Utilities Commission did not have jurisdiction.* The rule here is that the citizens of Los Angeles, through their chosen representatives, determine the public need for the plant and the rates they should pay to construct and operate it. There were no shareholders as there were with Southern California Edison who might be solely concerned about their own interests rather than those of the public. Furthermore, DEWAP's funding sources probably were more substantial than those of the private utilities who sought to build Kaiparowits, for the Department could issue high quality municipal bonds ultimately backed by the fee and tax revenues of the City and County of Los Angeles. Thus the expense of Intermountain could perhaps be borne more easily.

Obligations under the National Environmental Policy Act and the National Parks Organic Act were as formidable to Intermountain as they were to Kaiparowits. Moreover, impacts from widespread water diversions, with accompanying structures, storage areas, and transport facilities required for a 3,000-megawatt plant on the banks of the Fremont River, would be prodigious. The environmental community was as fully committed to the defeat of Intermountain as it had just been to the defeat of Kaiparowits, and the strategies used against the latter were quickly employed against this new threat. It was clear from the outset that the most immediate and one of the strongest legal remedies against

---

* DEWAP was the majority owner and the operating entity. Smaller municipalities in California and in Utah shared a minority interest.

Intermountain was based upon the Clean Air Act language forbidding significant degradation of existing clean air regions. While this was important in the Kaiparowits fight, particularly with the Environmental Protection Agency, it quickly became the principal legal remedy we would employ in hope of knocking out Intermountain early in the process.

The evolution of the principles and the regulatory structure to protect pristine air quality areas, the "prevention of significant deterioration" (PSD), is an important part of the environmental law story. It begins with the Clean Air Act of 1970, the first legislative attempt with sufficient muscle to begin addressing the country's burgeoning air pollution problems. After recognizing that air pollution was becoming a matter of serious public concern, Congress declared the purpose of the Act was "to protect and enhance the quality of the Nation's air resources." The one-year-old Environmental Protection Agency was given regulatory, oversight, and enforcement responsibilities. In the spring of 1971 EPA published draft regulations that forbade the "significant deterioration" of air quality in clean air regions. This was extremely important to the western part of the country, for it still had large regions, including most of the Colorado Plateau, where air quality was excellent. But this initiative was short-lived. Tom Turner, in his lively reportorial narrative of early Sierra Club Legal Defense Fund activities, *Wild By Law*, recounts —

> [O]n August 14 [1971], the EPA issued its final regulations, and PSD had disappeared. In its place was a paragraph saying quite frankly that clean-air areas could indeed be legally polluted, just so long as they didn't get dirtier than a certain standard. The sacrifice of the West's air was official policy.[20]

To the environmental community, the statutory mandate for "protect[ion] of the quality of the Nation's air resources" was clear. Pristine air sheds must remain pristine. It did not mean that they could be polluted to a certain level of deterioration arbitrarily determined by the EPA.

Sierra Club retained an experienced attorney in Washington DC who filed a lawsuit in the U.S. District Court for the District of Columbia seeking to overturn the EPA decision. After briefing and argument, Judge John Pratt ruled in favor of the Club in a four-page almost perfunctory opinion holding that the "protect and enhance" language of the Clean

Air Act meant protection of clean air locales from significant air quality deterioration. EPA appealed to the U.S. Court of Appeals for the District of Columbia, which affirmed Judge Pratt but did not write an opinion of its own. While it is very unusual for appellate courts to omit writing opinions explaining their decisions, it is not unprecedented. The government then took the case to the U.S. Supreme Court, which reviewed the matter and divided four for affirmation and four for reversal (one justice abstained), and again no opinion was written. A tie vote affirms the decision of the lower court, and with no other written opinion, Judge Pratt's four-page decision in District Court became the controlling interpretation of the law.[21]

The force and effect of PSD—this non-degradation mandate—would first be experienced in the western states with their remaining large areas of pristine air quality, and where rumors of potential developments drastically affecting that air quality were beginning to circulate. Because of my environmental law experience in the region and early familiarity with potential threats to its clean air, I became involved in the case at the appellate court level. Dr. Michael Williams, with whom I would work in the Kaiparowits fight, and Sierra Club volunteers and staff in the southwestern states were beginning to educate themselves on the issue. The rumors of large coal-fired power plants in the plans of West Coast utility companies were turning into publicly announced proposals. The PSD issue was becoming widely recognized in the environmental community as a critically important tool for protecting western parklands and their pristine air.[22]

A Whistle-Blower Gives Us Critical Help

While we were writing our appellate court brief, we received a telephone call from an individual who had become aware of the litigation and its importance to the protection of the Colorado Plateau. He informed us that EPA was making serious misrepresentations in the case and we should know about them. This was an exciting moment! Practically by definition it was unexpected, and it carried with it the possibility—indeed, maybe the probability—of a turning point in the case. It is not uncommon for public interest lawyers to be contacted by a whistle-blower; in fact, lawyers in many areas of practice experience such occurrences. You enjoy the intrigue and the sudden vulnerability of your opponent's position, but after your pulse quiets down, you have questions to ask: Will the whistle-blower's information, his revelations, be legitimate and measurably increase your chances of success? Why was the information avoided or suppressed?

The role of the "whistle-blower" in our government is a long and generally honorable one. Whistle-blowers are individuals who have inside knowledge of wrongdoing by a company or governmental agency and disclose that information to appropriate authorities. Whistle-blowers typically report misconduct to law enforcement and watchdog agencies, the media, or lawyers. In some instances, whistle-blowers are actively sought out or encouraged, and the individuals are subsequently rewarded. In other cases, whistle-blowers seek confidentiality to protect themselves from public exposure, workplace discrimination, and other forms of retaliation. In fact, there are federal and state statutes prohibiting such harassment, but enforcement can be involved and not wholly satisfactory. So we were not surprised that our contact sought confidentiality, though he seemed willing to bear the burdens of disclosure if absolutely necessary.

> [When] contacted by a whistle-blower ... you enjoy the intrigue ... but after your pulse quiets down, you have questions to ask....

We had three initial questions—questions any lawyer would ask: Was his information important to the issues we had before us? Was he in a position to be reasonably well informed of the particular circumstances involved? Did he seem credible? Although our whistle-blower was not an employee of EPA or the Department of Justice (the lawyers representing the government), his professional work gave him ready access to the matters he was disclosing, and the subject was clearly pertinent to the case. Due to the nature of his information, the matter of credibility would soon be answered. Of course, there were other important questions—particularly how to use the information disclosed. On that score, the nature of his information provided a clear path.

A critical aspect of any case taken on appeal is the record created in the district court below. Since the central question in the prevention of significant deterioration case was a question of statutory interpretation, a question of law, there was no trial in the district court, with the usual array of testimony, exhibits, and so forth. There was, however, an administrative record, the documents and information forming EPA's basis for drafting the regulations being challenged. When EPA filed its response to our lawsuit, it was required to designate or identify that record or those parts of it upon which EPA had based the regulations promulgated.

The administrative record can be especially important in a case like this, where both the issue and the applicable statutory language have not previously been reviewed by a court. Such cases of "first impression" rely foremost upon the statutory language and the legislative history—the hearings, committee reports, congressional debates, and the recorded evolution of the language finally passed. But the interpretation of the administrative agency charged with implementation can also be very important to judicial interpretation, especially when the statute and its legislative history are arguably not altogether clear when applied to the issue at hand. The Court of Appeals affirmation of the District Court without a written opinion, and the divided but unexpressed views of the Supreme Court, suggest the statutory language and its legislative history were thought to be less than definitive on the PSD issue.

In District Court EPA identified and listed an administrative record that recited the draft regulations, EPA's internal review, and its conclusion that nothing in the statutory language or its legislative history required more than minimal protection of existing clean air regions. References in the record to PSD were sparse, and what there were supported EPA's conclusion. Having no information to the contrary, we had accepted that "record" and went on to argue our view of the law. Judge Pratt agreed with us, but we knew we would have a tough job on appeal. Here the whistle-blower came to our aid. He informed us that EPA had not filed the entire administrative record. There were extensive internal files and documents reviewing and discussing protection of clean air areas, and the bulk of them concluded the statutory language should be interpreted as the District Court and we interpreted it. Furthermore, arrangements were being made for us to review and copy the documents.

This was a moment all lawyers treasure: all of a sudden, we held in our hands a powerful new tool reinforcing the arguments we were making! And we could use it immediately. We responded to the government's designation of the record on appeal with our own designation (a "counter designation") listing for several pages document after document of the newly acquired—and now complete—administrative record. Caught "red-handed," EPA was forced to acknowledge that its prior designation was woefully incomplete!

We could reasonably assume that the decision of the Court of Appeals not to write its own opinion and the tie vote of the Supreme Court indicated the question was very close. The affirming decisions could easily have hinged upon the contents of the administrative record. So it is quite possible the whistle-blower's disclosure became pivotal. The decisions confirming the prevention of significant deterioration doctrine that had served us so admirably in the Kaiparowits fight would give us critical assistance in the Intermountain contest. Consequently, on behalf of Sierra Club I filed a formal petition with the Secretary of the Interior asking that he deny the federal permits requested for the Intermountain Project. However, before he could act on the petition the PSD issue was back before Congress.

Lobbying Congress

The Clean Air Act was scheduled on the 1977 congressional calendar, and Congress expected to review all provisions of the Act for potential amendment and reauthorization, including the PSD doctrine. Pristine air quality regions around the country, including the Colorado Plateau, hung in the balance. Initially matters proceeded at an accelerated pace. The House of Representatives brought the legislation to the House floor for a vote so quickly that the environmental community was caught off guard. A bill was passed and sent to the Senate with comprehensive amendments, but it specifically omitted language protecting pristine air quality areas. This was serious, for the comprehensive congressional review and reauthorization of the Act likely insured that any important part of the 1970 Act purposefully excluded from the 1977 amendments and reauthorization would no longer be applicable law. An all-out campaign would have to be organized in the Senate, with lawyers and experts needed. Given our experience with this issue, Dr. Williams, our air pollution expert in the Kaiparowits fight, and I were recruited by Friends of the Earth and Sierra Club, leaders in the PSD campaign in the Senate, to come to Washington to help out.

Lawyers who regularly represent clients seeking to advance a public interest such as environmental protection are often called upon to review and interpret proposed legislative or regulatory provisions, draft such provisions themselves, and even advise and help conduct legislative or administrative lobbying campaigns. Existing laws are frequently amended as underlying circumstances or the political climate change. Furthermore, success in a court or in a formal administrative proceeding on an important public issue is often a prelude to renewed consideration by Congress or to new or amended regulations.

A working definition of a lobbyist is anyone who solicits or tries to influence the actions or votes of a member of a legislative body or the rule-making activities of an administrative agency. The word denotes the traditional large hall—the lobby—adjacent to the assembly room of a leg-islature, where the public or their representatives can meet and talk with the legislators. An earlier and definitely more interesting account has it that "lobbying" referred to the lobby of the historic Willard Hotel—the site of much government business in an earlier era—a couple of blocks east of the White House, where office-seekers and special petitioners sought an audience with President Ulysses Grant on his periodic visits there. An English visitor at that time described the close atmosphere of the Willard Lobby as compounded in equal parts of "heat, noise, dust, smoke, and expectoration."[23] There are professional paid lobbyists, but there are also "grassroots" lobbyists, individuals who lobby as volunteer or citizen activists on a particular issue. Writing letters or sending emails to Congressmen, or corralling them at an event in their districts to ask them to take action on an issue, is grassroots lobbying. At one time or another, many of us will engage in such lobbying activity.

The role of the professional or staff lobbyist usually becomes critical when a legislative or administrative campaign extends for weeks or months at a time. Monitoring the process on almost a daily basis, partic-ularly in intense legislative campaigns, is essential. There are hearings to attend and testimony to give, numerous meetings with legislative or agency staff, and congressional and administrative calendars to follow. Professional lobbyists serve as communications hubs, keeping grassroots supporters informed and advising them when to increase political pressure on the decision-makers. They promote, and even personally draft, statutory or regulatory language friendly to their clients. They field inquiries from the press and media. The ebb and flow of the politics of an environmental issue are constant, and the lobbyists are there to immediately evaluate changes. Furthermore, it is always helpful to have a good idea of what the opposition is doing. This list is not exhaustive. The lobbyists' daily fare can include practically anything that accompanies the writing of a law or a decision or rule-making of a governmental agency.

When Dr. Williams and I walked over to the Senate Office Building to discuss prevention of significant deterioration of air quality and pending amendments and reauthorization of the Clean Air Act, we were lobbyists. We were part of a well organized and intense national campaign of concerned citizens and their representative organizations writing letters to congressmen and senators, calling their offices, speaking at public meetings and hearings, getting press and media attention, and publicly advocating the air pollution issue whenever we could. All this was greatly enhanced by the support of our knowledgeable and experienced environmental lobbying staff in Washington. The strength of this grassroots base and its efforts is critical to the lobbying success of the public interest lawyer and his expert. Without the grassroots effort, without those grassroots lobbyists and the pressure they bring, we will not get the important appointments at congressional offices or the careful consideration we seek for our arguments.

The interests opposing the environmentalists have their own lobbyists, of course, ready to advocate their particular points of view. Thus, the issues are joined, facts are collected, positions developed, and remedies debated. Ideally, the legislators or the administrators become well informed on the matter at hand and in due course, after appropriate deliberation, make sound decisions. The ebb and flow of political currents naturally contribute their influence, but as long as the balance among legitimate interests remains reasonable the public business gets done. The legislation written and the decisions made may be imperfect, but in true democratic fashion all interested parties have participated, and the opportunity for amendment is there when subsequent experience recommends it. This is the way we want the process to work.

Unfortunately, today many private and corporate interests, with their seemingly unlimited financial resources, appear fixated on short-term ad hoc economic benefits for their narrow clientele. Frequently, worthy lobbying functions of education and assistance in writing good legislation are completely subordinated to purely private or political gain. Even when the public interest prevails, these private or corporate lobbies often immediately mount a campaign to reverse that success. They chip away with damaging anti-environmental "riders"—language tacked on to legislation on unrelated subjects—or attempt to befoul the implementation process by pushing confusing or contradictory phraseology for administrative rules, regulations, and formal administrative decisions. Legislators and government officials come and go, but corporate lobbyists remain almost as a shadow government, ever alert for vulnerabilities, ever ready to exploit loopholes, and endowed with seemingly unlimited financial resources. Much of their agenda and their actions may be hidden from the public, who only learns of them after the fact.

Since protection of the environment enjoys broad public support, opposition lobbyists avoid frontal attack where possible; artifice and subterfuge may yield more satisfactory results. Some of this is probably inevitable given the participatory nature of our system of government. All advocates are eager to push their point of view, and lobbyists are hired to do just that. However, when short-term objectives constantly override promising long-term solutions, and when lobbyists and allied media are rewarded for the degree of hostility they can foment or the damage they can inflict upon needed public policies and rational responses to pressing problems, the system becomes dangerously out of balance. Noise becomes the objective rather than good governance. And when raw politics or unbridled political philosophy becomes the dominant goal, there is little room for thoughtful deliberation and productive work. These conditions seem all too prevalent today.

But, in 1977, as Dr. Williams and I walked to our first appointment, such heavy thoughts were not on our minds. The Senate was seriously reviewing seven years of experience with the 1970 Clean Air Act, the existing state of the country's air quality, and amendments that would strengthen administration and effectiveness of the statute. We had important information to impart; senators and their staff wanted to hear us. Because of our experiences with the proposed Kaiparowits and Intermountain plants, there were fundamental issues that the two of us were particularly qualified to address. The first was whether any large project with significant air pollution emissions would be prohibited in pristine air quality areas or regions. We asserted that a number of mid-sized appropriately dispersed facilities that controlled their emissions with the latest and best technology could pass muster. Larger facilities or projects that were fundamentally "clean" or minimally polluting could also comply with a standard preventing significant deterioration. However, heavily polluting developments the size of a Kaiparowits or Intermountain would be prohibited. Dr. Williams could explain this very well, as we saw earlier in the Kaiparowits trip to Washington.

The second fundamental matter, the language of the statute and its developing legislative history, fell within my bailiwick. The courts had already determined that the 1970 statutory language mandated EPA to protect clean air quality areas. Thus our task was to maintain the strength of the language—framing directives in words of command: EPA "shall" protect pristine air quality areas as opposed to "may" or "should" protect them. We needed clear and supportive statements and arguments in the legislative history—the written reports of congressional committees, statements and interpretations of sponsoring senators, and colloquies on the Senate floor—regarding the meaning of the PSD language of the Clean Air Act Amendments. Our job was to press for direct and unmistakable references to the proposed statute and its terms, not just generalized political or philosophical rhetoric. We wanted a judge examining the statute in the future to find specific support in the legislative history confirming a strong policy of protection of clean air regions.

The third important task was to assure senators there was a reasonable and workable regulatory structure that could be implemented. The environmentalists' position would be in serious jeopardy if there was no legal route to achieve their objective. Dr. Williams explained air quality measuring technologies available to determine ambient air quality circumstances in pristine areas, monitoring technologies for measuring deteriorating or potentially deteriorating conditions, and available pollution control technology. I addressed the reasonableness and appropriateness of the regulatory framework—the air quality classification approach—that actually could be implemented. While Congress might not want to write specific details of the regulatory structure, it legitimately needed to know whether the basic objectives of its amendments and reauthorization could be realized in a practical manner. With that assurance, Congress could rely upon EPA to use its expertise to flesh out the actual regulations.

While we did speak briefly with several senators, we spent the bulk of our time talking to senatorial staff, both the personal staff of senators and staff of the Senate committees having jurisdiction. These conversations were generally lengthy, giving us time to address the details and complexities of the PSD subject. The four or five days we were on Capitol Hill gave us the opportunity to talk with most of the staff who were working with the senators sponsoring the legislation and who would bring it to the Senate floor for debate and passage. After our departure, our environmental staff lobbyists would carry on through the weeks ahead with the overall Clean Air Act agenda — including PSD — providing the continuity that we must have for most of our important legislative campaigns. Meanwhile, vital national grassroots efforts described earlier continued unabated.

A few months later, on August 7, 1977, comprehensive Clean Air Act Amendments passed both houses of Congress and were signed into law by President Jimmy Carter. Included was strong language protecting the pristine air quality of national parks and monuments, wilderness areas, and other preserves.[24] While Dr. Williams' and my efforts were important, they were just a part of a multi-faceted national campaign encompassing all Clean Air Act issues being addressed, and many professional lobbyists, lawyers, and staff of other organizations in the environmental community were involved. Speaking collectively, our lobbying campaign was a great success. As a result, the Clean Air Act became a more powerful force in protecting our environment and, not coincidentally, an important new layer of protection for the Golden Circle of National Parks on the Colorado Plateau was assured.

Intermountain Victory: A Presidential Order

A couple of weeks after passage of the new amendments, we experienced another remarkable surprise. We received a telephone call from the principal lawyer for the Department of Water and Power. He informed us that DEWAP had decided not to build Intermountain at the Fremont River site and was considering alternate plans for a 1500-megawatt plant—one-half the original project's size—at Lyndall, Utah, one hundred miles to the northwest in the Sevier River drainage. What did we think? .... Victory again! We called our clients and told them to begin celebrating once again. Certainly PSD was critical, but it also must be noted that by then we had a new Secretary of the Interior—Cecil Andrus, a past governor of Idaho—who was more receptive to environmental positions than his predecessor, Secretary Kleppe. If the fight had continued, Secretary Andrus had already informally indicated he favored protecting the parks over building Intermountain Power Plant on the banks of the Fremont River.[25]

Similarly, the Utah State Engineer seemed to be reluctant to ease the path for the Intermountain utilities. The principal lawyer for the State Engineer informally told our local counsel in Salt Lake City that the State would act on our water planning petition, filed back in the early days of the Kaiparowits fight, before granting Intermountain the water appropriations it sought. The implication seemed clear: an appropriation of water for Intermountain as proposed for the Fremont River site was by no means assured. Indeed, throughout the Kaiparowits and Intermountain fights I had a lingering suspicion that while Utah wanted development in the southern part of the State, the State as a whole was never truly convinced it wanted these monstrosities located within the Golden Circle of National Parks on the Colorado Plateau.

Kaiparowits and *Intermountain* were both signal victories. However, the advocates of exploitation of the West's natural resources and related development in extremely sensitive areas always seem ready with yet another plan. The proposed Allen-Warner Valley Project was a notable sequel to Kaiparowits and Intermountain. Coal was to be strip-mined from the Alton Hills formation in full view of overlooks at Bryce Canyon National Park, and thence transported to a 500-megawatt power plant west of Zion National Park and a larger plant near Las Vegas, Nevada. Ably contested by a Sierra Club Legal Defense Fund colleague, this proposal was also abandoned, but only for a time. On the western doorstep of Bryce, the Coal Hollow Mine site was opened and now planned expansion of the mine is well advanced. Nevertheless, the environmental community and its lawyers are fighting hard to mitigate its impact, writing yet another chapter in the continuous struggle to protect the priceless lands at stake.

In recent years, recurrent threats have come from proposals for development of scores of miles of paved highways and the creation or extension of innumerable unimproved roads for four-wheel drive vehicles. Local and state politicians want to extend four-wheel drive access to areas actually inside national park lands. Particularly notable today is pending litigation by the State of Utah against the United States seeking title to thousands of miles of "roadway"— so-called "ghost roads"— across federal lands, including national parks and monuments. Obviously this litigation is being vigorously contested by the United States and the environmentalists.[26] The pressure for oil and gas leasing and drilling is unremitting. Uranium exploration and mining periodically become a serious threat. Litigation on one or more of these issues is practically continuous. The environmental community must maintain a continuous lobbying presence to preserve gains made and victories enjoyed, to counter unrelenting and indiscriminate lobbying by resource developers, and to protect uniquely deserving lands not yet protected by park, monument, or wilderness status.

President William J. Clinton brought us an enormous way forward in the fall of 1996. On September 18, seated at a small table on the South Rim of Grand Canyon near where Teddy Roosevelt spoke in defense of the canyon in 1903, President Clinton signed an Executive Order establishing the Grand Staircase-Escalante National Monument.[27] This order protected 1.7 million acres of government-owned land in the center of the Golden Circle of National Parks — in the felicitous words of Greer Chesher, "The Heart of the Desert Wild!" As a result, the incomparable Escalante River is now largely protected from its source to its mouth. The Kaiparowits Plateau is included within the monument boundaries. Indeed, an immediate catalyst for President Clinton's Proclamation was the threat that the Kaiparowits coal beds—still with hungry suitors twenty years after the power plant fight—would finally surrender to the miner's pick and shovel. A company called Andalex Resources proposed to remove 14,000 tons of coal every two days and truck it over 200 miles through Glen Canyon National Recreation Area—requiring 300 huge trucks moving round the clock—to rail heads at Iron Springs, Utah, and Moapa, Nevada. From there the coal

A Dance in the Desert

One thousand head of livestock, 83 wagons, stacks of supplies, 250 men, women, and children—the San Juan Mission. By 1878 the Mormons had explored and settled most of Utah Territory, excepting only that country lying east of the Colorado River and north of the San Juan. This wedge of land was occupied by outlaws, a few ranchers, restive Indians, and gentile (not of Mormon faith) prospectors and miners. Mormon settlement was indicated, so in November 1879 the pioneering mission party rendezvoused at Forty Mile Spring— 40 miles southeast of the town of Escalante—preparatory to seeking a good location for settlement in that unsecured region.

These pioneers were experienced at this sort of thing, and their purpose was firm as they awaited final preparations. They were also exuberant. Nearby was a massive sandstone rock formation. A huge overhang partially embraced a large flat sandstone platform. Given the high spirits of the group, this natural amphitheater, and the presence of three violins in the party it was probably inevitable that these musical pioneers would gather there after dinner and commence to dance. And what a wonderful picture this made—the moon and stars above, the massive rocks looming up, the flickering light from the lanterns, the music echoing from the rock walls, the rustle of the dancers' feet, and their shouts of joy and approval! Dance Hall Rock.

The spirit of those evenings carried over during the harrowing journey that followed through some of the roughest country in the Southwest to the site of Bluff, Utah, reached in April of 1880—the number of pioneers augmented by three babies born on the trail.

Long a dedicated national historic site, Dance Hall Rock and Forty Mile Spring now lie within the boundary of Grand Staircase-Escalante National Monument. It is not just the spectacular unforgettable natural wonders of Red Rock Country which are protected in the National Monument; it also celebrates that very appealing moment of significant regional history and it salutes those hardy pioneers.[28]

would be shipped to the Pacific Coast and then across the ocean to power plants in Asia. This threat was finally put to rest with the President's proclamation and with the later government acquisition of the outstanding leaseholder rights.[29]

One can argue that the protection given to the lands within the National Monument is minimal. Existing private use privileges, such as grazing permits, were not terminated, and use of existing primitive roads could continue, at least until a transportation plan for the Monument could be developed. But the decision was made to henceforth protect this land, and now the landowner—the government—is charged with preserving its natural beauty and its natural condition. This is the way we protect our valued public lands. We turn from wringing all we can from the land to preserving in perpetuity those lands best suited for public enjoyment and spiritual inspiration. The transition and the journey are hard, and concerned citizens and their lawyers must force most of the important steps. Moreover, these advocates must remain in the field, protecting what we have saved from persistent and rapacious private interests, abetted by allied government officials, who never cease trying to compromise the protected lands. But the reward is great, for the route we now travel in the Grand Staircase-Escalante National Monument and the parks that surround it leads toward public enjoyment of their unique qualities and preservation of their wonders.

CHAPTER VI

It Takes an Expert

Defending the Wild of East Meadow Creek

We were in the fourth day of trial in the U.S. District Court for Colorado in the *East Meadow Creek* wilderness case. Plaintiffs and other individuals had already testified to the wilderness character of the forests slated for logging, other Forest Service lands in the vicinity, and the contiguous Gore Range-Eagles Nest Primitive Area. They spoke eloquently of the undisturbed nature of the forest, the gorgeous scenery, rushing streams and pristine lakes, the presence of wildlife, and the rugged crest of the Gore Range rising just beyond. They shared the strong emotions they felt of release and serenity, and the sense of physical well being when they hiked up the trails into the forest. We had questioned Forest Service witnesses about their wilderness review process mandated by the recently passed Wilderness Act. Now we were ready to call our most important witness.

The Forest Service and the timber industry resisted our evidence every step of the way—mere citizens, they implied, could not speak with the authority and expertise of the United States Forest Service or the tested veterans of the timber industry. But the judge heard our testimony, examined our exhibits, and admitted them into evidence. However, we knew the Forest Service and the industry would be offering contrary testimony when their turn came to present their own case. While we felt our witnesses had presented convincing evidence that the area was overwhelmingly wilderness in character, we were not sure we could prevail in the end if it was just our lay witnesses against experienced Forest Service officials. And we had to win this point if we were going to succeed.

As plaintiffs, we had the burden of proof; we had to persuade the judge that the facts upon which we relied had been established by a preponderance of the evidence. A "tie" or "draw" would result in judgment for the defendants. It was also 1969—only four years since the *Scenic Hudson* case gave public interest advocates the opportunity to go to federal

Alpine lake, Eagles Nest Wilderness Area, Colorado

court and only five years since passage of the Wilderness Act. We were asking the court to make decisions in uncharted legal territory. The judge would want to be confident we had a good case. We had to do more before we rested and turned the case over to our opponents. We needed a witness of established credibility who could bring together everything we had said.

This called for a witness with special experience in wilderness identification and classification matters and who was familiar with East Meadow Creek and its environs, a witness who because of his special qualifications could testify authoritatively that the timber sale area met the definition of wilderness set forth in the Wilderness Act. We needed an expert who could testify that the graded road leading to the edge of the East Meadow Creek area, and the remains of an old abandoned "bug road" pushed into the area in the 1930s for forest fire control, did not disqualify the East Meadow Creek area as a whole from meeting the definition of wilderness. In that event, we argued, the Wilderness Act required that East Meadow Creek remain in its existing wild state and not be logged until the President and Congress decided whether it should be formally designated and protected as a wilderness area. We needed an expert to tip the balance. We needed Clif Merritt.

We think of a trial or a formal hearing as a forum for determining the facts of a case, and indeed this is fundamental to any court or administrative process. Witnesses are needed to tell us what actually happened, what were the observable facts. The general rule is that the opinions of witnesses are excluded. But as with many aspects of the law, the general rule does not always suffice. This is particularly true where the events or circumstances observed and related require more information and explanation for them to be interpreted or understood. Then an expert or a specialist on the subject at hand may give a meaningful interpretation or view of the events or circumstances and thus materially assist in the determination of the "facts" and their significance. The interpretations—the "opinions"—of the expert can help the trier of fact, whether it is judge or jury, better relate to the facts presented and see them in the context of the case at hand.

The law has developed rules that help insure that expert testimony is appropriate. Article VII of the Federal Rules of Evidence addresses Opinions and Expert Testimony in federal courts:

Rule 702. Testimony by Experts

If scientific, technical, or other specialized knowledge will assist the trier of fact to understand the evidence or to determine a fact in issue, a witness qualified as an expert by knowledge, skill, experience, training, or education, may testify thereto in the form of an opinion or otherwise, if:

    (a)   The expert's scientific, technical, or other specialized knowledge will help the trier of fact to understand the evidence or to determine a fact in issue;

    (b)   The testimony is based on sufficient facts or data;

    (c)   The testimony is the product of reliable principles and methods;

    (d)   The expert has reliably applied the principles and methods to the facts of the case.

The Advisory Committee Notes* logically continue: "An intelligent evaluation of facts is often difficult or impossible without the application of some scientific, technical, or other specialized knowledge." The fields of knowledge which may be drawn upon "are not limited merely to the 'scientific' and 'technical' but extend to all 'specialized' knowledge. Similarly, the expert is viewed, not in the narrow sense, but as a person qualified by knowledge, training or education."[1]

The first fundamental question in the *East Meadow Creek* trial was whether the area met the definition of wilderness under the Wilderness Act of 1964. As we have seen, in 1969 there were no published court decisions interpreting any of the Act's provisions. Thus there had been no judicial review measuring the condition of any of our public lands, including our National Forests, against the definition of wilderness set forth in the Act. The Act speaks of lands of "primeval character," lands which "generally appear to [be] affected primarily by the forces of nature," and "where the earth and its community of life are untrammeled by man." Noble sentiments surely, but what did they mean in reality, particularly in the forests of East Meadow Creek?

We believed the experiences and perspectives Clifton Merritt could bring to this new land management question—the review and classification of wilderness—would be valuable. A hundred years ago the famous jurist Learned Hand succinctly wrote, "The whole object of the expert is to tell the [court], not facts, [...] but general truths derived from his specialized experience."[2] We believed Clif would do this extremely well; he knew East Meadow Creek and he knew wilderness. We have already met Michael Williams and Ronald Doctor, each an expert in his own right, in the Kaiparowits struggle. Clif Merritt could similarly serve us here, providing crucial testimony precisely where needed. Clif hailed from Montana and was already a seasoned veteran in the rapidly evolving wilderness review process under the Wilderness Act, which included review of the Gore Range-Eagles Nest Primitive Area and its contiguous wilderness qualifying lands. He was the Regional Director for The Wilderness Society stationed in Denver, and in 1969 he probably knew more about wilderness review in the Rocky Mountains than any other person. Hiking out from the end of the graded access road, he had thoroughly

---

* Official interpretive notes that follow the published statement of each rule.

explored East Meadow Creek; he was also familiar with the "bug road" trace and had followed its path. He knew the alpine meadows and the rugged peaks of the contiguous primitive area.

When I called Clif Merritt to the witness stand we had already satisfied the first requirement for offering expert testimony: the usefulness to the court of the opinion of an expert on the question of whether the timber sale area in East Meadow Creek met the definition of wilderness in the Wilderness Act. For three days lay witnesses and a wilderness trip outfitter had related their experiences in East Meadow Creek, emphasizing its "wild" and undisturbed nature. This was valuable evidence, but it was largely personal—the individual observations of those who visited the area. In cross-examination, the defendants suggested that this testimony amounted to no more than personal sentiment. The effect of the access road and the visible remnants of the old bug road on the wilderness character of the area remained an open question, and defendants were prepared to rebut our testimony when their turn came to present their own evidence. The court was ready to hear more from us on this subject.

Our second task was to establish that Clif was an expert, that he had relevant "specialized knowledge" beyond that of the public at large. In fact, his detailed knowledge of western lands that were wilderness candidates and the nature and complexities of on-going wilderness reviews across Montana, Idaho, and down through Wyoming and Colorado, was unequalled. Not even Forest Service witnesses had his comprehensive region-wide perspective of current wilderness review matters. Thirdly, we had to be sure appropriate evidence establishing the underlying facts and circumstances—the "foundation" evidence upon which Clif would offer his opinions—was in the record.

Opposing counsel will first test an expert's qualifications if he thinks they may be vulnerable. Then he may challenge the testimony on the grounds that the evidence adduced is based upon incomplete or erroneous facts; he will try to impeach the foundation of the expert's testimony. Of course, he will also point out that equally qualified and informed experts—his experts naturally—draw different opinions or conclusions from the same evidence. This is why laying the foundation and qualifying the expert is key. Often the expert's opinions themselves flow naturally once this all-important preliminary work is done. If the expert's credentials are truly outstanding, or if his experiences are uniquely or intimately related to the issue at hand, the lawyer wants to be sure to develop this background in detail, for he wants the court to know that his expert is particularly well qualified. The hope is that he has been present for the preceding days of testimony, for this enhances his understanding of the case and his role in it. Obviously the better the expert's qualifications and the more comprehensive and thorough the foundation, the more credible his testimony will be.

In *East Meadow Creek*, there were two critical questions we called upon Clif Merritt to address:

- The condition of the land itself: Was East Meadow Creek wilderness in character? An existing graded and maintained access road extended three-quarters of a mile into the sale area where it abruptly ended. In addition, traversing a part of the area was an old primitive road—in 1969 little more than a trace—used in the 1930s for bark beetle control efforts and for forest fire control. This "bug road" had been abandoned for decades and was reverting to a natural state, but its track was still visible in several places. Defendants argued that these intrusions were inconsistent with the meaning and definition of wilderness in the Wilderness Act.
- Was East Meadow Creek an integral part of the Gore Range Primitive Area and its contiguous wilderness qualifying lands? Was the "whole" worthy of wilderness consideration? If so, it was a candidate for formal wilderness designation.

If these two questions were decided in our favor, then we were a long way toward winning the case. The timber sale and accompanying road construction would be prohibited, and East Meadow Creek would be included in the mandated wilderness review for the Gore Range Primitive Area and its qualifying contiguous lands. Then Congress would make the decision whether East Meadow Creek would be permanently protected as part of an Eagles Nest Wilderness Area.

Clif's demeanor in the witness box was compelling. He sat straight and gave counsel and the judge his full attention. A balding man in his late fifties, he was noticeably deliberate in his answers. When he warmed to a question he became more intense, more animated, but he still did not rush his response. When I developed his qualifications, he neither bragged about them nor deprecated them. Rather, he seemed to be saying that he wished everyone could be so fortunate as he to explore as much of America's remaining wilderness as he had done. I asked Clif about the access road and the "bug road." Had he been there? Yes, he had. The flow of question and answer was good. He testified on point and with confidence. He firmly believed the sale area was of high wilderness quality and value.

As I moved into the second subject, East Meadow Creek's relation to the Primitive Area, Judge Doyle interrupted me and began asking the questions. He turned his chair so that he was directly facing Mr. Merritt. An extended colloquy developed—the judge and the witness in comfortable conversation, both seeming to understand well what the other was saying. Clif repeated his view that East Meadow Creek qualified for wilderness review under the Wilderness Act, that the present and past road intrusions did not disqualify the timber sale area and the larger area around it from wilderness consideration.

As Judge Doyle moved to questions of the area's relation to the Primitive Area, Clif became more animated. He drew verbal images of the forests, the streams and lakes, and the peaks just beyond; together the whole made a wilderness to be treasured and protected. The judge listened intently, occasionally nodding as if to say, "This is what I want to know." By this time I had moved well back from the lectern and was leaning against the edge of the counsel table. I wanted to remove myself as an immediate presence and just let the conversation continue. When Judge Doyle's questions ended, a comfortable silence ensued between the two men, Clif waiting patiently and the judge reflecting on what he had heard. After a few moments, the judge pivoted his chair back to face the courtroom.

JUDGE: Anything further, Mr. Ruckel?

ME: No, your honor.

JUDGE (*looking at defendants' counsel*): Do you have any questions?

DEFENDANTS' COUNSEL: No questions, your honor.

JUDGE (*to the witness*): Thank you sir, you may step down.[3]

What a moment! Of course, there was a temptation to jump in with more questions. Clif could have covered this point or that point a little more comprehensively, or a detail here or there could have been topped off a little better. But these thoughts were small concerns; they were not worthy of the moment. Our case had just been made in the best possible manner: an extremely able expert establishing an excellent rapport with the judge and in his own fashion conversationally addressing the two basic subjects for which we called him to the stand. I wanted Judge Doyle's recollection of this crucial testimony to be his conversation with the witness, followed by that comfortable silence as the judge mulled over what he heard and what he learned, not a hectic search by me for perfect answers.

Defendants' counsel also wanted to let Mr. Merritt alone. The last thing they wanted was to give him a second opportunity to articulate his views, a second opportunity to engage in another friendly conversation with the court. Defendants had nothing in their arsenal that through cross-examination would immediately challenge Clif's credibility. They would have their opportunity the next day or the day after to put on their own witnesses to rebut his testimony. This was their best strategy now, but clearly that task had just become a lot more difficult than defendants imagined when Clif Merritt first walked up to the witness stand earlier in the day. Defendants tried their best over the following day and one-half, but their witnesses never equaled Clif's range of expertise or his ability to relate to the court. At the end of the trial, Judge Doyle took the matter "under advisement." He indicated he would issue his findings and judgment as soon as practicable, but he intended to review everything very carefully. The issue was important and one of first impression; thorough review of the facts and the meaning of the Wilderness Act were necessary.

We waited anxiously. The Court's decision would have far-reaching impact upon wilderness reviews and designations across the West. The thirty plus Forest Service primitive areas, with a few exceptions, were comparatively small and often largely restricted to alpine areas above timberline. We believed Congress intended full wilderness review of sur-rounding qualifying lands—the forests, the sub-alpine meadows, the lakes, and the larger streams—not just the rocks and peaks above. We were satisfied with our arguments on the law and the intent of Congress, but a decision against us on the facts—whether East Meadow Creek was wilderness in fact and eligible for review—would not only substantially reduce the size of a Gore Range or Eagles Nest Wilderness, but would also encourage truncated wilderness reviews elsewhere.

On February 27, 1970, Judge Doyle ruled in favor of the Plaintiffs. He agreed with our interpretation of the Wilderness Act, and he held that East Meadow Creek met the definition of wilderness set forth in the Act:

- The access road itself was not proposed for wilderness and "due to the dense forest condition, this road is substantially unnoticeable from approximately 100 yards away." Beyond the road itself, East Meadow Creek "is untrammeled by man."
- The "bug road" was blocked off and could not be used by motorized vehicles. "In some places the vegetation has camouflaged the 'bug road' so that it is substantially unnoticeable."
- East Meadow Creek was "significantly interrelated to the Gore [Range] Primitive Area." It is contiguous to the primitive area, and "the evidence shows that it is desirable to have both alpine and sub-alpine [areas] within a wilderness area."

Judge Doyle concluded, "The East Meadow Creek region meets the minimum requirements for suitability for wilderness classification and must, therefore, be included in the study report to the President and Congress." Therefore, "[i]f the proposed sale and harvesting of timber proceeds, it will frustrate the purpose of the Wilderness Act to vest the ultimate decision as to wilderness classification in the President and Congress, rather than the Forest Service."[4]

Victory on all points! It was also a major victory for the public: those millions who enjoy our wilderness areas each year. Looking back, I believe the half-day of testimony by Clifton Merritt was the clincher. And history tells us the ultimate outcome: when Congress established the Eagles Nest Wilderness Area in 1976, via Public Law 94-352, it included East Meadow Creek.

Teton Dam, a Monument to Bureaucratic Hubris

On the west side of the Grand Teton Mountain Range in northwestern Wyoming, Teton Creek, Darby Creek, and smaller streams draining the west slopes of the range join Trail Creek coming in from the Caribou-Targhee National Forest to the south to form Idaho's Teton River. The river flows north in a slow meandering course through a broad flat valley now called the Teton Basin. The valley was known as Pierre's Hole in the fur-trading days of the nineteenth century, and in 1832 it was the site of the brief but sanguinary Battle of Pierre's Hole between American fur trappers, led by the legendary William Sublette, and their Indian allies against the Gros Ventres Indians. At the north end of the valley the river turns west into the twenty-five mile long Teton Canyon where it is joined by Badger and Bitch Creeks flowing from the east. Leaving the canyon, the river flows out into the basin of Henry's Fork, a major tributary of the Snake River to the south and west.

In the early 1970s, the bench lands above the canyon were given over almost wholly to agriculture, and the potatoes and other crops depended almost entirely on irrigation water. There were a few towns along the Teton; Rexburg, population about 8,000 people, was the largest in the immediate vicinity. Idaho Falls, an even larger town, was sixty miles farther downstream. Since the 1920s the farmers had talked of building a dam somewhere along the river to supplement their existing water supplies. By the late 1960s and early 1970s, political pressure to build the dam had reached a crescendo, and such a dam, to be built with federal money by the U.S. Bureau of Reclamation, was finally authorized and funded by Congress. The site selected was six miles above the mouth of Teton Canyon, and the resulting reservoir would extend seventeen miles upstream.

Idaho environmentalists led by two citizens groups, the Idaho Environmental Council and Trout Unlimited, opposed the project. The Teton River was a priceless blue-ribbon wild trout stream and offered wonderful river running opportunities. The citizens questioned the sacrifice of the river's natural state and the expense of millions of federal dollars to benefit only a small number of nearby farmers and ranchers. The environmental costs were too great: two-thirds of the wild and scenic river would disappear beneath a still reservoir, and the superb trout fishery would be drastically reduced. There also were rumors that the dam site, an area of unstable and fissured volcanic rocks, could present challenging engineering and design problems. In 1974, the environmentalists filed suit in the U.S. District Court for Idaho alleging that the Bureau had prepared an environmental impact statement—required by the new National Environmental Policy Act—which was totally inadequate.[5]

For several reasons the *Teton Dam* litigation was difficult from the outset. Regional newspapers and local and state politicians were clamoring for the dam. Construction work at the dam site had already begun, so the litigation got off to a late start, and there was little time to develop plaintiffs' case. The Sierra Club Legal Defense Fund was approached by the plaintiffs to conduct the trial with little more than 60 days for preparation. It was an uphill battle, but the trial and construction of the dam itself became dramatic events in their own right. The drama came from a single witness in something less than two hours of testimony—and from a tragic event two years later.

A few days before the trial began we heard about Shirley Pytlak, a young geologist who had spent the summer of 1973 working for the Bureau of Reclamation at the Teton Dam site. She had just come to the attention of the Idaho conservationists, and after conferring with our team, they flew her down to Boise from Alaska, where she was then living. Upon interviewing her the day before trial began, we discovered that she had a fascinating story to tell. There seemed to be a legitimate question whether the dam could actually hold back the waters of the Teton River! Marc Reisner, in *Cadillac Desert*, his compelling exposé of water projects and their politics in the West, summarizes her testimony:

> [Ms. Pytlak] had worked briefly on the Teton project during the summer of 1973, drilling test holes at the dam site and injecting water into them. The idea was to see how fast the holes filled, which would allow the Bureau to gauge—"guess" is a better word—the extent to which the surrounding rock was fissured and fractured and concomitantly leak-prone. For weeks, Pytlak said, the boreholes had been pumped with water at a rate of three hundred gallons per minute, which was like sticking a fire hose in them and turning it on full-blast. The holes never filled. If test holes leaked at such a rate, Pytlak asked her supervisors, how much water would seep out of the reservoir and try to get around the dam?[6]

Obviously, this was a very serious question. But the Bureau of Reclamation had been in the water business for more than 60 years, building some 300 major dams, most of them earth-filled like Teton Dam. None had failed. Significantly, however, by the 1960s most of the best dam sites had been built out. Despite this, demand for new projects was as intense as ever. These massive public works projects built with federal money were just too tempting to local promoters, contractors, and businessmen, to agricultural interests, and to the commercial instincts of growing villages and towns. This was a formidable political constituency. Consequently, dam projects were being authorized and built on increasingly questionable sites.[7] Nevertheless, the Bureau of Reclamation was confident it was ready for any geological or engineering challenge. The environmental impact statement (EIS) for Teton Dam did not discuss the issue, defendants belittled Pytlak's testimony, and the judge did not deem the issue sufficiently important to render the EIS inadequate. The U.S. Court of Appeals agreed, and the dam project went ahead.[8]

By the spring of 1976, Morrison-Knudson, the government contractor, had completed the dam and the reservoir was filling rapidly, the river's flow augmented by spring snowmelt from the mountains upstream. The engineers had designed extensive grout curtains* in the "bedrock" under the dam and in the abutments on each side. They were confident these would successfully protect against any geological hazards. The dam stood 310 feet high and stretched 3,000 feet across the Teton River Canyon. Quiet clear water, 270 feet deep at the dam, stretched for miles upstream. Everything seemed normal. Beneath the surface, however, powerful forces were at work. On the morning of June 3rd, an equipment operator reporting for work at the dam site noticed a small leak in the north canyon wall about a third of a mile below the dam. Over the next twenty-four hours, two more leaks appeared from the canyon wall closer to the dam. On-site Bureau of Reclamation employees began monitoring the leaks.

June 5th dawned, promising a bright warm late spring day. But at Teton Dam, events were quickly accelerating toward devastation and tragedy. At 7:30 A.M., an employee of Morrison-Knudson noticed a roiling stream of muddy water emerging from the north abutment adjacent to

---

* Mixtures of concrete, clay and other materials forced into the canyon abutments to fill fissures in the rock and create water impermeable layers preventing water flow beyond them.

the dam. Subsequent events are best related by the clock:

7:30–9:30 A.M.: The Bureau of Reclamation on-site supervisor ordered a bulldozer into action attempting to plug the flow.

9:30 A.M.: A hole opened in the downstream face of the dam itself approximately twenty feet out from the north abutment. A few minutes later, it had become a creek, and the volume of roiling water steadily increased.

9:30–11:00 A.M.: A second bulldozer was sent into action. The sheriffs of Madison and Fremont counties were alerted to prepare to evacuate thousands of people downstream.

11:00 A.M.: A whirlpool appeared in the reservoir directly upstream from the dam, and two more bulldozers were sent to the upstream face of the dam to shove riprap from the embankment into the swirling hole. The Bureau advised the county sheriffs to begin evacuations.

11:20–11:50 A.M.: The hole on the downstream side of the dam grew much larger, swallowing the two bulldozers there, the operators jumping free and assisted to safety by ropes tied around their waists. The upstream bulldozers abandoned their efforts and quickly retreated.

11:50 A.M.: The now massive hole on the downstream side neared the crest of the dam.

11:55 A.M.: The dam breached.[9]

Approximately 250,000 acre-feet of water and four million cubic yards of embankment, and dam material swept downstream in about six hours. The leading wave was 20 feet high. Destruction reached all the way to the upper end of American Falls Reservoir 95 miles downstream. The small communities of Wilford and Sugar City were wiped out; Wilford would never be rebuilt. Massive quantities of floodwaters choked with eroded topsoil, logs from a local timber mill, and remnants of the upstream towns devastated the lower sections of Rexburg. Estimated monetary damages exceeded one billion dollars. Eleven people lost their lives. Ironically, the irrigating farmers on the benches above the river, for whose benefit the dam was mainly authorized, were unscathed. Of course, they would miss out on the promised five inches (average) of additional irrigation water—on top of the several feet they already used each year.[10]

Investigations were mounted and reports were prepared. Subcommittees of Congress convened hearings. Bureau of Reclamation files revealed that concerns about the geology at the dam site had been persistent for several years. Before Shirley Pytlak's drilling, the Bureau had drilled other test holes with similar results. Enough concern was raised that a test-grouting program was carried out, although this was done on the south side of the canyon wall, not the north side where Pytlak had drilled and where the failure occurred. Again and again, the concerns were viewed as problems to be overcome with engineering fixes, not as reasons for not building the dam in the first place. In the *East Meadow Creek* case, Clif Merritt's expertise and experience out-matched the Forest Service witnesses; his testimony compelled attention. Here in the *Teton Dam* fight Shirley Pytlak, although well versed in the science of geology, was young and lacked the years of experience brought by Bureau of Reclamation scientists and engineers. When the issue was on the line, she was alone. No one in authority recommended that the Bureau step back and review its assumptions and justifications. After all, the Bureau of Reclamation had the best engineers in the world....

Hubris is defined as "bold or unreasonable pride or self-confidence." With 70 years' experience, the best engineers in the world, and 300 dams to its credit, the Bureau was not to be stopped by a single young geologist, no matter how damaging her testimony.[11] The Bureau was in the business of building dams, and the resulting bureaucratic momentum created over the decades was overwhelming. The Idaho political establishment was committed, the dam was authorized and funded, and therefore it would be built; the court was not going to intervene. Doubt was not allowed to intrude into such a world. So we lost the case. Of course citizens of the Teton River Valley lost so much more: their property, in many cases their livelihoods, and eleven people lost their lives. The Bureau of Reclamation's reputation as master engineers was devastated.

The Teton Dam fiasco should have provided a lasting lesson about the consequences of hubris and of the unbridled confluence of politics and bureaucracy. But in the spring of 2008, the Idaho legislature unanimously passed Senate Bill 1511, which articulates two purposes: "[I]t funds $10 million for water projects in FY 2008 and $1.8 million for water storage studies in FY 2009." The fiscal notes to the legislation declare that $400,000 of the latter appropriation represents the "estimated costs of studying the replacement of Teton Dam."[12]

How far this will really go is not clear as of this writing. It now appears the study will also include non-structural alternatives to supplementing existing water supply in the area. It is clear that local economic forces and the political instincts that build from them usually remain in place, regardless of the most severe setbacks, ready to move again when they perceive another opportunity. Once more, a consistent theme of this book is highlighted: the environmental community must always be ready to rise to the occasion. Indeed local environmentalists are already on the job. They have spoken out against a new dam and in defense of the present free-flowing river and its canyon and the marvelous trout fishery and white-water rafting values it holds.

Nuclear Wastes—Where to Put Them

Standing on an old slate-walled squash court beneath the west stands of Stagg Field, the University of Chicago's old football stadium, Dr. Enrico Fermi looked down at his five inch hand held slide rule and made a final calculation. It was 3:25 P.M. on December 2, 1942, the day after wartime gasoline rationing began across the country. Fermi turned to his colleague George Weill, who was gradually pulling cadmium safety rods from an atomic pile of 12,000 pounds of uranium metal shaped like an oblated spheroid flattened on the top—like a doorknob. Weill was down to the last rod. A small number of scientists had gathered. Robert Leckie, in his World War II history *Delivered From Evil*, describes the moment:

> Fermi called to Weill: "Pull it another foot, George. This is going to do it." He turned to Compton [a fellow physicist]. "Now it will become self-sustaining." He pointed toward the recording meter. "The track will climb, and continue to climb," he said softly. "It will not level off."
>
> It did not level off. Minutes later, as the chain reaction continued and the energy and radiation levels rose, the safety rods were slammed home.[13]

The Atomic Age had begun.

After the war, the peacetime promise of atomic energy was the generation of electric power. The United States began building nuclear power plants, and today we have 104 of them, accounting for 20% of the country's electric power generation. While nuclear plants do not have the obvious air-pollution emission problems of fossil fuel burning plants, and associated water pollution problems are different, each mode of power generation presents its own particular challenges. At the top of the list for nuclear power, of course, is radiation, and a critical challenge here is the disposal of highly radioactive waste products from the plants, particularly spent or partially burned fuel rods. This material no longer has the strength to maintain an atomic reaction and generate electric power, but it retains an extremely dangerous level of radioactivity—indeed, it is among the most toxic substances known to man—and it must be kept from the environment (the biosphere) until the radiation declines to benign levels. This decay process takes tens of thousands of years—more than a hundred thousand for some of the waste elements—yet temporary surface storage at power plant sites is measured by decades. There must be safe permanent repositories. Unfortunately, the technology for building nuclear plants has far outpaced development of processes and procedures for handling the wastes. But ignoring them will not make them disappear.

In the late 1950s, the National Academy of Sciences (NAS) recommended burial of high-level nuclear waste in underground salt formations. The Academy thought these formations were geologically and structurally stable, free of circulating groundwater, isolated from underground aquifers by impermeable shale, and that any fractures that might develop would be sealed by the plasticity of the salt. In the 1960s, the Atomic Energy Commission began testing salt beds near Lyons, Kansas, but this effort was abandoned in 1973 because it appeared that old oil and gas boreholes in the area could not be sufficiently plugged, and a significant and unexpected movement of water beneath the surface brought the geological integrity of the site into question. As the wastes continued to accumulate, the industry resorted to "temporarily" storing them on the surface in contained pools of constantly cycling cooling water or recently in dry cask storage—steel and concrete casks with water and air replaced by inert gas—at operating or decommissioned plant sites.[14] Indeed, potential dangers of above-ground temporary cold water storage were dramatically brought home in April 2011 in the Fukushima Daiichi nuclear plant disaster following Japan's Tohoku Earthquake.[15]

> [T]he technology for building nuclear plants has far outpaced development of processes and procedures for handling the wastes.

In 1983, Congress passed the Nuclear Waste Policy Act (NWPA), directing the Department of Energy (DOE) to pursue permanent underground geologic disposal of the high-level nuclear wastes. NWPA required that DOE review potential sites using specific statutory criteria in a detailed site screening process.[16] At the conclusion of this process, DOE was to recommend a specific site to Congress for approval and funding. Despite the experience at Lyons, salt deposits continued to draw maximum attention, and the thick beds of salt in the Paradox Formation in southern Utah became favored sites. Surely these were better formations than those found at Lyons. Paradox Formation salt beds underlie Canyonlands National Park near Moab, Utah, and reach their greatest thickness—up to 3,000 feet—just east of the Park boundary. Three "promising" sites for review were identified in David and Lavender Canyons approximately one to three miles east of the Park boundary. The two canyons are an integral part of the popular Needles District of Canyonlands and were originally proposed by the Park Service for inclusion within the park.[17]

Sierra Club and Utah environmentalists were alarmed at the impact a repository would have upon the Canyonlands environment and the experience of visitors to the Park. In early spring of 1984, they decided it was time to investigate legal options. Construction of the repository would be a massive undertaking, and until it was completed—certainly several years—the activity and disturbance would be extreme. While the nuclear wastes would be stored underground, the permanent surface presence—access points and operations, transportation, and maintenance facilities—would constitute a huge industrial complex coming right up to the boundary of the park. Despite these consequences, however, all of this would be located outside the park boundary, and above ground physical impacts, although severe, were not likely to be as intense as the daily above ground impacts of a massive Kaiparowits or Intermountain Power Plant. Comprehensive environmental reviews and procedures* would certainly apply, and the strictures of the National Park Organic Act would have to be honored, but these constraints alone might not ultimately disqualify a waste repository. It was necessary to widen our investigation.

> # The lawyer's job is to be sure the expert addresses the critical issues ... in a form the decision-makers can understand and appreciate.

Lawyers handling a complex environmental case usually need to research more than just the law. They have to gain at least some familiarity with the critical scientific and technical aspects. In this Nuclear Waste Repository matter, we naturally researched the geology. We discovered three interesting things. First, there was surprisingly little basic information in available records discussing the specific nature of the Paradox Formation and its suitability for a repository—assumptions yes, empirical review, no.

Second, what we could find on our own made us wonder whether the condition of the formation actually met the government's assumptions. If it did not, we could be dealing with extremely serious long-term environmental consequences wholly apart from surface impacts on adjacent parklands. Third, we learned that a gentleman in Laramie, Wyoming, was a recognized authority on the geology of southern Utah. Dr. Peter Huntoon was a professor at the University of Wyoming and a

---

* NWPA itself specifies an environmental review process that for practical purposes is a mirror image of NEPA processes.

highly regarded geologist and hydrologist. He knew Canyonlands well; in fact, he collaborated on the authoritative geologic map of the entire park and nearby lands.[18]

I called Dr. Huntoon, made an appointment with him, and drove up to Laramie. Over lunch I outlined the situation and asked him if he could help us out. He was delighted and enthusiastic. Indeed, he already felt the geologic state of the whole Canyonlands region with its active faulting and movement of surface rocks and formations—influenced to a considerable degree by the plasticity of the underlying salt formations—rendered the region unsuitable for a waste repository that must remain secure for tens of thousands of years. Before going further and refining his opinions, though, he wanted to review source material and travel again to the area. My timing was good, for he said he would get on it right away.

I returned to Denver and immediately began tackling the task of figuring out how best to use his expertise and where and when to apply it. Broadly speaking the expert's role is to conduct his review and articulate his findings and conclusions. The lawyer's job is to be sure the expert addresses the critical issues, and that his report and its presentation are in a form the decision-makers can understand and appreciate. If the arguments will be made to administrators or to an administrative forum, the lawyer must determine when and where the biggest impact can be made. This was not an easy task because the NWPA process for selecting a site or sites for long-term high-level nuclear wastes was incredibly complex. Three independent federal agencies had jurisdiction:

- The Department of Energy (DOE) was concerned with site evaluation and the recommendation of a site or sites to Congress which had to give final approval;
- The Environmental Protection Agency (EPA) would determine the standards necessary to protect the biosphere—the "accessible environment"—and the limitations on releases of radioactivity which would insure such protection;
- The Nuclear Regulatory Commission (NRC) was charged with licensing a completed waste repository facility.

All three agencies had adopted regulations or were considering proposed regulations in rule-making proceedings. In addition, the U.S. Department of the Interior, particularly the National Park Service and the U.S. Geological Survey, were interested participants. A number of other parties in interest were involved on a continuing basis: the nuclear energy industry; the state of Utah; the states of Washington, Nevada, Texas, Mississippi, and Louisiana with candidate sites of their own; and other environmental organizations. Lawyers were not quite as numerous as scientists, engineers, and federal and state agency representatives, but all principal parties were represented by counsel, the states through their attorney generals. A number of appeal petitions were filed in U.S. Courts of Appeal against the government alleging its failure to comply with, or its direct violation of, one or more applicable statutory provisions or regulatory standards or procedures. On behalf of Sierra Club, we joined this opposition. Three other states filed actions based on the secondary but nonetheless important issue of the transport of high-level nuclear wastes through their jurisdictions. Obviously all of the legal intersections were going to be crowded.

Meanwhile, Dr. Huntoon was keeping us advised of his efforts. During the summer of 1984, Peter made field trips to the area, and we were growing increasingly excited about the data he was gathering and the conclusions he was beginning to form. Significant aspects of the geology of the Paradox evaporites, or salt beds, and their surrounding geology were emerging. It was also becoming clear that we would have to know this geology well and be able to argue its importance with clarity and force. Was the Paradox a suitable place to entomb extremely toxic high-level nuclear wastes? Could we be assured that once there they would remain isolated from the biosphere for the tens of thousands of years it would take for them to decay to benign levels? Furthermore, the margin of error had to be extremely narrow, for once movement of radioactive wastes away from a repository began—with the likelihood that much of that movement would be via groundwater—the job of interdicting the site breach would probably be extraordinarily difficult and expensive, and it might prove impossible.

The Paradox salt beds began forming more than 300 million years ago on top of a layer of limestone, the Madison Formation, as inland seas repeatedly covered the region and evaporated, all the while depositing layers of salt. At the same time, erosion material from the nearby

Uncompahgre Uplift to the east added dark bands of shale. After about 30 million years, the Paradox Formation had been laid down. Over the next 100 million years, marine and terrestrial sediments were deposited on top of the salts—the sandstones so dramatically displayed today across the canyonlands region. For another 140 million years, five thousand additional feet of rock and sediment were deposited, but these have eroded away leaving the red, white, and yellow sandstones now at the surface. Crustal movement and continuing erosion, working on top of the plastic or "squishy" salts of the Paradox, have combined to shape the magnificent cliffs, amphitheaters, and canyons, the spires, arches, and other landforms of Canyonlands at which we marvel today.[19]

The Department of Energy assumed the Paradox salts were an excellent candidate for the nuclear wastes. By virtue of their existence, these "evaporites" presumably met the National Academy of Sciences' view that salt deposits were geologically and structurally stable, free of circulating groundwater, and isolated from underground aquifers. The belief was that even if groundwater—thought to be the greatest potential threat to the integrity of an underground salt bed repository—were to appear in the Paradox beds, it would drain down to and along the relatively impermeable Madison Limestone, and that formation only reached the surface two hundred miles away at the Grand Canyon in Arizona. Over the hundreds of thousands of years it would take to get there, any radioactive material that escaped the repository would have decayed to safe levels. Furthermore, existing EPA regulations only required that a repository be capable of keeping radioactive wastes from the accessible environment (the biosphere) for ten thousand years. The "accessible environment" was any point beyond a very generous ten kilometer radius from the repository location. Superficially, the Davis and Lavender Canyon sites seemed ideal.[20]

As Peter's review continued, his doubts grew. He originally suspected the Madison Limestone reached the surface much closer to the Canyonlands sites than the Grand Canyon. Sure enough, his field research found that the formation reached the Colorado River at the mouth of Dark Canyon in Glen Canyon National Recreation Area—barely twenty-five miles away. This drastically changed the picture, undermining what was probably the most important government assumption. Not only would escaped wastes get to the environment much sooner than expected, but as a result their level of radioactivity would be appreciably greater when they got there. And their point of egress into the environment would be the Colorado River, ready to distribute them for potentially hundreds of miles.

> [Our expert] believed the Paradox salt beds were over-pressurized, but he had not yet figured out how to prove it.

There was more. After one of his days in the field, Huntoon stopped at a bar and restaurant in Paige, Arizona, just below the Utah border, for refreshment and a meal. He fell into conversation with another patron who proved to be a fellow geologist. They started one of those friendly discussions people have when they meet a fellow professional in a convivial atmosphere. Peter explained what he was doing in the area and, after further conversation, allowed that a particular problem was bothering him. He believed the Paradox salt beds were over-pressurized, but he had not yet figured out how to prove it. This over-pressurization characteristic was important, for it meant that any waste that escaped a containment vessel in the repository could move either up to the surface or down to the Madison Limestone through faults or cracks by virtue of methane under pressure in the host salt bed. And the expected life span of the containment vessels was considerably less than the time it would take for the radioactive wastes to decay to acceptable levels. Adding to the geological and hydrological problems was the ability of the hot containment vessels—a by-product of nuclear decay is heat—to attract water present in the salt itself. Resulting brine pockets would provide a ready medium for the transport of radioactive material through any faults or cracks in the formation.

Then an amazing coincidence occurred—the kind we read about, while shaking our heads over its improbability. Peter's new acquaintance agreed the salt beds were under substantial pressure and explained that he had seen real physical evidence nearby. The next morning, he and

Peter drove out to an old oil and gas exploratory well drill site. Lying on the ground was an old rusted drill bit, bent and twisted almost precisely into the shape of a corkscrew. Only the force of great pressure released when the drill penetrated the salt formation below could have so completely twisted that drill bit as it was thrown out of the well hole. Peter took out his camera and took several photographs. One became known to us as "the slide." Now we were even better armed. But how could we best use Peter's findings?

The appeal petitions pending before the circuit courts involved regulatory problems such as the promulgation of site selection guidelines and deficiencies in their standards and requirements. All parties, ourselves included, were vigorously arguing these issues. However, at that point in the process these appeals did not lend themselves to direct site-specific challenges, and none of the other parties were yet concentrating on specific conditions at individual candidate sites. We believed Peter's evidence could knock the Davis and Lavender Canyon sites off the candidate list, and we needed a way to present Peter's work and conclusions to the government decision makers. We wanted quality professional time with these individuals—one-on-one—without the distraction of all the other issues and parties. Consequently, as with the fight against Kaiparowits, we decided to head to Washington, DC. We scheduled meetings with the regulatory players: the Department of Energy, the Environmental Protection Agency, and the Nuclear Regulatory Commission.

We arrived in Washington on December 13, 1984. Our first stop was the Department of Energy. Unlike the Kaiparowits trip, our party was small—Dr. Huntoon, a volunteer activist from Utah, one of Sierra Club's Washington lobbyists, and myself. DOE, however, had a large number in attendance. We kept introductions, procedural, and legal matters very brief for we wanted as much time as possible for Peter to explain his work and findings. Peter broke out his slides and maps (one being his published geologic map of Canyonlands) and went to work. I knew he was an experienced expert witness and that his expertise in geological and hydrological matters was widely acknowledged, but I was unprepared for just how good he was. He had a "western" look to him—expressions, clothing, boots, mannerisms—the look of a person who spent more time in the field than he did in the office or the classroom. *He looked like a geologist.* While his voice was not loud, it was confident and penetrating.

Peter first addressed the active geological nature of the Canyonlands region. He explained in considerable detail the importance of where the Madison limestones and associated groundwater reached the "accessible environment"—the Colorado River only twenty-miles from the repository sites. He discussed his field investigations and his findings. He addressed the probability that the Paradox salts at the Davis and Lavender Canyon sites were over-pressurized and the significance of that condition. Peter urged DOE to look for repository sites in the less geologically active granites of the Precambrian shield, the ancient basement rocks of the continent deep below the surface of the mid-continent region of the country. The DOE representatives were extremely interested, asked a lot of questions, and at the end told us that Huntoon's work would clearly be very important to their site selection review. They were also pleased that we had come forward with a detailed professional analysis of the geology and hydrology of a specific site; indeed, they voiced surprise that none of the other parties affected by the site-selection process had yet done this. The legal arguments over guidelines and attenuated procedural matters were interesting and would ultimately be critical in the selection of any site, but the DOE representatives meeting with us were eager to learn more about the specifics of individual sites themselves. They were pleased we were "cutting to the chase."

The following day we met with Dan Egan, the Deputy Administrator of EPA for regulatory matters. Egan told us at the outset he personally favored the Utah sites over the other candidates, but he wanted to hear what we had to say. Our presentation was a bit different here. As mentioned earlier, we believed EPA's proposed radioactive waste containment standards were too weak. Using a ten-thousand-year time period and defining "accessible environment"—that point where radioactive wastes could come to the surface—in terms of a ten kilometer radius from the repository were completely inadequate. Some of the wastes would be dangerous for more than 100,000 years. Allowing those which escaped their entombment to go ten kilometers before they were deemed a threat practically guaranteed that, in the event of a breach, a large amount of waste at dangerous radioactive levels would escape to the accessible environment; after all, they already would have traveled ten kilometers in just 10,000 years.

Egan responded that personally he was not completely comfortable with those standards and thus was glad to hear from us on this point and listen to Huntoon's presentation. As with DOE, Egan was pleased to have this opportunity to review site-specific information. This was an excellent way to assess the potential effectiveness of new and untried standards and regulations that specifically fell within his direct responsibilities. Egan had obviously thoroughly reviewed the "file," and our discussion was comprehensive. We urged EPA to substantially strengthen the standards. Egan assured us reexamination of the standards would be a priority for his office.

Interestingly, Dan Egan met with us alone in his office, without the usual complement of aides and advisors. This is the only time in my years of environmental work that I can recall an official in such a high-level position with such direct regulatory responsibilities doing this. We were not so naïve as to suppose he would be making critical regulatory decisions alone, but we were impressed by the man's confidence and his grasp of the issues. And we strongly suspected he would be rethinking his prior preference for the Canyonlands sites.

Our final meeting was at the Nuclear Regulatory Commission's offices in suburban Silver Spring, Maryland. We walked into a large conference room, a larger copy of that drab hearing room in Los Angeles used by the California PUC in the Kaiparowits fight—no pictures, no color, and very basic furnishings. Large rectangular well-used tables had been unfolded and placed in a square with a large space in the middle occupied by a slide projector. The projector was a nice touch, but we carried our own—we wanted to avoid the possibility of any operating or mechanical "hitches." After we were seated, some ten NRC officials and experts entered the room and we exchanged greetings. A large amount of time was blocked out for us, so the meeting began with informal introductions and friendly conversation. Then we got down to business. The NRC representatives explained their individual areas of expertise and the roles each would likely play in the final repository permitting process. NRC had heard about our activities and was obviously well prepared.

This was the picture: We were facing no fewer than seven scientists and engineers—the best NRC had. It was obvious that this was going to be quite a session; we would have to do our very best job. Rather, Peter would have to do his best work. The other three of us—the activist, the lobbyist, and me—were merely outriders here. We began with the usual adjustment of chairs so that everyone had a clear view of the screen. Pads of paper, pens, and pencils came out. Huntoon set up his projector and adjusted the focus. The rest of our contingent pushed our chairs back and moved away from the tables. Brooks Yeager, the Club's lobbyist, and I took neighboring chairs over against the west wall of the room. Peter was alone at his table with the NRC experts sitting at the adjoining tables to his left and his right—between him and the screen above the remaining table opposite him. We were not overly concerned, for we had already seen Peter in action, but we realized his expertise and his interpretations and opinions were going to be tested more critically than heretofore.

Peter's briefing took on the nature of a lengthy seminar. As each slide succeeded another, one or more NRC experts had questions— detailed questions. A few pictures stayed up on the screen four or five minutes as Peter explained the subject and responded to the inquiries. The geologic instability of the Canyonlands area, the nature of the Paradox Formation, and the significance of the surface exposure of the underlying Madison Limestone in the Colorado River only twenty-five miles from the proposed repository sites were covered in depth. Peter often put his remarks in the form of a question and then answered it, particularly when he was summing up a particular point. About thirty minutes into this, Yeager leaned over to me and in a quiet voice—which, however, did not disguise the respect in his voice—asked, "We are doing well, are we not?" I nodded emphatically and whispered back, "You're damned right we are!"

Peter moved to the subject of the over-pressurization of the Paradox salts and the potential ramifications of this condition. The slide of the twisted drill bit came on. Huntoon's audience was already impressed and increasingly convinced, but I suspect that picture removed any lingering doubts. Peter described the subsurface escape route—the Madison Limestone and its accompanying groundwater that would convey escaped waste (escaped from the containment vessels) away from the repository. He emphasized the close proximity of where that route would reach the surface environment, and the over-pressurization of the formation which could readily put the wastes in motion either to the Madison below or directly above to the surface through fissures or cracks in the overlying rocks. His presentation was clear and impressive. Peter mentioned again the potential suitability of a repository deep underground in the mid-continent basement rock.

As Peter concluded, the expressions and body language of his audience left no doubt that he had made a considerable impression. The NRC experts also realized that the burden had just increased enormously for any who would contest his conclusions. Peter's findings could not be waived aside as solely one man's opinion. At a minimum, challenges would have to at least equal his effort, and obviously the actual geology of the salt formations and their surrounding landscape could not be changed or brushed aside. The geology and hydrology could not be "adjusted" to fit preconceived ideas. Moreover, the margin of error was ever so small—the wastes had to remain entombed for tens of thousands of years.

> ## The NRC experts also realized that the burden had just increased enormously for any who would contest [our expert's] conclusions.

Sometimes a brief action or exclamation, or a single question, can alone communicate volumes of information, and so it was at the Nuclear Regulatory Commission that day. One of the small ceremonies or courtesies at the beginning of meetings such as this is for petitioners such as ourselves to pass out our professional cards to our hosts, and this we had done. Usually, a representative of the host delegation will give us his card, although most of his colleagues may not. This routine was also followed. But on this day something more took place: when Peter finished, the NRC experts came up almost as one and handed him their cards. This was immediately followed by two questions: "May I call you up later?" and "Are you available for consulting?" No one was questioning his conclusions! In context, this was convincing confirmation that Dr. Huntoon's presentation had a profound effect upon his audience.

We left Washington satisfied that we had done well. The three federal agencies involved now knew there was impressive evidence that the Canyonlands sites were unsuitable for a long-term high-level nuclear waste repository. Sure enough, not long after we returned home I received a telephone call from Dan Egan: *EPA's final waste containment regulations would be revised to meet many of our concerns!* The ten-kilometer radius within which all radioactive waste must be contained was formally reduced to five kilometers.[21] This was a significant victory. While the ten-thousand-year timeline remained the same, the reduced radius meant that the geologic and hydrologic characteristics of a repository site would have to be considerably better than before. As a result, the Davis and Lavender Canyon sites would certainly fall from the first rank of DOE's repository candidate sites, and might be eliminated from serious consideration altogether.

The site review process already underway at the Department of Energy continued, and on May 28, 1986, the final environmental assessments on five sites—one each in the states of Mississippi, Nevada, Texas, Utah (Davis Canyon), and Washington—were published. On that same day, the Secretary announced he was recommending three sites to the President as required by the Nuclear Waste Policy Act: the existing atomic energy site at Hanford, Washington, the Yucca Mountain test site in Nevada eighty miles northwest of Las Vegas, and a bedded salt site in Deaf Smith County, Texas. The Secretary also announced that the President approved those recommendations.[22]

The final environmental assessment for the Davis Canyon site—selected by DOE as marginally better than Lavender Canyon—recognized, for the first time in an important government document, the geologic and hydrologic complexity of the Paradox Formation and the active geologic nature of the surface rocks above it. The problems noted by Dr. Huntoon were prominently featured and discussed. While DOE did not publicly accept all of Peter's conclusions, the fact remains that neither of the Canyonlands sites was selected for the final three recommended candidates. Of those three, only the Deaf Smith County site was a salt site. Davis and Lavender Canyons were out of the picture.[23]

Dr. Huntoon's work was pivotal. It attacked the basic assumptions upon which the presumed suitability of the Canyonlands sites rested. This was critical, for it moved the argument from differences of opinion or interpretation of preexisting data and information to a formidable challenge of the underlying facts upon which those opinions or interpretations had previously been based. This is the best of all positions for the advocate: he undermines the opposition's position rather than engage in a battle of differing expert opinions. This is especially true for the environmental lawyer who in his usual role of petitioner or plaintiff must win these points to succeed. A battle of experts fought to a draw is usually a battle lost. Once the fundamental facts behind a proposition are found to be materially different from those previously assumed, old opinions must be rejected, new investigations of the necessary facts must take place, and new interpretations will have to be made. Peter did precisely this. He went out into the field, gathered the data himself, and recorded his findings. He then transposed his work and his conclusions into a thorough, coherent, convincing presentation.

At this point we need to recall the appreciation specifically expressed by DOE, Deputy EPA Administrator Egan, and the Nuclear Regulatory Commission representatives that we had thoroughly investigated one of the candidate repository sites and come to Washington with our results. This is worthy of comment. The roster of interested parties across the country—the industry, the states, the federal government departments, and the environmentalists—made quite a crowd. We were all getting organized and sharpening our advocacy points for the recently filed appellate court actions, which promised to be lengthy and complicated. We were also keeping a weather eye on each other: Who would be our allies? Who would be our toughest opponents? Did anyone have a significant political advantage? Who would be devoting the greatest resources—in the vernacular, the "big bucks"—to their effort? All of this was keeping everyone pretty busy.

The individual officials and professional personnel of the regulating agencies, however, had a more focused view. The legislation and the regulations, really draft regulations, were new, and the subject matter—permanent underground disposal of high-level nuclear wastes—was not well developed. How, for instance, would the developing regulatory systems measure up to realities on the ground? The agencies were still feeling their way and testing their preliminary conclusions; they were hungry for more site-specific information and eager to listen to someone like Dr. Huntoon who could provide valuable insights based on hard data. I claim no prescience myself; I did not know our trip would be so timely. I was only thinking we had an excellent expert who had important things to say, and I wanted to get him to Washington DC and into the mix as soon as I could. Maybe we could beat everyone else to the punch. We lawyers try to understand our opponents' position: we try to anticipate. Doubtless, all of us would have come to these considerations before matters progressed much further. It was our good fortune to arrive at precisely the right place at the right time before the right people with the right information. But the lesson is clear: there is often much to be gained by understanding early the potential vulnerabilities, as well as the positions and concerns of one's opponents.

The site selection process continued with intensive scientific study of the three recommended sites. Meanwhile we environmentalists—still concerned with the nature of the process, but also worried about the viability of the three final candidate sites—and the affected states continued prosecuting our several appeals in the courts. In the spring of 1986, President Ronald Reagan approved the Yucca Mountain site for site characterization—the repository design step—and in December 1987, he signed Congressional amendments to the Nuclear Waste Policy Act which specifically selected Yucca Mountain for the nation's first geological long-term nuclear waste repository and phased-out review of all other candidate sites.[24] At this point the initial pending court appeals were withdrawn.

Over the next fifteen years DOE spent hundreds of millions of dollars on studies and site preparation activities. Nevada continually fought this, and finally in April 2002 the Governor, exercising power reserved by Congress to any selected state, vetoed Yucca Mountain. Congress overrode this veto, and the President signed the Yucca Mountain Development Act in July. DOE continued its work, and in June 2008, after spending more hundreds of millions, submitted a license application to the Nuclear Regulatory Commission for Yucca Mountain. Nevada continued its implacable opposition. In 2009, President Obama's administration terminated the Yucca Mountain program and established a blue ribbon commission to recommend a new strategy for high-level nuclear waste disposal.[25] The Blue Ribbon Commission released its final report in January 2012 recommending a new strategy for addressing high-level nuclear wastes, including creation of a new organization solely dedicated to the task and independent of the Department of Energy. Additionally, the Commission urged immediate efforts to develop at least one geologic disposal facility and at least one consolidated storage facility.[26]

Observers have noted from the beginning of the development of nuclear power that it seemed the industry and the government hoped to solve the waste problem by quickly identifying suitable, readily accessible, and relatively shallow geological disposal sites. They would be underground and out of sight, radiation impacts would be removed from the surface environment, and at shallow depth capital costs would be manageable, especially when compared with the total investments involved in making nuclear power an important part of the nation's electric power generation picture. Furthermore, the industry already had to overcome committed opposition just to get enough of the public to at least begrudgingly accept nuclear power plants. So neither the industry nor the government wanted to dwell upon the disposal subject; they did not want the public to think that waste disposal itself would pose particularly significant health and environmental problems or add materially to the overall financial costs of nuclear power. Besides, nuclear power generation technology was new and exciting, and it promised "clean" electric power without the formidable air pollution problems of conventional fossil-fueled plants. The waste problems could be satisfactorily addressed later as the industry got underway and public acceptance grew. There would be ample time, industry and government leaders thought, because the waste stream would not build up for many years.

Shortsighted approaches such as these often come to grief, and this has been the doleful experience of our efforts to address high-level nuclear waste disposal.

- It has been more than fifty years now since the National Academy of Sciences suggested salt formations for waste disposal.
- Forty years ago the Lyons, Kansas, experimental efforts with underground salt deposits failed.
- Thirty years ago the Nuclear Waste Policy Act was passed, directing a concerted effort to solve the problem.
- Twenty-eight years ago the Yucca Mountain site in Nevada was recommended.
- It has been twelve years since the Governor of Nevada's veto of

Yucca Mountain was overridden by Congress.

- Five years ago the President directed that work cease on Yucca Mountain and that a specially appointed blue ribbon commission review the problem and come up with a recommended strategy for the permanent disposal of high-level nuclear wastes.
- Two years ago the Blue Ribbon Commission submitted its final report recommending substantial administrative changes in the disposal program and immediate development of a geologic site, together with a consolidated temporary storage facility.

Billions of dollars have been spent, and we have come full circle without arriving at a long-term solution, with uncounted billions still to be spent. We now have over 75,000 metric tons of highly radioactive wastes—enough to fill an entire football field to a depth of more than twenty feet—stranded in temporary surface storage at dozens of nuclear sites across the country awaiting safe and permanent disposal. And the amount grows inexorably day-by-day.

CHAPTER VII

Reflections

In the following few words the constitutional scholar, Edward S. Corwin, succinctly describes the authority and the powers of our judicial system:

> Judicial power is the power to decide cases and controversies in conformity with law and by methods established by the usages and principles of law. [...] Like legislative and executive power under the Constitution, judicial power, too, is thought to connote certain incidental or inherent attributes. One of these is the ability to interpret the standing law, whether the Constitution, acts of Congress, or judicial precedents, with an authority to which both the other departments are constitutionally obliged to defer.[1]

We have talked about this structure and these principles. More importantly, we have seen them at work in the environmental cases and disputes we have examined in these pages.

I have emphasized that this system, as we practice it, has the institutional capability to adjust to, and become an integral part of, the pursuit of new priorities arising from developing needs and desires of the public. In the 1960s and 1970s, the judicial system could not avoid dealing with burgeoning environmental issues. With their intimate relationship to the interests of the people, and their ready accessibility to contending parties affected by the rapidly growing environmental protection ethic, the courts were certain to become involved. Once involved, their structure and their procedures required them to respond. Out of their response came a new jurisprudence: environmental law.

Of course, once we begin talking about the breadth of influence of the judicial system, or its reach beyond the traditional and the familiar, we touch the realms of political discourse and philosophy of government. And debates over the scope of judicial power and authority seem inexhaustible. We have only to open our morning newspapers or tune in to our favorite news media to become a part of these debates. While it would be disingenuous for me to say I have no opinions of my own on such matters (I am sure most of us do) I have tried to avoid these arguments here and focus upon individual cases and campaigns. These give us, I believe, the best view of how the judicial system works in actual practice, and in even broader context a look at the legal system itself. My aim has been to impart understanding rather than score political or philosophical points.

Conflicts among interested parties regarding protection of a national park or a wilderness, or the establishment of a far-reaching clean air standard, and the resolution of policies, interpretations, and disputes at issue—or the failure to resolve them—may provide our best instruction. The lawyers, the experts, the civil servants and governmental officials, the corporate interests, and above all concerned citizens—the plaintiffs—show us the system in action. *East Meadow Creek*, *Uncompahgre*, *Beaver Creek*, *Kaiparowits*, *Grand Canyon*, the *River of No Return*, and each of the other cases give flesh to the spartan but penetrating sentences of Professor Corwin.

We draw many lessons from the cases: we see how parties can frame the issues at stake, present their own case, and test the strength of their opponents. We learn that the public interest advocate—the environmentalist—can confront rigid governmental authorities and narrow corporate interests on a relatively level playing field; a place where facts are actually tested and determined, where laws are interpreted using well understood precepts, and where decisions are made and enforced. It is useful to recall some of the basic components that distinguish this process:

- Our judicial system is independent; decisions in a specific case can only be reviewed by a higher court, not by the legislative or executive branches of the government;
- The judicial process is a public process and records are kept; it is not a private affair conducted behind closed doors;
- The process strives to be fair: each party has his say, and all are subject to the same rules of procedure and evidence;
- These rules of procedure and evidence have been refined by countless years of experience, and they are admirably suited to test the facts and identify the important issues;
- Everyone may have legal representation—their own lawyer—skilled in the ways and processes of the law;

- Decisions are rendered; they are articulated in an order of the court or the administrative authority; and they are enforceable;

- And, for the most part, these decisions are based upon the weight of the evidence and applicable law, not extraneous emotions, philosophy, or political agenda.

Errors will be made and digressions will occur; the complexities involved and human nature teach us this will be so. Interpretations which do not stand the tests of experience and practicality—the tests of time—will need to be changed. Courts do not always get it right. Laws will need to be amended, and new laws will be written. But what environmentalist, faced with an action damaging to the environment and in need of adequate and timely remedy and the prospect of fair review, would fail to seek relief in such a forum?

We have only to call the roll of the cases here to see the broad sweep of matters addressed and the breadth of resolutions and decisions reached. Comprehensive and nationally applicable issues were confronted in the *Prevention of Significant Deterioration* litigation, and in the precedent determining the *East Meadow Creek* wilderness dispute. Weighing in the balance were congressional objectives to protect clean air and pristine wilderness. In contrast, *Indian Peaks* and *Holy Cross* wilderness matters focused on very site-specific questions. *Beaver Creek, Viavant,* and *Uncompahgre* illustrated the critical importance of a court's power to immediately enjoin threatening events on the ground until deliberate reasoned decisions could be made on the merits of the litigation. Without that intervention, irreparable damage would have occurred and any decision earned by plaintiffs would likely have had substantially diminished value.

In *Uncompahgre* and the *Carlsbad Mountain Lions* cases, the courts provided the platform for exposing abrupt, even aberrant governmental actions. They derailed a devious maneuver by the U.S. Forest Service in Uncompahgre to avoid a mandate of the Wilderness Act by re-writing the rules. They also prevented an altogether capricious and regressive decision by an Assistant Secretary of Interior, who was pandering to disgruntled ranchers at the expense of a consequential resource and value of our national parks (most immediately at Carlsbad Caverns, but presumably threatening all national parks). Testimony in open court in *Viavant* exposed federal land managers—the National Park Service itself—who were seemingly oblivious to what was about to happen in the southern part of Capitol Reef National Park. In *Conundrum Creek*, deep within the Maroon Bells-Snowmass Wilderness, the environmental community would not let the Forest Service escape the conflict between yesterday's destructive mining traditions and tomorrow's promise of wilderness appreciation and recreation—the beauty and harmony of wilderness, and its challenges—in one of our finest mountain treasures. The Forest Service and Congress decided for wilderness; they decided for the future.

The *River of No Return Wilderness* matter brought out the best from the contending parties, the legal and procedural backdrop providing the incentive for the government and environmentalists to sit down at the table and agree on fundamental ground rules for the long wilderness review process that followed. We should not forget that interested parties working with their lawyers in the broad context of the law and its varied processes—not just in the courtroom itself—can often put a controversy on a path to ultimate resolution short of actual litigation. Of course, the knowledge that a complaining party has recourse to the courthouse provides a powerful impetus, but this is not a bad circumstance if it leads to resolution of difficult public questions.

Protection of the *Redwoods* in a national park took a different course. Here no comprehensive agreement was possible—there would be little meeting of the minds—and ultimately the federal district court, despite intervention three separate times, could only achieve limited success. However, the litigation framed the outstanding issues well and clearly pointed the way to congressional solutions. Valuable forests were lost in the interim, but the eventual legislation not only strengthened protection of remaining redwood stands but in addition significantly reinforced the heart of the National Park Organic Act, the buttress of all national park lands.

When we look back at the *Kaiparowits* and *Intermountain* power plant struggles, we cannot help being impressed again by the kaleidoscope of issues, venues (state and federal), parties, and applicable laws. It is difficult to picture the prodigious size of the projects, but even they would have been dwarfed by the extent and severity of environmental and natural resource impacts if the plants had been built as proposed. We must acknowledge the advantages and benefits derived from the roles of the multiple jurisdictions involved. The circumstances called for the most comprehensive and detailed examination of all the major impacts: environmental reviews, assessment of consumption or impairment of natural resources such as water and clean air, and thorough scrutiny of the need for the projects. Fundamental questions included: If we were going to harm or destroy so much, should we not be sure we had no alternative? And what sacrifices must we endure for what advantages?

Experts—scientists, engineers, and economists—came forward to assist the prosecution of these cases and give needed interpretation to observed facts. We saw them at work in *Kaiparowits, Intermountain, East Meadow Creek, Teton Dam*, in the *Prevention of Significant Deterioration* of clean air quality issue, and in the high-level *Nuclear Waste Repository* matter. In *East Meadow Creek*, the judge in open court worked comfortably with our expert to understand the nuances of wilderness qualification of the lands in question. Their dialogue—the judge and Clif Merritt earnestly considering and exchanging questions and answers—cut to the chase in decisive fashion. In the *Nuclear Waste* matter Peter Huntoon explored the geology and hydrology involved, meeting with government experts and officials face-to-face around the table. Important regulations were significantly changed. The nature of the geologic strata encountered at the proposed Canyonlands repository, its unsuitable condition, and the ensuing implications came to light in significant and convincing detail. Unfortunately, in the *Teton Dam* case, our young expert witness could not convince the Bureau of Reclamation of the error of its ways; tradition and over-confidence prevailed. But the truth of her testimony was tragically borne out three years later when the dam ruptured. The public interest does not always win.

Sometimes the process yields only partial results, but these can themselves be important. For example, the *Nuclear Waste* issue has gone through many phases over its fifty-year life—administrative, legislative, and legal; all have played a central role at one time or another—but achievement has been limited to tightening some regulations and disqualifying individual proposed repository sites. These achievements are substantial, but the country seems no closer to a "permanent" solution to the waste problem than it was at the outset. Obviously there are many chapters yet to be written.

Then there is the *Grand Canyon*. There seems no end to the legal disputes; in fact, the conflicts and their persistence appear undiminished from that moment when the battle over dams in the canyon was joined fifty years ago. Moreover, river-running management and airspace regulation seem destined to be contentious well into the forseeable future. Whenever there is a lull in these issues, other disputes move to the fore: water release regimes of Glen Canyon Dam, protection of endangered species, uranium leasing and mining on adjacent lands, or timber management on the adjoining forest lands of the Kaibab Plateau. But at least now the government must make its decisions within the mandate to protect Grand Canyon and its treasures.

Today's reader, reflecting on this summary and looking back through the cases we have visited, might say, "All this is fine. And much was accomplished in those last decades of the Twentieth Century. But in the very recent past matters haven't been as promising. Hostility to the environmental agenda seems widespread. Our political and governmental institutions have difficulty finding solutions to acknowledged problems, even problems of pressing priority. Too many view short-term political advantage as more important than reaching solutions." It's hard to argue with these observations. The worst representatives of that combination of corporate interests do focus preemptively on financial return, their well-paid ubiquitous lobbyists and influence peddlers are dedicated solely to that objective, and their political friends frequently seem to dominate public debate.

While recognition of and sensitivity to environmental matters have comparatively improved of late, real progress remains halting and sporadic. The array of forces referenced above is still in the field pushing its agenda for all it is worth. And for all intents and purposes, the financial and lobbying resources of the players are practically infinite. So, the struggle continues to be intense.

Yes. But the public-interest community—the environmentalists— have always had to overcome committed opponents and entrenched interests. The political environment has been hostile before. Elimination of the Environmental Protection Agency has been a cornerstone of ill-considered political platforms from the moment President Nixon signed the National Environmental Policy Act creating EPA in 1969. From their inception, protective air, water, and waste disposal standards and regulations have been anathema to many interests. Laws protecting the environment and mandating management of public lands with respect and sensitivity are frequently under severe, even irrational, attack.

It is good that we talk about these things. We measure again the strengths and the vulnerabilities of our systems, our processes, and our environmental laws, standards, and regulations. Are they up to the tasks before them? We need to reflect upon the structure of our government; we need to think about its ability to function well in difficult and disputatious times. The cases we have reviewed help us understand how the legal and judicial systems can work for the benefit of all; we see them working through difficult environmental and resource management questions in real time and reaching actual decisions. But saying all of this does not quite complete the picture. One more component—probably the most important component—must again be recognized.

Standing out in bold relief are the citizen environmentalists. They must put the system in play. They, their compatriots and supporters, their non-profit advocacy organizations, their staff, experts, and lawyers—the collective voices for the earth—must take the initiative. And as we have seen, they have done it time and time again. They are knowledgeable, committed, and indefatigable. They enthusiastically challenge the hostile dogmas of those who view environmental protection as a needless roadblock—an impediment to brush aside or dismiss—in the pursuit of narrow and selfish private or corporate goals.

We have met some of these individuals and seen them in action. We know something of their mettle and their range. We have seen how effective they can be in protecting the natural world in which we live. We also know how necessary they are; we recognize they are the ultimate guardians of environmental values and interests. They carry the torch through the difficult moments. They are the ones who advocate foremost the environmental ethic—the public interest—when legislation is written and the laws put in place. Today they campaign for their issues knowing they can be sure the laws they value will be implemented upon appropriate complaint or petition to a court or an administrative reviewing authority, and decisions in favor of the environment will be enforced. They do this today, and they will be doing it tomorrow, the day after tomorrow, and long into the future.

Notes

General

The most important recorded reference material for this book is the collection of annual reports of the Rocky Mountain Office of Sierra Legal Defense Fund (now Earth Justice). These comprehensive recitations of the legal program and the active cases of the office were carefully prepared and checked thoroughly for accuracy. They were sent to selected Club leaders and used by the San Francisco Office of SCLDF for monitoring and fund raising purposes. Given this informed and interested audience, there was little room for error. The reliability of these reports as competent authority is manifested at several levels:

- Active cases were reviewed from inception to conclusion. Many cases were reported over a span of several years; others appear in only two or three reports. Continuity was thus maintained through the life of each case.
- Cases were reported in detail: where a specific case had been, where it was going, and the case objectives.
- The reports were prepared contemporaneously with the events related. Case documents, research, writings and the myriad conversations, discussions, and deliberations with clients, counsel, and other concerned parties were all fresh.
- They had to address client needs for tactical and strategic information.
- The reports were read and critically reviewed by client leaders.
- They were written as straight reporting; editorial and argument were minimal.

These reports constituted critical reference for all cases discussed in Voices, excepting only the Scenic Hudson, Mineral King, and Redwoods cases. Consequently repeated citation to the reports does not seem merited. The three exceptions are adequately covered in publicly available published court decisions. Reference to these will appear in appropriate notes below.

Case files were also important. Of course they include everything assembled during the life of a case and even afterward, so discrimination was required. It is difficult to imagine a nonfiction writer with no debt to the internet and its plethora of sources, references, websites, articles, and commentary. Certainly my debt is considerable. And an appropriate nod is necessary to Wikipedia and family for their broad coverage of the lands and issues addressed in Voices.

The cases I selected for review in Voices are only a part of the docket of the Rocky Mountain Office over the years covered. Many highly competent colleagues were simultaneously pursuing important cases throughout the Rocky Mountain Region. My selection is based first upon the ability of a particular case to contribute to the objectives of the book, to tell the story. Secondly, I feel that my personal involvement assures accuracy, at least as I saw it then, and, also, see it now. Three cases—*Scenic Hudson, Mineral King,* and the *Redwoods* cases— are exceptions. I had no participation or role in their prosecution. But, they are included for they are necessary to explain critical portions of the text; indeed, their "landmark" character makes this inevitable.

Prologue

1   Powell, J. W. *Canyons of the Colorado* (1895), republished unabridged as *The Exploration of the Colorado River and Its Canyons* (New York: Dover Publications, 1961), 247. Powell's *Canyons of the Colorado* is the publication of his 1869 Journal. It is likely that *Canyons*, as edited and published by Powell, was influenced by his experiences and records from his second expedition, 1871–1872. See Frederick S. Dellenbaugh, *A Canyon Voyage* (New York: G. P. Putnam's & Sons, 1908), republished Yale University Press (New Haven, 1926). Two excellent works, both biographical, addressing Powell's adventure and in larger context the story and significance of his life are Wallace Stegner's classic *Beyond the Hundredth Meridian* (Boston: Houghton Mifflin, 1953, 1954); and Donald Worster, *A River Running West* (New York: Oxford University Press, 2001).

2   Ibid.

3   Ibid.

4   Stegner, Wallace. *Beyond the Hundredth Meridian* (Boston: Houghton Mifflin, 1953), 110.

5   Powell, op. cit., 256. My research discloses that this passage appears in different sources with markedly different punctuation and, on occasion, slightly

different wording. I have used the Dover edition here, represented as the unabridged and unaltered republication of the work first published by Flood and Vincent in 1895 under the title *Canyons of the Colorado*.

Chapter I: Origins

1   Nash, Roderick. *Wilderness and the American Mind* (New Haven: Yale Press, 4th edition, 2001), 331–334 and footnotes; Wikimedia Website, "Rafting Grand Canyon," updated 2013.

2   Beaver Creek Wilderness, "wilderness.net," University of Montana 2013; Eastern Wilderness Areas Act, Public Law 93-622, 16 U.S. 1132 (1975); Forest Service website.

3   Ibid.

4   Cahn, Edmund. *Confronting Injustice*, Lenore L. Cahn, Editor (Boston: Little, Brown, 1962, 1966), 25.

5   Some of the early conservation law efforts, including several related in Voices, are well captured in Tom Turner's *Wild By Law* (San Francisco: Sierra Club, 1990). Turner's informative and engaging text is enhanced by marvelous photographs by Carr Clifton strikingly presented through the "exhibit format" presentation of the book. See also Joseph L. Sax, *Defending the Environment* (New York: Alfred A. Knopf, 1971).

6   Haines, Aubrey L. *The Yellowstone Story*, Volume One (Niwot, Colorado: University Press of Colorado, 1977, 1996), 214-215, 324-325. Readers seeking a comprehensive history of a national park will find Haines' two volumes on the world's first national park fascinating.

7   The Wilderness Act, Public Law 88-577, 16 U.S.C. 1131 (1964). Legislative History references found at "wilderness.net," University of Montana.

8   The history regarding the 1960s and early 1970s is related in detail in James Patterson's comprehensive *Grand Expectations, The United States, 1945–1974* (New York, Oxford University Press, 1996).

9   *Baker v. Carr*, 369 U.S. 186 (1962).

10 Voting Rights Act of 1965, Public Law 89-110 (1965), 42 U.S.C. 1973.

11 Grand Canyon National Park, 40 Stat. 1175 (1919), 16 U.S.C. 221; Public Law 93-620, (1975), 16 U.S.C. 228a.

12 Redwood National Park, Public Law 90-545, (1968), 16 U.S.C. 790; Public Law 95-250 (1978), 16 U.S.C. 79b.

13 Endangered Species Act, Public Law 93-205 (1973), 16 USC. 1531.

14 National Environmental Policy Act, Public Law 91-190 (1970), 42 U.S.C. 4321.

15 Clean Air Act, Public Law 91-604 (1970), Public Law 95-95 (1977); 42 U.S.C. 7401.

16 Clean Water Act, Public Law 92-50 (1972), Public Law 95-217 (1977); 33 U.S.C. 1251.

17   Muir, John. *Our National Parks* (Boston: Houghton Mifflin, 1901); Sierra
      Club edition (San Francisco, 1991), 42. Muir—interpreter of glaciers, voice
      of the Sierra Nevada—was the late 19th and early 20th century sage of
      wilderness and scenic park lands and the father of activism on their behalf.
      His name and deeds are familiar to all today, and his inspiration lives on.
      Among his classic works is *My First Summer in the Sierra* (Boston:
      Houghton Mifflin, 1911), edited and republished in the beautiful exhibit
      format book *Gentle Wilderness* (San Francisco: Sierra Club, 1967). For biog-
      raphical information and the significance of his work, see Donald Worster,
      A Passion for Nature: The Life of John Muir (New York: Oxford University
      Press, 2008) and Stephen Fox, *John Muir and His Legacy* (Boston: Little,
      Brown, 1981).

18   Jeffers, Robinson. "The Answer" (1936), reprinted in *Not Man Apart*, David
      Brower, editor (San Francisco: Sierra Club, 1965), 20.

19   Carson, Rachel. *Silent Spring* (Boston: Houghton Mifflin, 1962).

20   Leopold, Aldo, *A Sand County Almanac and Sketches Here and There* (New
      York: Oxford University Press, 1949), 114. Leopold's seminal writings on
      ecology and conservation were recently published as *A Sand County
      Almanac & Other Writings on Ecology and Conservation* (New York: The
      Library of America, 2013), Curt Meine, editor.

21   I found this Stilwell wisdom early in my research and writing. It hit the mark,
      characterizing the times referenced in the text in penetrating fashion. I feel
      it needs to here. Unfortunately, my reference has disappeared into the mas-
      sive thicket of notes and drafts forming the soil from which *Voices* grew. If
      any reader can enlighten me, his or her guidance on the source for this quo-
      tation will be gratefully received.

22   This famous quote is attributed to Margaret Mead, but there are no definitive
      references. She did write and make statements very similar to this passage,
      and it is entirely in character in sentiment and style. Wikiquote notes: "Ralph
      Keyes, in the introduction to *The Quote Verifier* (2006), xvi, "gives this
      [quote] as an example where derivative sources merely cite each other and
      no one knows the original sources."

23   Guthrie, Woody. "This Land is Your Land" (1940), recorded 1944, first pub-
      lished 1945; first professional printed publication, Ludlow Music, 1956. We
      all know and have sung the words.

24   *Scenic Hudson Preservation Conference v. Federal Power Commission*,
      354 F.2d 608 (2d Cir. 1965). After subsequent administrative and judicial pro-
      ceedings, settlement was finally reached in 1980 when Consolidated Edison
      agreed to terminate the Storm King plans.

25   Ibid.

26   *Sierra Club v. Morton*, 405 U.S. 727 (1972). Ultimately Mineral King was
      never developed, and it was annexed into Sequoia National Park in 1978,
      Public Law 95-625 (1978), 16 U.S.C. 45f..

27 *McCullough v. Maryland*, 17 U.S. (4 Wheaton) 316, 415 (1819).

28 Holmes, Oliver Wendell, Jr. *The Common Law* (Boston: Little, Brown, 1881), 1.

Chapter 2: There Must Be Advocates

1 Williams, Terry Tempest. *An Unspoken Hunger* (New York: Random House, 1994), 73, 78. Words used again in an expansion of the thoughts conveyed in Williams's essay "The Coyote Clan" in *Red* (New York: Random House, 2001), 23-26. Williams is a fierce advocate of the Colorado Plateau and an eloquent guide to the spiritual and the wild of the Redrock Country—a worthy successor to Ed Abbey. Publication of the environmental and preservation ethic must reach a broad audience if these values are to enjoy continued success, and Williams does an admirable job of this in her article "This Land is Your Land" (referring to the Colorado Plateau, naturally) in the popular magazine *Condé Nast Traveler*, April 2012: 81.

2 *Viavant, Frear and Sierra Club v. Trans-Delta Oil and Gas Co., et al.*, No. 367-73, U.S. District Court for Utah (1973).

3 See U.S. General Services Administration website, "Frank E. Moss U.S. Courthouse, Salt Lake City, UT," 2009, for comprehensive description of the courthouse, its architecture and interior design.

4 *Viavant et.al.*, Transcript of Proceedings, December 11, 1973. Honorable Willis Ritter, Judge. The hearing testimony related in the following pages is taken from this transcript

5 Two important recently published memoirs give perceptive and authoritative insight to the work of the full time committed environmentalist: Edgar Wayburn's *Your Land and Mine* (San Francisco: Sierra Club, 2004) and Michael McCloskey's *In the Thick of It* (Washington DC: Island Press, 2005). They do more than that: they take the reader inside national campaigns and explore the processes, organizations, judgments, and decisions involved. Nationally recognized environmentalist leaders, these gentlemen were indeed at the center of many of the most important environmental struggles and accomplishments of the second half of the Twentieth Century. On a more narrow front, Carl Pope and Paul Rauber's *Strategic Ignorance* (San Francisco: Sierra Club, 2004) explores the conflict between the administration of Presidnet George W. Bush and the environment.

6 National Parks Organic Act, 390 Stat, 535 (1916) 16 U.S.C. 1 et seq, as amended.

7 Denver, John. "Rocky Mountain High," in *The Authentic Guitar Style of John Denver* (Port Chester, NY: Cherry Lane Music Company, Inc., 1988), 11. Recorded and released 1972.

Chapter 3: The Grand Canyon

Altogether there must be thousands of books and significant articles on United States national parks. Our National Park System is the envy of the world; thus the audience seeking information on the parks is legion. While most of the literature is likely guides and natural histories—important, of course, in their own right—there are probably scores, if not hundreds, which address the matters raised in *Voices*.

While recognizing that I am leaving out many excellent works, two recent titles critical to the writing of Chapter III must be underscored: Richard West Seller's *Preserving Nature in the National Parks: A History* (New Haven, CT: Yale University Press, 1997), already a classic and an indispensable history of the national parks, the National Park Service, and the evolution of park management policies; and Dayton Duncan and Ken Burns' *The National Parks: America's Best Idea* (New York: Alfred A. Knopf, 2009), together with the marvelous companion film by Ken Burns, the most comprehensive recent overview and history of the parks. Of early historical interest is John Muir's *Our National Parks* (Boston: Houghton Mifflin, 1901), written in his lyrical and flowing style.

Three references specific to Grand Canyon were important background and will be rewarding and instructive to anyone interested in learning more about the park and its wonders: *The Grand Colorado: The Story of a River and its Canyons,* T. H Watkins and Contributors (Palo Alto, CA: American West Publishing Company, 1969); *Grand Canyon Country*, Seymour L. Fishbein (Washington DC: National Geographic Society, 1991, 1997); and *Time and the River Flowing: Grand Canyon*, Francois Leydet (San Francisco: Sierra Club, 1964, 1968).

This Grand Canyon chapter focuses upon two very significant park management responsibilities: protection of the Colorado River environment within the canyon from destructive river-running practices and activities, and regulation of airspace above the park in a manner compatible with other park values. Over the past forty years, regulatory decisions and actions have been practically continuous. Furthermore, Congress periodically wades in with new or amended governing legislation. *Voices* addresses the early years of the effort to protect the river environment and the airspace. Regulatory responses are cited below, and I have tried to include the important and distinguishing management efforts and rules then in play. However, through the succeeding years there have been many studies, continued regulatory pronouncements, and periodic changes in applicable statutory law. Referencing all of these would be needlessly burdensome, especially since the only real certainty is that the playing field is and will be constantly in flux. Readers seeking more information can find this on the internet, the websites of the two federal agencies, and the various park management plan iterations. These are all accessible to the public.

1   Nash, Roderick. *Wilderness and the American Mind,* 4th Edition (New Haven: Yale University Press, 2001), 331.

2 *University of Northern Arizona Preliminary Report*, 1976. Scientific analyses and accompanying written reports are recurring features of federal land management agencies. They catalogue environmental conditions, pinpoint harm, real or threatened, and suggest remedies. Frequently they undergird management policies and plans for the lands or resources involved. In the present instance, no permanent or final report was issued during the life of the case; UNA's Preliminary Report served admirably.

3 Abbey, Edward. *The Monkey Wrench Gang* (Philadelphia: Lippincott, 1975).

4 Management plans underlie the daily operation of the lands or resources involved. Consequently, they are constantly interpreted and re-interpreted as time goes by and circumstances change. If conditions merit more involved treatment, plans may be significantly supplemented or amended. The current Colorado River Management Plan for Grand Canyon, adopted in 2006, supersedes earlier plans and revisions dated 1979-1980 (the plan emanating from the subject litigation), 1981, and 1989. While statutory authority and criteria have been present since creation of the National Park Service in 1916, the 1998 National Parks Omnibus Management Act, Public Law 105-391, 16 U.S.C. 5931, 5951, provides recent expanded guidance.

5 Yellowstone National Park Establishment Act, 17 Stat 32 (1872), 16 U.S.C. 21.

6 National Parks Organic Act, 39 Stat. 535 (1916), 16 U.S.C. 1.

7 Sellers, Richard. *Preserving Nature in the National Parks: A History* (New Haven, CT: Yale University Press, 1997) 282. This is probably the best history of National Parks management in print.

8 Section 2 of the Establishment Act, 17 Stat 32; the quoted passage is now codified at 16 U.S.C. 22. While the code does not include all the language Congress adopted in 1872, the quoted passage is included.

9 16 U.S.C. 1.

10 Redwood National Park Establishment Act, Public Law 90-545 (1968), expanded, Public Law 95-250 (1978), codified at 16 U.S.C. 79a.

11 *Sierra Club v. U.S. Department of Interior,* 376 F. Supp. 90 (N.D. Cal. 1974), 398 F. Supp. 284 (N.D. Cal. 1975), 425 F. Supp. 172 (N.D. Cal. 1976). These decisions and the carefully crafted opinions of Judge William Sweigert are pivotal in the evolution of National Park Service management imperatives.

12 16 U.S.C. 1a-1.

13 National Park Service *Management Policies 2006*, Section 1.4.3. "The NPS Obligation to Conserve and Provide for Enjoyment of Park Resources and Values." www.nps.gov/policy/mp2006.pdf.

14 See note 4, Chapter 3, above.

15 Colorado River Management Plan 2006 (www.nps.gov/grca/parkmgmt/upload/CRMPIF_ s.pdf). See also Colorado River Management Plan 2012 Commercial Operating Requirements (nps.gov/grca/parkmgmt/upload/2012-final-COR.pdf).

16 See National Park Service, *Grand Canyon National Park: Overflights— Chronology of Significant Events,* 2012 (www.nps.gov/grca/naturescience/ airoverflights_chrono.htm). This comprehensive chronology is an absolutely necessary resource for the interested reader. Also see Grand Canyon Historical Society, Inc., *The Bulletin* 12:3 (2008): www.GrandCanyonHistory.org.

17 The National Park Service has many written accounts of the impact of air tour operations in and over the Grand Canyon prior to the mid-air collision (covered later in this chapter) between two air tour flights in 1986. Reference: *Overflights, and Soundscape Preservation and Noise Management* (www.hps.gov/policy). See also *Overflights—Chronology* in the just previous note.

18 Grand Canyon National Park Enlargement Act, Public Law 93-620, 16 U.S.C. 228a; Section 8 at 16 U.S.C. 228g.

19 National Parks Overflights Act, Public Law 100-91 (1987), 49 U.S.C. 40128. FAA regulations: Special Federal Aviation Regulation SFAR 50 (March 1987) and SFAR 50-1 (June 1987). Federal Aviation Regulations (FARs) are part of Title 14 of the Code of Federal Regulations (CFR). SFARs can be directly reached on the internet via Google.

20 SFAR 50-2 (June 1988). An excellent graphic representation of the flight free zones, special flight zones, and special flight rules areas, together with aviation corridors, is found in High Country News, June 13, 2011. See website: www.hcn.org. The Park Service publishes up-to-date graphics (charts) available on the Grand Canyon National Park website (www.ups.gov/grca) under "Science Center".

21 *U.S. Air Tour Association, et al. v. FAA,* 298 F.3d 997 (2002).

22 National Parks Air Tour Management Act, Public Law 106-181, 49 U.S.C. 40128 (2000), as amended.

23 Public Law 112-141 (2012), 126 Stat. 842. See language in notes to 49 U.S.C. 40128, as amended, 2013 edition.

24 President Theodore Roosevelt at the Grand Canyon, May 6, 1903; quoted in Duncan and Burns, *The National Parks: America's Best Idea* (New York: Knopf, 2009), 94.

25 Brinkley, Douglas. *The Wilderness Warrior* (New York: Harper Collins 2009), 536-544.

Chapter IV: Protecting Wilderness

Descriptions of each wilderness area in this chapter are taken from Wikipedia and U.S. Forest Service websites, augmented by my own personal experiences. These sources explain the character and size of each area, their unique characteristics, and some of their history. Since this is uniformly true for each "case," there does not seem to be a need for specific citation to these references. See also United States Geological Survey (USGS) maps and National Geographic Society "Trails Illustrated Maps."

Two references are indispensable to the inquirer seeking to know more about the evolution and development of the wilderness ethic into the Wilderness Act of 1964 and, thereby, the National Wilderness System of the United States. They are essential to the researcher or commentator seeking to explore the Act's origins, evolution, drafting, and interpretation. Doug Scott's thorough and scholarly *The Enduring Wilderness* (Golden, CO: Fulcrum Publishing, 2004) ably relates the ripening of the early ideas of wilderness preservation of Thoreau, Muir, and Roosevelt, through halting but original administrative efforts (stimulated by the work of Aldo Leopold), on to the drafting of legislation, and, finally, passage of the Act. The University of Denver *College of Law Symposium, Wilderness Act of 1964: Reflection, Application, and Prediction*, Marinda K. Peterson, editor, Denver University Law Review, Vol. 76, No. 2 (1999), examines in comprehensive fashion the first thirty-five years of interpretation and administration of the Wilderness Act; and this transcription of the Symposium is as relevant and useful today as it was fifteen years ago.

In a broader context, Roderick Frazier Nash's *Wilderness and the American Mind* (New Haven, CT: Yale University Press, 1967, 2001) explores in sweeping fashion the role of wilderness in our history and in our lives today. Dave Foreman, in *Rewilding North America* (Washington DC: Island Press, 2004), presents thought-provoking and expansive vision and challenges for the role of wildlands in our world, both today and in the future. For excellent background on the U.S. Forest Service, see Harold K. Steen's *The U.S. Forest Service: A History* (Seattle: University of Washington Press, 1976, 1977).

1   Wayburn, Edgar. *Your Land and Mine* (San Francisco: Sierra Club, 2004), 312.

2   The Wilderness Act of 1964, Public Law 88-577 (1964), 16 U.S.C. 1131.

3   Review of the history and evolution here and over the next few pages leans heavily on Scott's *Enduring Wilderness*.

4   Scott, *Enduring Wilderness*, 35-39.

5   16 U.S.C. 1131, 1132.

6   Theodore Roosevelt, excerpt from the speech "Citizenship in A Republic," delivered at the Sorbonne in Paris, France, April 23, 1910 (design.caltech.edu/erik/Misc/Citizenship_in_a_Republic).

7   *Parker v. United States*, 309 F.Supp. 593 (D. Colo. 1970), affirmed 448 F. 2d 793 (10th Cir. 1971).

8   Adams, Ansel and Nancy Newhall, *This is The American Earth* (San Francisco: Sierra Club, 1960), 78-83.

9   Central Idaho Wilderness Act of 1980, Public Law 96-312; Gospel Hump Wilderness, Public Law 95-237 (1978); Selway-Bitterroot Wilderness, designated by the Wilderness Act of 1964 itself.

10 Brower, David. "Wilderness Conflict and Conscience," *Wildlands in Our Civilization*, John Collier, editor (San Francisco: Sierra Club, 1964), 52.

11 Scapegoat Wilderness, Public Law 92-395 (1972).

12 National Environmental Policy Act (NEPA), Public Law 91-90: 42 U.S.C. 4321 (1969).

13 Fielder, John and Mark Pearson, *Colorado's Wilderness Areas* (Englewood, CO: Westcliffe Publishers, 1994), 57-58. This volume is an exemplary treatment of its subject, including data, history, and issues, advice, maps, physical descriptions, features, trails and hikes, and wonderful photographs for each wilderness area in the state. Altogether, it is an outstanding reference.

14 16 U.S.C. 1131 (c).

15 Eastern Wilderness Areas Act, Public Law 93-622 (1975), 16 U.S.C. 1132.

16 Federal Land Policy and Management Act of 1976, Public Law 94-579, Sec. 603, 43 U.S.C. 1782.

Chapter V: Sculptured Lands

1 Dutton, Clarence. *Report on the Geology of the High Plateaus of Utah* (Washington, DC: USGS Survey, US Government Printing Office, 1880); an early geological classic on the Colorado Plateau, written with color and verve.

2 Thybony, Scott. *Canyon Country Parklands* (Washington, DC: National Geographic Society, 1998), 42. This conversational narrative is a useful introduction to the lands of the Colorado Plateau, including the national parks featured in this chapter.

3 Chesher, Greer. Photographs by Liz Hymans. *Heart of the Desert Wild* (Bryce Canyon, UT: Bryce Canyon Natural History Association, 2000), 43. This is an excellent reference work for those seeking guidance to the issues surrounding Grand Staircase-Escalante National Monument and understanding of the magnificent lands it encompasses. There is much written material on the Colorado Plateau, its parks, monuments, and natural areas, and its unforgettable land forms; photography books of this country have become an art form. For the descriptive and historical in addition to Thybony and Chesher, I recommend: *Wilderness at the Edge* (Salt Lake City: Utah Wilderness Coalition, editors and publisher, 1990); *Slickrock*, Edward Abbey and Philip Hyde (San Francisco: Sierra Club, 1973); *Standing Up Country*, C. Gregory Crampton (New York: Alfred A. Knopf and the University of Utah, 1965). For advocacy, philosophy, poetry, and fire, the works of Edward Abbey and Terry Tempest Williams, referenced elsewhere in these notes, stand apart.

4 Abbey, Edward. *Desert Solitaire* (New York: Simon & Schuster, 1968), 47. This is Abbey's finest. He was iconoclastic, often outrageous, but always trenchant and penetrating. He spoke directly and movingly to conservationists rising to the defense of the Colorado Plateau in the 1960s, Seventies, and Eighties,

and his influence is still widely felt today.

5   In re *The Matter of Public Service Company of New Mexico*, Case No. 1216, New Mexico Public Service Commission, 1973.

6   National Environmental Policy Act (NEPA), Public Law 91-190 (1970), 42 U.S.C. 4321.

7   NEPA, 42 U.S.C. 4332 (2) (c).

8   Council on Environmental Quality (CEQ), Guidelines for Implementing NEPA, 40 CFR Parts 1500-1508 (2005). Heavily relied upon by the courts, the fundamental processes and requirements of implementation and compliance with NEPA are set forth in these regulations and guidelines.

9   *Audubon Magazine* xxx.

10   Abbey, Edward and Philip Hyde. *Slickrock* (San Francisco: Sierra Club, 1973).

11   Clean Air Act (CAA), Public Law 95-95 (1977), 42 U.S.C. 7401. See "Historical and Statutory Notes" following the statutory language.

12   CAA, 42 U.S.C. 7470 et seq., particularly section 7472, and "Historical and Statutory Notes" in the Annotations.

13   Section 309 of the Clean Air Act, 42 U.S.C. 7609.

14   The National Park Service maintains a couple of informative websites on Lafayette Square; reference "Lafayette Square Historic District."

15   CAA, 42 U.S.C. 7609 (b).

16   CEQ Guidelines, 40 CFR 1504.2 (7).

17   *Application No. 35818* (89-74) before the Division of Water Rights, Utah Department of Natural Resources, specifically Application for Permanent Change of Point of Diversion Place and Nature of Use of Water and Request Extension of Time, variously bearing dates of July 13 and 15, 1976, and supporting exhibits and documents.

18   *In the Matter of the Participation of Southern California Edison Company and San Diego Gas and Electric Company in the Proposed Kaiparowits Electric Generating Plant*, before the Public Utilities Commission of the State of California, Application No. 56050; Decision and Opinion and Findings, No. 88005, October 18, 1977.

19   Ibid., 25.

20   Turner, Tom. *Wild By Law* (San Francisco: Sierra Club, 1990), 50.

21   *Sierra Club v. Ruckelshaus*, 344 F. Supp. 253 (D.D.C. 1972), affirmed per curiam, 2 ELR 20656 (DC Cir. 1972), affirmed per curium and sub nominee, Fri v. Sierra Club, 412 U.S. 541/1973).

22   For explanatory treatment of the subject of prevention of significant deterioration of air quality and its evolution over some thirty years, an excellent reference work is Arnold W. Rietze, Jr.'s *Stationary Source Air Pollution Law* (Washington, DC: Environmental Law Institute, 2005), 175–182 in particular.

23   Googling "Willard Hotel," and specifically its lobby, yields a number of Web sites and blogs with historical and entertaining references to the interesting history of this Washington, DC, landmark.

24 CAA, 42 U.S.C. 7470, 7472.

25 Indeed a 1900 megawatt Intermountain Power Plant went online in 1988-89 at Delta, Utah, 20 miles from Lyndall. An additional 900 MWt unit planned for 2012 was scrapped when Los Angeles declared it would be "carbon free" by 2020. The existing units are scheduled to be converted to less polluting natural gas by 2025.

26 The best source for the details and progress of this litigation is the website of the Southern Utah Wilderness Alliance. SUWA's Web postings and newsletters give it constant and thorough attention. See www.suwa.org.

27 Proclamation No. 6920, 61 Federal Register 50:223 (September 18, 1996). President Clinton's authority was derived from the Antiquities Act of 1906, 34 Stat. 225, 16 U.S.C. 431.

28 Crampton, C. Gregory. *Standing Up Country* (New York: Alfred A. Knopf, University of Utah, 1965), 103-107.

29 Chesher, Greer K. *Heart of the Desert Wild* (Bryce Canyon, Utah: Bryce Canyon Natural History Association, 2000), 42.

Chapter VI: It Takes an Expert

1 Rule 702, Rules of Evidence for United States Courts and Magistrates, Public Law 93-595, 88 Stat. 1926 (1975), as amended. Advisory Committee Notes immediately follow official publication of the Rule. See further on expert testimony, Rules 703-706.

2 Hand, Learned. *Historical and Practical Considerations Regarding Expert Testimony*, 15 Harvard Law Review 40 (1901), republished in part in *Selected Writings on the Law of Evidence and Trial*, William T. Fryer, editor (St. Paul: West Publishing Co., 1957), 481.

3 Unfortunately, I cannot locate the actual transcript of the trial. Thus this narrative is the product of my memory, reinforced by Judge Doyle's findings and opinion and by other commentary gleaned from files and related contemporaneous materials. It is worth noting that critical impact moments, such as Clif Merritt's testimony and the court's response, are firmly embedded within the memories of the direct participants. This is certainly so with myself in this instance.

4 *Parker v. United States*, 309 F.2d 593, 599-602 (D. Colo. 1970), affirmed 448 F.2d 793 (10th Cir. 1971). See H. Anthony Ruckel, "The Wilderness Act and The Courts," *Symposium, Wilderness Act of 1964*, Denver Law Review 76:2 (2009): 611, 612-614 and Joseph L. Sax, *Defending the Environment* (New York: Alfred A. Knopf, 1971), 193-205, 208-209, where various aspects of the Parker case are discussed.

5 *Trout Unlimited v. Morton*, 509 F 2d 1276 (9th Cir. 1974).

6 Reisner, Marc. *Cadillac Desert* (New York: Penguin Books, 1986, 1993), 395.

Reisner's masterful, alarming, and meticulously researched work on water in the American West is a true classic. It is a must read for political leaders, government administrators, environmentalists, and the general public— anyone interested in western water development and use. The Teton Dam is covered exhaustively, see pages 383-410.

7   Reisner, 382–383.

8   *Trout Unlimited v. Morton.*

9   American Society of Civil Engineers (ASCE). *Teton Dam Failure Case Study.* Proceedings of the Third ASCE Forensics Congress in San Diego, October 19-21, 2003 (http:matdl.org/failure cases/Dam%20Cases/%.htm). This is a basic, detailed review from a well-regarded professional society and a non-governmental agency. By incredible coincidence, a party of tourists had arrived at a point just above the dam on the morning of the 5th, and—as Reisner notes (page 402): "On the seat of their car was a movie camera loaded with film." Sequences of photos of the collapse have appeared in many reviews and reports, including in the ASCE Proceedings referenced above. A well-reproduced sequence of these photos, labeled with specific time intervals, can be found at http://ponce.sdsu.edu/teton_dam_failure_photos.html, posted under the title of College of Engineering, Dr. Victor Miguel Ponce, and labeled "Teton Dam Failure." The interested reader will find many sources on the Teton Dam and its failure, including federal government reviews and investigation.

10 Reisner, *Cadillac Desert,* 387.

11 ASCE Proceedings, supra, page 5.

12 Idaho Senate Bill No. 1511 (2008). See text and report of the Senate Finance Committee, particularly the "Fiscal Note" at the end of the posting. www.legislature.idaho.gov/legislation/2008/S1511.html. And see: Idaho Water Resource Board 2010 presentation, Statewide Surface Water Storage Project Studies, particularly the "House Joint Memorial 8" part.

13 Leckie, Robert. *Delivered From Evil* (New York: Harper & Row, 1987) 491-492.

14 Two useful surveys of the country's policies, programs, and projects—or aborted programs and projects—regarding disposal of high level nuclear wastes are: James M. Hylko, *The U.S. Nuclear Waste Disposal Policy: The Long Road Traveled from Lyons to Yucca Mountain, and Points in Between* (Nevada: U.S. Nuclear Energy Foundation, www.usnuclearenergy.org/ hylko.htm. Last modified 2013); and "Nuclear Waste Policy Act" (http://en.wikipedia.org/ wiki/Nuclear_Waste_Policy_Act), last modified in 2014. The State of Nevada has published on the Internet a helpful chronology from 1945 (first nuclear weapons) through 1999, titled "Nuclear Waste Policy Dilemma, The First Fifty Years: A Chronology" (www.state.nv.us/nucwaste/yucca/nwchron/.htm).

15 The Fukushima Daiichi disaster, including the nuclear waste storage ramifications, has been treated exhaustively by three press or media sources: *The New York Times, The Wall Street Journal,* and *The Economist.* For two years, articles and commentary appeared constantly. Particularly notable was a

comprehensive "Special Report: Nuclear Energy," addressing the entire subject of nuclear energy in *The Economist*, March 10, 2012.

16 The Nuclear Waste Policy Act, Public Law 97-425, 42 U.S.C. 1010 (1983).

17 The geology of Southern Utah, with its arresting surface manifestations, and the Colorado River, has been the subject of many geological books. The reader will find three particularly useful: Robert Fillmore, *Geological Evolution of the Colorado Plateau of Eastern Utah and Western Colorado* (Salt Lake: University of Utah Press, 2011); Douglas A. Sprinkel, Thomas C. Chidsey, Jr., and Paul B. Anderson, Editors, *Geology of Utah's Parks and Monument* (Salt LakeCity: Utah Geological Association and Bryce Canyon Natural History Association, 2003); and Donald L. Baars, *Canyonlands Country* (Salt Lake City: University of Utah Press, 1993).

18 Peter W. Huntoon, George H. Billingsley, Jr., and William J. Breed, *Geologic Map of Canyonlands National Park and Vicinity, Utah* (Moab, Utah: The Canyonlands Natural History Association, 1982). Also see Peter W. Huntoon, *The Meander Anticline, Canyonlands, Utah: An Unloading Structure Resulting From Horizontal Sliding on Salt*, Geological Society of America, Bulletin, 10 (1988), 941; Peter W. Huntoon, *Late Cenozoic Gravity Tectonic Deformation Related to the Paradox Salts in the Canyonlands Area of Utah*, Utah Geological and Mineral Survey Bulletin 122 (1988) 80ff.

19 For geology of the Paradox Formation, see Baars, *Canyonlands Country*, 33-36. See also Fillmore, *Geological Evolution of the Colorado Plateau*, 43-48, and Sprinkel, et al., *Geology of Utah's Parks*, 77-78, all supra.

20 See Hylko, *U.S. Nuclear Waste Disposal*, 1-5, for assumptions. See Wikipedia, :Nuclear Waste Policy Act" for description of the U.S. Department of Energy Guidelines for selection of a repository site. For DOE's Guidelines themselves, see 10 CFR Part 960 and appendices.

21 50 FR 38084, September 19, 1985, 40 CFR191.11 and 191.12. See Subpart B —Environmental Standards for Disposal:

   i.   191.11 Applicability.

      (b) This subpart applies to:

         (1) Radioactive materials released into the accessible environment as a result of the disposal of spent nuclear fuel or high-level or transuranic radioactive wastes;

   ii. 191.12 Definitions.

      (1) *Accessible environment* means: (1) The atmosphere; (2) land surfaces: (3) surface waters; (4) oceans; all of the lithosphere that is beyond the controlled area.

      (2) *Controlled area* means: (1) A surface location ... that encompasses no more than 100 square kilometers and *extends horizontally no more than five kilometers in any direction from the outer boundary* [italics mine] of the original location of the radioactive wastes in a disposal system; and (2) the subsurface underlying such a

surface location.

22 *Recommendation by Secretary of Energy of Candidate Sites for Site Characterization for First Radioactive Waste Repository*, May 1986. www.cyberceme-
tery.unt.edu/archive/brc..._recommendation_document_s.pdf.

23 *Environmental Assessment: Davis Canyon Site, Utah*, U.S. Department of
Energy, Office of Civilian Radioactive Waste Management, 1986.

24 NWPA Amendment, Public Law 100-203, 42 U.S.C. 10172 (1987).

25 Presidential Memorandum, 75 FR 5485, January 29, 2010.

26 Blue Ribbon Commission, Report to the Secretary of Energy, January 26,
2012. www.cybercemetery.unt.edu/brc_finalreport_jan2012pdf.

Chapter VII: Reflections

1   Corwin, Edward S. *The Constitution and What It Means Today*. Revised by
Harold W. Chase and Craig R. Ducat (Princeton: Princeton University Press,
13th Edition, 1973, 1920).

Bibliography

Abbey, Edward. *Desert Solitaire.* New York: Simon & Schuster, 1968.

Abbey, Edward and Hyde, Phillip. *Slick Rock.* San Francisco: Sierra Club, 1971.

Adkinson, Ron. *Utah's National Parks.* Berkeley: Wilderness Press, 1991, 2001.

ASCE Forensics Congress. *Proceedings: Teton Dam Failure Case Study.* San Diego: American Society of Civil Engineers, 2003. See particularly citations: matdl.org/failurecases/Dam%20Cases/Teton%20Dam.htm.

Ash, Roderick Frazier. *Wilderness & the American Mind.* New Haven, CT: Yale University Press, 1967, 1982.

Brinkley, Douglas. *The Wilderness Warrior: Theodore Roosevelt and the Crusade for America.* New York: Harper Perennial, 2009.

Chemerinsky, Erwin. *Constitutional Law: Principles and Policies.* New York: Aspen, 2006, 2008.

Chesher, Greer K. *Heart of the Desert Wild.* Bryce Canyon, Utah: Bryce Canyon Natural History Association, 2000.

Coggins, George C. and Wilkinson, Charles F. *Federal Public Land and Resources Law.* Mineola, MN: Foundation Press, 1981.

Crampton, C. Gregory. *Land of Living Rock.* New York: Alfred A. Knopf, 1972.

Crampton, C. Gregory. *Standing Up Country.* New York: Alfred A. Knopf and University of Utah Press, 1964.

Duncan, Dayton and Burns, Ken. *The National Parks: America's Best Idea.* New York: Alfred A. Knopf, 2009.

Evarts, John and Marjory Popper, Editors. *Coast Redwood: A Natural and Cultural History.* Los Olivos, California: Cachuma Press, 2001.

Fielder, John and Mark Pearson. *Colorado's Wilderness Areas.* Englewood, CO: Westcliffe Publishers, 1994.

Fillmore, Robert. *Geological Evolution of the Colorado Plateau.* Salt Lake City: University of Utah Press, 2011.

Fishbein, Seymour L. *Grand Canyon Country.* Washington, D.C.: National Geographic Society, 1981, 1997.

Foreman, Dave. *Rewilding North America.* Washington D.C.: Island Press, 2004.

Fox, Stephen. *John Muir and His Legacy: the American Conservation Movement.* Boston: Little, Brown, 1981.

Haines, Aubrey L. *The Yellowstone Story.* Two Volumes. Niwot, CO: Colorado University Press, 1977, 1996.

Hylko, James M. *The U.S. Nuclear Waste Policy: The Long Road Traveled.* Sparks, NV: U.S. Nuclear Energy Foundation, 2005, 2013. See also: usnuclearenergy.org.

Leopold, Aldo. *A Sand County Almanac and Sketches Here and There.* New York: Oxford University Press, 1949.

Leopold, Aldo. *A Sand County Almanac & Other Writings on Ecology and Conservation.* Curt Meine, editor. New York: The Library of America, 2013.

Marian, Nancy E. *Making Environmental Law: The Politics of Protecting the Earth.* Westport, CT: Praeger, 2011.

McCloskey, Michael. *In the Thick of It.* Washington, D.C.: Island Press, 2005.

Muir, John. *Our National Parks.* Boston: Houghton Mifflin, 1901.

Muir, John. *My First Summer in the Sierra.* Boston: Houghton Mifflin, 1911.

Nash, Roderick Frazier. *Wilderness & the American Mind.* New Haven: Yale University Press, 1967, 1982.

Patterson, James. *Grand Expectations: The United States, 1945-1974.* New York: Oxford University Press, 1996.

Peterson, Marinda K., Editor. *Symposium: Wilderness Act of 1964.* Denver: University of Denver Law Review, Vol. 76, No. 2, 1999.

Powell, John W. *The Exploration of the Colorado River and Its Canyons.* New York: Dover, 1961. Republication of the work first published by Flood & Vincent in 1895 under the title Canyons of the Colorado.

Reisner, Marc. *Cadillac Desert.* New York: Penguin, 1987, 1993.

Reported Cases:

Baker v. Carr, 369 U.S. 186 (1962).

Parker v. United States, 309 F. Supp. 593 (D. Colo. 1970), affirmed 448 F.2d 793 (10th Cir. 1971).

Scenic Hudson Preservation Conference v. Federal Power Commission, 354 F.2d 608 (2nd Cir. 1965).

Sierra Club v. Morton, 405 US 727 (1972)

Sierra Club v. Ruckelshaus, 344 F. Supp. 253 (D.D.C. 1972), affirmed per curiam, 2 ELR 20656 (D.C. Cir. 1972), affirmed per curiam and sub nominee, Fri v. Sierra Club, 412 U.S. 541 (1973).

Sierra Club v. U.S. Department of Interior, 376 F. Supp. 90 (N.D. Cal. 1974), 398 F. Supp 284 (N.D. Cal. 1975), 424 F. Supp. 172 (N.D. Cal. 1976).

Trout Unlimited v. Morton, 509 F 2d 1276 (9th Cir. 1974).ington Press, 1976

Rietze, Arnold W., Jr. *Stationary Source Air Pollution Law*. Washington, DC: Environmental Law Institute, 2005.

Ruckel, H. Anthony. "The Wilderness Act and the Courts, in Symposium: Wilderness Act of 1964." *University of Denver Law Review* 76, No. 2 (1999): 611.

Sax, Joseph L. *Defending the Environment*. New York: Alfred A. Knopf, 1971.

Scott, Doug. *The Enduring Wilderness*. Golden, CO: Fulcrum Publishing, 2004.

Sellars, Richard West. *Preserving Nature in the National Parks*. New Haven, CT: Yale University Press, 1997.

Sprinkel, Douglas A., Thomas C. Chidsey, Jr., and Paul V. Anderson, Editors. *Geology of Utah's Parks and Monuments*. Salt Lake City: Utah Geological Association and Bryce Canyon Natural History Association, 2003.

Steen, Harold K. *The U.S. Forest Service: A History*. Seattle, WA: University of Washington Press, 1976.

Stegner, Wallace. *Beyond the Hundredth Meridian*. Boston: Houghton Mifflin, 1953.

Thybony, Scott. *Canyon Country Parklands*. Washington, DC: National Geographic Society, 1998.

Turner, Tom, photographs by Carr Clifton. *Wild by Law*. San Francisco: Sierra Club, 1990.

United States Code (Annotated):

Antiquities Act, 16 U.S.C. 431 (1906), as amended.

Clean Air Act, Public Law 91-64 (1970), Public Law 95-95 (1977), 42 U.S.C. 7401.

Clean Water Act, Public Law 92-50 (1972), Public Law 95-217 (1977), 33 U.S.C. 1251.

Eastern Wilderness Areas Act, Public Law 93-622, 16 U.S.C. 1632 (1975).

Endangered Species Act, Public Law 93-205 (1973), 16 U.S.C. 1531.

Federal Land Policy and Management Act, Public Law 94-579 (1976), 43 U.S.C. 1782.

National Environmental Policy Act, Public Law 91-190, 42 U.S.C. 4321 (1970).

National Parks Air Tour Management Act, Public Law 106-181, 49 U.S.C. 40128 (2000).

National Parks Omnibus Management Act, Public Law 105-391 (1998), 16 U.S.C. 5931, 5951.

National Parks Organic Act, 39 Stat. 535, 16 U.S.C. 1 (1916). See particularly amendments in Public Law 95-250, codified at 1 U.S.C. 1a-1 (the Redwoods Act amendments, 1978).

National Parks Overflight Act, Public Law 100-91, 49 U.S.C. 40128 (1987).

Nuclear Waste Policy Act, Public Law 97-425, 42 U.S.C. 10101 (1982, 1987).

The Wilderness Act, Public Law 88-577, 16 U.S.C. 1131 (1964).

Utah Wilderness Coalition, Editors. *Wilderness at the Edge.* Salt Lake City: Utah Wilderness Coalition, 1990.

Watkins, T. H. *The Grand Colorado.* Palo Alto: American West Publishing Co., 1969.

Watts, David A. *Canyonlands National Park and the Organic Act: Balancing Resource Protection and Visitor Use.* Washington D.C.: National Park Service, Environmental Quality Division, 2008. nps.gov/… /resource_protection.pdf

Wayburn, Edgar. *Your Land and Mine.* San Francisco: Sierra Club, 2004.

Wilkinson, Charles F. *Crossing the Next Meridian.* Washington, D.C.: Island Press, 1992.

Williams, Terry Tempest. *Red: Passion and Patience in the Desert.* New York: Random House, 2001.

Winks, Robin W. *The National Park Service Act of 1916: A Contradictory Mandate?* Denver: 74 University of Denver Law Review 575, 1997.

Worster, Donald. *A Passion for Nature: The Life of John Muir.* New York: Oxford University Press, 2011.

Worster, Donald. *A River Running West: The Life of John Wesley Powell.* New York: Oxford University Press, 2001.

Index

CPSIA information can be obtained at www.ICGtesting.com
Printed in the USA
BVOW04s1150180516

448604BV00011B/47/P